Madaurensis Apuleius, William Adlington

The Golden Ass of Apuleius

Madaurensis Apuleius, William Adlington

The Golden Ass of Apuleius

ISBN/EAN: 9783743313705

Manufactured in Europe, USA, Canada, Australia, Japa

Cover: Foto ©ninafisch / pixelio.de

Manufactured and distributed by brebook publishing software (www.brebook.com)

Madaurensis Apuleius, William Adlington

The Golden Ass of Apuleius

THE GOLDEN ASS OF
APULEIUS

TRANSLATED OUT OF LATIN BY

WILLIAM ADLINGTON

ANNO 1566

With an Introduction by

CHARLES WHIBLEY

LONDON
Published by DAVID NUTT
IN THE STRAND
1893

Edinburgh: T. and A. CONSTABLE, Printers to Her Majesty

TO

STÉPHANE MALLARMÉ

THIS METAMORPHOSIS OF

AN ANTIENT DECADENT

INTRODUCTION

HE GOLDEN ASS of Apuleius is, so to say, a beginning of modern literature. From this brilliant medley of reality and romance, of wit and pathos, of fantasy and observation, was born that new art, complex in thought, various in expression, which gives a semblance of frigidity to perfection itself. An indefatigable youthfulness is its distinction. As it was fresh when Adlington translated it 'out of Latine' three centuries since, so it is familiar to-day, and is like to prove an influence to-morrow. Indeed, it is among the marvels of history that an alien of twenty-five —and Apuleius was no more when he wrote his *Metamorphoses*—should have revolutionised a language not his own, and bequeathed us a freedom which, a thousand times abused, has never since been taken away.

Apuleius

A barbarian born, a Greek by education, Apuleius only acquired the Latin tongue by painful effort. Now, a foreigner, not prejudiced by an inveterate habit of speech, seldom escapes a curiosity of phrase. Where the language is the same, whether written or spoken, art is wont to lapse into nature. But there was no reason why Apuleius, who could

His Style

THE GOLDEN ASSE

INTRO-
DUCTION
not but be conscious of his diction, should ever deviate from artifice. His style, in truth, he put on as a garment, and it fitted the matter without a crease. His exotic vocabulary was the fruit of the widest research. He ransacked the ancient plays for long-forgotten words. He cared not where he picked up his neologisms, so they were dazzling and bizarre. Greece, his own Carthage, the gutters of Rome, contribute to the wealth of his diction, for he knew naught of that pedantry which would cramp expression for authority's sake. The literary use of slang was almost his own invention. He would twist the vulgar words of every day into quaint, unheard-of meanings, nor did he ever deny shelter to those loafers and footpads of speech which inspire the grammarian with horror. On every page you encounter a proverb, a catchword, a literary allusion, a flagrant redundancy. One quality only was distasteful to him: the commonplace. He is ever the literary fop, conscious of his trappings and assured of a handsome effect. In brief, he belonged to the African School, for which elaboration was the first and last law of taste. He may even have been a pupil of Fronto, the prime champion of the *elocutio novella*, the rhetorician who condemned Cicero in that he was not scrupulous in his search for effect, and urged upon his pupils the use of *insperata atque inopinata verba*. No wonder poor Adlington, whose equipment of Latin was of the lightest, hesitated for a while! No wonder he complained that ' the
' Author had written his work in so darke and high a stile,
' in so strange and absurd words, and in such new invented
' phrases, as hee seemed rather to set it forth to shew his
' magnificencie of prose, than to participate his doings to

OF LUCIUS APULEIUS

' others'! But the difficulty is not invincible; and the adventurous have their reward. The prose sparkles with light and colour. Not a page but is rich inlaid with jewels of fantastic speech. For Apuleius realised centuries before Baudelaire that a vocabulary is a palette, and he employed his own with incomparable daring and extravagance.

INTRODUCTION

Though his style be personal, the machinery of his story is frankly borrowed. The hero who, transformed by magic to an ass, recovers human shape by eating roses was no new invention. He had already supplied two writers with a motive; and the learned have not decided whether it was from Lucian (so-called) or from Lucius of Patrae that Apuleius got his inspiration.[1] But a comparison of the Latin version with its Greek forerunner, commonly attributed to Lucian, proves the debt a feather's weight. Whatever Apuleius conveyed, he so boldly changed and elaborated, as to make the material his own. His method is a miracle of simplicity. He accepts the Λούκιος ἢ Ὄνος

His Debt to Lucian

---

[1] That the hero transformed to an ass was the motive of two Greek romances can hardly be doubted after Photius' statement. The one, he says, was the work of Lucius of Patrae (who wrote μεταμορφώσεων λόγους διαφόρους), the other the work of Lucian. The Λούκιος ἢ Ὄνος, preserved in the works of Lucian, is doubtless one of the romances known to Photius. But its style and impartiality never for an instant suggest Lucian, who would have made the metamorphosis a peg for satire. And modern scholars are for the most part agreed that Lucian was not the author. Other considerations prevent our assigning it to Lucius, who, it is said, ran to a greater length, and it would be difficult to set forth the story in briefer terms than are employed by the author of Λούκιος ἢ Ὄνος. Probably it is the work of neither, though it may well be the romance attributed to Lucian by Photius. The only sure fact is that in the Λούκιος ἢ Ὄνος are to be found the dry bones of *The Golden Ass*. The curious may consult Professor Rohde's *Ueber Lucian's Schrift* Λούκιος ἢ Ὄνος *und ihr Verhaeltniss zu Lucius von Patrae und den Metamorphosen des Apuleius*.

THE GOLDEN ASSE

INTRO-
DUCTION

as a framework, sometimes following it word for word, yet decorating it with so lavish an array of phrases, tricking it out with episodes so fertile and ingenious, as to force you to forget the original in the copy. Only in a single incident does his fancy lag behind. His hero's interview with the serving-maid is chastened and curtailed. The professionally elaborate detail, wherewith Lucian enhances this famous episode, is touched by Apuleius with a light and summary hand. But elsewhere he appropriates to adorn. Though again and again the transference is verbal, the added ornament is entirely characteristic, and it is as unjust to charge the author with plagiarism as it were to condemn the Greek tragedians for their treatment of familiar themes. Indeed the two writers approach the matter from opposite points of view. Lucian's austere concision is purely classical. He has a certain story to present, and he reaches the climax by the shortest possible route. The progress is interrupted neither by phrase nor interlude, and at the end you chiefly admire the cold elegance, wherewith the misfortunes of Lucius are expressed, so to say, in their lowest terms. Apuleius, on the other hand, is unrestrainedly romantic. He cares not how he loiters by the way; he is always ready

The *Sermo Milesius*

to beguile his reader with a Milesian story—one of those quaint and witty interludes, which have travelled the world over, and become part, not merely of every literature, but of every life. Our new fashion of analysis, our ineradicable modesty, have at last denied them literary expression, and to-day they eke out a beggarly and formless existence by the aid of oral tradition. But time was they were respectable as well as joyous. What reproach is attached to the Widow of

OF LUCIUS APULEIUS

Ephesus, who has wandered from Petronius even unto Rabelais? To what admirable purpose is the *Sermo Milesius* handled in the *Decamerone*, to which Apuleius himself contributed one delectable tale! Did not the genius of Balzac devise a monument proper to its honourable antiquity in the *Contes Drolatiques*? And yet the second century was its golden age, and none so generously enhanced its repute as Apuleius. His masterpiece, in truth, is magnificently interlaced with jests, sometimes bound to the purpose of the story by the thinnest of thin threads, more often attached merely for their own or for ornament's sake. But not only thus is he separate from his model. Though he is romantic in style and temper alike—and romanticism is an affair of treatment rather than of material—he never loses touch with actuality. He wrote with an eye upon the realities of life. Observation was a force more potent with him than tradition. If his personages and incidents are wholly imaginary, he could still give them a living semblance by a touch of intimacy or a suggestion of familiar detail. Compare his characters to Lucian's, and measure the gulf between the two! Lucian's Abrœa is a warning voice—that, and no more. Byrrhena, on the other hand, is a great lady, sketched, with a quick perception of her kind, centuries before literature concerned itself with the individual. And is not Milo, the miser, leagues nearer the possibility of life than Hipparchus? Even Palæstra, despite the ingenuity of one episode, is not for an instant comparable in charm and humour to Fotis, most complaisant of serving-maids. Nor is it only in the pourtrayal of character that Apuleius proves his observation. There are many scenes

INTRODUCTION

The Book's touch with Life

The Dramatis Personæ

THE GOLDEN ASSE

INTRO-
DUCTION
whose truthful simplicity is evidence of experience. When Lucius, arrived in Hypata, goes to the market to buy him fish, he encounters an old fellow-student—Pythias by name—already invested with the authority and insignia of an ædile. Now he, being a veritable jack-in-office, is enraged that Lucius has made so ill a bargain, and overturning his fish, bids his attendants stamp it under foot, so that the traveller loses supper and money too. The incident is neither apposite nor romantic; it is no more Milesian than mystical; but it bears the very pressure of life, and you feel that it was transferred straight from a note-book. Again, where shall you find a franker piece of realism than the picture of the mill, whereto the luckless Ass was bound? Very ugly and evil-favoured were the men, covered only with ragged clouts; and how horrible a spectacle the horses, with their raw necks, their hollow flanks, their broken ribs!

The Witches
of Thessaly
The Greek author, disdaining atmosphere, is content to set out his incidents in a logical sequence. Apuleius has enveloped his world of marvels in a heavy air of witchery and romance. You wander with Lucius across the hills and through the dales of Thessaly. With all the delight of a fresh curiosity you approach its far-seen towns. You journey at midnight under the stars, listening in terror for the howling of the wolves, or the stealthy ambush. At other whiles, you sit in the robbers' cave, and hear the ancient legends of Greece retold. The spring comes on, and 'the little birds chirp 'and sing their steven melodiously.' Secret raids, ravished brides, valiant rescues, the gayest of intrigues—these are the diverse matters of this many-coloured book. The play of fancy, the variety of style, the fertility of resource are inex-

OF LUCIUS APULEIUS

haustible. Mythology is lifted into life, and life itself transformed to mystery at the wizard's touch. The misery and terror of the Ass's life are intercepted by the story of Cupid and Psyche, set forth with rare beauty and distinction of style. And yet this interlude, exquisitely planned and phrased, which suggested a worthless play[1] to Tom Heywood, and has been an inspiration to many poets from Mrs. Tighe to Mr. Bridges, is the one conspicuous fault of the book. Admirable in itself, it is out of proportion as well as out of key, and though you turn to it again and again for its own sake, you skip it industriously when it keeps you from robbery and witchcraft. But the most remarkable characteristic of *The Golden Ass* is the ever-present element of sorcery, of the *Macabre* as Mr. Pater calls it. Grim spectres and horrid ghosts stalk through its pages. The merriest Milesian jest turns sudden to the terror of death and corruption. The very story which Boccaccio borrowed is shifted by Apuleius to a weird conclusion. The baker, having most wittily avenged his wife's deceit, is lured into a chamber by a meagre, ragged, ill-favoured woman, her hair scattering upon her face, and when the servants burst open the door to find their master, behold! no woman, but only the baker hanging from a rafter dead! And where for pure horror will you match Meroe's mutilation of Socrates? Secretly the witch attacks him in his sleep, drives her sword deep into his neck, and dragging out his heart, stops the wound with a sponge. Aristomenes, unwilling witness

INTRODUCTION

Cupid and Psyche

The *Macabre* Element

---

[1] *Loves Maistresse: or, the Queens Masque.* As it was three times presented before their two EXCELLENT MAJESTIES, within the space of eight dayes. In the presence of sundry forraigne AMBASSADORS. 1636.

THE GOLDEN ASSE

INTRO-
DUCTION

of the cruelty, half believes it a dream, and gladly they resume the journey, until, when Socrates goes to the river to drink, the sponge falls out and with it the last, faint pulse of life. Again, when Thelyphron watches in the chamber of the dead, lest witches should bite off morsels of the dead man's face, and, falling asleep at sight of a weasel, loses his ears and nose, who so callous as to feel no shudder of alarm ? But the most terrific apparition of all is the obscene priest of the Syrian Goddess, with his filthy companions carrying the Divine Image from village to village, and clanging their cymbals to call the charitable. This grimy episode, with its sequent orgies, is related with an incomparably full humour which, despite its Oriental barbarity, is unmatched in literature.

Indeed there is scarce a scene without its ghostly enchantment, its supernatural intervention. And herein you may

Apuleius
the Man

detect the personal predilection of Apuleius. The infinite curiosity wherewith Lucius pries into witchcraft and sorcery was shared by his author. The hero transformed suffered his many and grievous buffetings because he always coveted an understanding of wizardry and spells; and Apuleius, in an age devoted to mysticism, was notorious for a magic-monger. Seriously it was debated, *teste* St. Augustine, whether Christ or he wrought the greater marvels: and though the shape wherein the romance is cast induced a confusion of author and hero, it is recorded that Apuleius was a zealous magician, and doubtless it is himself, not Lucius, he pictures in his last book among the initiate. In

Autobio-
graphy

the admirable description of Isis and her visitation, as of the ceremonies wherein he was admitted to the secret worship of the Goddess, he departs entirely from his Greek

OF LUCIUS APULEIUS

original. Here, indeed, we have a fragment of autobiography. When in 158 A.D., at the dramatic moment of an adventurous career, Apuleius delivered his Apology—*pro se de magia*—before Claudius Maximus, he confessed that he had been initiated into all the sacred rites of Greece, and had squandered the better part of a comfortable fortune in mysticism and the grand tour. The main accusation was that he had won his wife—a respectable and wealthy widow—by magic arts. He was also charged with other acts of witchcraft and enchantment. Thattus, it was said, and a free-born woman had swooned in his presence: a piece of superstition which reminds you of Cotton Mather. But, replied Apuleius, with excellent humour and a scepticism worthy of Reginald Scot, they were epileptics, who could stand in the presence of none save a magician. In brief, we cannot appreciate *The Golden Ass*, until we realise the modern spirit of curiosity which possessed its author. The lecturer's fame well-nigh outran the writer's. Apuleius travelled the length of civilised Africa with his orations, as the popular lecturer of to-day invades America; and the Majesty of Æsculapius, a favourite subject, was an excellent occasion for his familiar mysticism. He had been as intimately at home in the nineteenth century as in the second. Were he alive to-day Paris would have been his field, and he the undisputed master of Decadence and Symbolism. The comparison is close at all points. Would he not have delighted in the Black Mass, as celebrated on the heights of Mont Parnasse? Like too many among the makers of modern French literature he was an alien writing an alien tongue. His curiosity of diction, his unfailing

THE GOLDEN ASSE

INTRO- loyalty to speech, his eager search after the strange—and
DUCTION living—word, his love of an art which knows no conceal-
ment—these qualities proclaim the Decadent. And that
Symbolist is wayward indeed who finds not matter for his
fancy in the countless stories, which a perverse ingenuity
has twisted a hundred times into allegory.

Adlington Such the author and his book. And when William
Adlington, in the untried youth of English prose, undertook
the translation of *The Golden Asse*, you would have thought
no apter enterprise possible. Primitive and Decadent
approach art in the same temper. Each is of necessity
inclined to Euphuism. In the sixteenth century the slang,
the proverb, the gutter phrase, which Apuleius brought
back to the Latin tongue were not yet sifted from English
by the pedantry of scholars. But William Adlington,
His Purism though an Elizabethan, was something of a purist. To
be sure, he was unable to purge his diction of colour and
variety, and his manner was far better suited to the rendering of Apuleius than the prose of to-day, which has
passed through the sieve of the eighteenth century. But
with an excellent modesty he pleads acceptance for his
'simple translation.' Though he applauds the 'franke and
' flourishing stile' of his author, 'as he seems to have the
' Muses at his will to feed and maintaine his pen,' he uses of
deliberation ' more common and familiar words '—the phrase
proves the essential recognition of his own style—' fearing lest
' the book should appear very obscure and darke, and thereby
His simple ' consequently loathsome to the reader.' Indeed, he elected
Diction to translate the one book of the world which demanded the
free employment of strange terms, and set himself incontinent

OF LUCIUS APULEIUS

to avoid slang and to simplify redundancies. And his restraint is the more unexpected when you recall the habit of contemporary translators. Barnaby Rich studded Herodotus thick with colloquialisms and fresh-minted words. Philemon Holland made no attempt to chasten his vocabulary. But Adlington, his opportunity being the higher, fell the more marvellously below it. For the most part, then, you will ransack his version in vain for obsolete words or exotic flowers of speech. And yet not even his love of simplicity has kept his vocabulary entirely pure. Again and again a coined phrase, a strange form shows, like a dash of colour, upon his page. 'The roperipe boy'—thus he renders *puer ille peremptor meus* by a happy inspiration, which Apuleius himself might envy. Fresh and unhackneyed is 'the gleed 'of the sun' for *jubaris orbe*. How exquisitely does 'a 'swathell of red silke' represent *russea fasceola*! 'Traffe or 'baggage' is more pleasantly picturesque than *sarcinam vel laciniam*, and one's heart rejoices to hear a churl styled 'a 'rich chuffe.' Again, 'ungles' is far more expressive, if less common, than 'claws'; and who would write 'niggardly' when 'niggish' is ready to his hand? And is not 'a carraine 'stinke' a high-sounding version of *fetore nimio*? To encounter so sturdy and wholesome a phrase as 'I smelling his 'crafty and subtil fetch'—though it be a poor echo of *ego perspiciens malum istum verberonem blaterantem et inconcinne causificantem*—is to regret the impoverishment of our English tongue. But not often are we rejoiced by the unexpected, and for the most part Adlington is a scrupulous critic of his diction. As he makes no attempt to represent in English his author's vocabulary, so is he wont to shirk the imagery,

Margin notes: INTRODUCTION. Coined Words. The Imagery shirked

THE GOLDEN ASSE

INTRODUCTION

and curtail the redundancy affected by Apuleius, repressing the hyperbolical ostentations of his original, save only when he indulges in exaggerations of his own. When the miserable Thelyphron is protecting a dead man from the witch women, thus does Apuleius, with his admirable sense of words, enhance the horror of crawling minutes: *cum ecce crepusculum et nox provecta et nox altior et dein concubia altiora; et jam nox intempesta* for which Adlington writes in all brevity 'midnight.' Apuleius again has a dozen fantastical notions of the dawn, and Adlington cuts them all down to the colourless level of 'when morning ' was come.' Thus even does he reduce so garishly purple a piece of imagery as: *Commodum punicantibus phaleris Aurora roseum quatiens lacertum cœlum inequitabat.* When the thieves return to their den after the sack of Milo's house, and sit them down to revelry, Apuleius surpasses even his own habit of opulent description. *Estur ac potatur*—thus he writes—*incondite pulmentis acervatim, panibus aggeratim, poculis agminatim ingestis.* 'Cups in battalions!' 'Tis a pretty conceit, and for Adlington it means no more than 'they drank and eat exceedingly.' But having accustomed you to a chaste severity of language, he will break out

His rare Ornament

suddenly into a decorative passage, for which the Latin gives no warrant. 'Moreover there be divers that will cast off ' their partlets, collars, habiliments, fronts, cornets, and krip- ' pins': thus he turns a perfectly simple sentence—*lacinias omnes exuunt, amicula dimovent*—proving his quietude of phrase the effect of design rather than of necessity. So also he is wont to clip and crop his author's metaphors. 'While I considered these things' is a withered, nerveless rendering of *cum isto cogitationis salo fluctuarem*; yet is it entirely characteristic of his method. Indeed, from beginning to end he treats his author with the freest hand, and never permits the form and colour of the Latin to interrupt his conception of English prose.

But if he sacrificed something by too scrupulous a restraint, he sacrificed still more by his scanty knowledge of Latin. Scholarship was as little fashionable in Tudor England as pedantry, the defect corresponding to its quality; and Adlington laid no claim to profound erudition. He did but purpose 'according to his slender knowledge (though 'it were rudely, and farre disagreeing from the fine and 'excellent doings now-adayes),' to translate 'the delectable 'jeasts of Lucius Apuleius into our vulgar tongue.' Nor is the confession of 'slender knowledge' a mere parade of modesty: it is wholly justified by the event. To compile a list of errors were superfluous. In truth there is no page without its blunder, though, as we shall presently see, the translator commonly manages to tumble not only into sense but into distinction. Now and again the mistakes are so serious as to pervert the meaning, and then one regrets that Adlington was not more wisely guided. For instance, the servants of Philebus, the priest of the Syrian Goddess, are called *puellæ* by Apuleius in contempt of their miserable profession, and the translator impenetrably obscures the episode by rendering the word 'daughters' without a hint of explanation. Still, all are not so grave, though you are constantly driven to wonder at the ingenuity of error. When Byrrhena, in her panegyric of Hypata, tells Lucius that there the merchant may encounter the bustle of

THE GOLDEN ASSE

INTRO- Rome, the quiet visitor enjoy the peace of a country-house,
DUCTION Adlington thus heroically misses the mark: 'When the
'Roman merchants arrive in this city they are gently and
'quietly entertained, and all that dwell within this province
'(when they purpose to solace and repose themselves) do come
'to this city!' Verily there is magnificence (of a kind) in
such confusion; and how shall one reproach a translator,
upon whom accuracy sets so light a burden? Again, with
a sublime recklessness Adlington perverts *extorta dentibus
ferarum trunca calvaria* into 'the jaw-bones and teeth of
'wilde beasts,' not pausing to consider the mere formality of
grammatical concord. And when Fotis relates how Pam-
phile, having failed to advance her suit by other arts (*quod
nihil etiam tunc in suos amores ceteris artibus promoveret*),
designs to assume the shape and feathers of a bird, Adlington so carelessly confounds cause and effect as to say that the
transformation was intended 'to worke her sorceries on such
'as she loved.' *Tune solus ignoras longe faciliores ad ex-
pugnandum domus esse majores?* asks one of the robbers;
and Adlington, with the twisted cleverness of a fourth form
boy, extorts therefrom this platitude: 'Why are you only
'ignorant that the greater the number is, the sooner they may
'rob and spoil the house?' When one of Psyche's wicked
sisters threatens to go hang herself if Psyche prove the
mother of a god (*si divini puelli—quod absit—hæc mater
audierit, statim me laqueo nexili suspendam*), 'if it be a divine
'babe,' says the sister in the translation, 'and fortune to
'come to the ears of the mother (as God forbid it should)
'then may I go and hang my selfe': thus ignorant was our
Englishman of the commonest idiom. Once, at the marriage

OF LUCIUS APULEIUS

of Charite—good fortune seemed to wait upon the Ass, and his mistress promised him hay enough for a Bactrian camel (*fœnum camelo Bactrinæ sufficiens*): a promise misinterpreted by a masterpiece of grotesquerie into 'she would call me her 'little camell.' With his very easy baggage of Latin, the translator lost the point of every *Sprichwort*, and turned the literary allusion into nonsense. In the phrase *non cervam pro virgine sed hominem pro homine*, the reference to Iphigenia is patent, and yet our excellent Adlington gets no nearer the truth than 'not a servant for his maidens, 'but rather an Asse for himselfe.' {INTRODUCTION}

So much must be said in dispraise of what after all is a masterpiece of prose. The translator, said Dr. Johnson, 'is 'to exhibit his author's thoughts in such a dress as the author 'would have given them had his language been English.' Now, Adlington has failed, with the rest of the world, to reach this high standard. Under no conceivable circumstances could Apuleius have written in his terms and with his significance. For the perfect translation a knowledge of two languages is necessary. The modern translator is commonly endowed with a complete apprehension of Latin or Greek, and is withal lamentably ignorant of English. Adlington, on the other hand, was sadly to seek in Latin, but he more than atoned for his slender knowledge by an admirable treatment of his own language. Though he abandoned the colour and variety of Apuleius, he turned his author into as handsome a piece of prose as you are like to meet. From the first page to the last you will not find a trace of foreign idiom. The result is not so much a fine translation as a noble original, fitted to endure by {The Ideal Translation} {Adlington's English}

THE GOLDEN ASSE

INTRO-
DUCTION

its vigorous diction and excellent rhythm. The manner is perfectly adapted to narration, and there are few can handle a story with better delicacy and point. The style, if simple for its age, has all the distinction of simplicity. The cadences are a perpetual pleasure to the ear. There is a stateliness, a dignity of effect, which proves that the prose of the Authorised Version was no invention, but a growth. Though Adlington does not pretend to echo the locutions of

His Mastery of Phrase

Apuleius, he is, after his own method, a master of phrase. 'Girded with her beautiful skarfe of love'—is it not an exquisite idea? How more nearly or more adroitly would you turn *tamen nisi capillum distinxerit* than in these terms: 'if her hair be not curiously set forth'? If only the modern translator dared to represent *ementita lassitudo* by 'feigned 'and coloured weariness,' there were hope that his craft might rise above journey-work. Who would complain that the original was embroidered when it is to such admirable purpose as: 'Thus she cried and lamented, and after 'she had wearied herself with sorrow and blubbered her 'face with teares, she closed the windows of her hollow eyes, 'and laid her down to sleep.' Here is prose, ever vivid and alert, ever absolved from the suspicion of the stereotyped phrase. In Adlington's day 'good taste' had not banned freshness and eccentricity from the language. A century later it had been impossible to translate *glebosa camporum* into 'cloggy, fallowed fields'; yet this is Adlington's expression, and it may be matched or bettered on every

His Sustained Rhythm

page. Above all, his work is distinguished by that sustained nobility of rhythm which makes the Tudor prose the best of good reading. 'And while I considered these things, I

OF LUCIUS APULEIUS

'looked about, and behold I saw a farre off a shadowed
'valley adjoyning nigh unto a wood, where amongst divers
'other hearbes and pleasant verdures, me thought I saw
'divers flourishing Roses of bright damaske colour; and said
'within my beastiall mind, Verily that place is the place of
'Venus and the Graces, where secretly glistereth the royall
'hew, of so lively and delectable a floure': here are no exotic
words, no long-sought images; the rare effect is attained by
a harmony, which not even the sternest simplicity can impoverish. Or take a passage in another key: 'In the meane
'season while I was fed with dainty morsels, I gathered
'together my flesh, my skin waxed soft, my haire began to
'shine, and was gallant on every part, but such faire and
'comely shape of my body, was cause of my dishonour, for the
'Baker and Cooke marvelled to see me so slick and fine, con-
'sidering I did eat no hay at all.' True, the word 'slick'
(aptly suggested by *nitore*) is, so to say, a high light; but the
beauty still depends upon the rhythm, to which Adlington's
ear is ever attuned. In brief, whatever defects of scholarship and restraint mar the translation, it remains a model of
that large, untrammelled prose which, before the triumph of
common-sense, seemed within the reach of all. But is it not
the strangest paradox of literary history that they who lived
in the golden age of translation sought their original at
second hand, or fumbled for their meaning in the dark?

One advantage at least was enjoyed by Adlington. He
studied Apuleius in the native Latin, using, we may believe, the famous folio of 1500 (*cum Beroaldi commentariis*),
prefaced by that *Vita Lucii Apuleii summatim relata*, which
he paraphrased in English with his accustomed inaccuracy.

THE GOLDEN ASSE

INTRO- Howbeit, he did not 'so exactly pass through the author,
DUCTION ' as to point every sentence according as it is in Latine ':
for so, he adds, 'the French and Spanish translators have
' not done.' Nor is there any doubt that he attempted
to amend his ignorance of Latin by the aid of a French
version. It is some proof of the early popularity of *The
Golden Ass* that Spain, Italy, and France had each its
translation into the vulgar tongue, before Adlington under-
Two French took the work. In 1522 there appeared a tiny quarto
Versions bearing this legend upon its title-page : 'Lucius Apuleius
' de Lasne dore ... On les vend a Paris en la grand
' rue St. Jacques, Par Philippe le noir.' It was by one
Guillaume Michel; and though before the English translation was a-making there had appeared another version by
Georges de la Bouthiere (Lyons, 1553), adorned with cuts in
the manner of Bernard Salmon, the earlier book was a guide,
and too often a blind guide, unto Adlington's footsteps. The
Guillaume Frenchman, indeed, was the riper scholar, but not only did
Michel he indulge the tiresome habit of commenting by the way,
and without warning, upon his text, but he was also guilty
His Mislead- of the most ingenious blunders, which Adlington, as though
ing of Adling- his own errors were not sufficient, too readily followed. A
ton
comparison of the versions sets the matter beyond un-
certainty. If again and again the same inaccuracy glares in
English and French, it is obvious that the one was borrowed
from the other. At the very outset there is a clear clue.
Guillaume Michel, according to his habit of expansion,
paraphrases *hæc me suadente* in half a dozen lines ; and
Adlington,[1] turning his invigilant eye from the Latin, is

[1] P. 27.

OF LUCIUS APULEIUS

guilty of the like unwarranted prolixity. Moreover, when Apuleius by a quip says of Meroe, *sic reapse nomen ejus tunc fabulis Socratis convenire sentiebam*, you are puzzled by the ingenuity of Adlington's rendering[1]: 'being so named because 'she was a Taverner,' until you turn to the French and find in *tavernière* the source of error. Again, Diophanes, the magician in Milo's story, is consulted by a certain merchant, Cerdo by name. (The Latin is unmistakable: *Cerdo quidam nomine negotiator.*) Now, Adlington boldly translates 'a 'certaine Cobler,'[2] and instantly the Frenchman's *quelque savatier* explains the blunder. *Toutfoys mon cheval et lautre beste lasne de Milo ne me voulurent souffrir avec eulx paistre*: so Michel at the beginning of the Fourth Book. And thus Adlington: 'but myne own horse and Miloes Asse 'would not suffer me to feed there with them, but I must seeke 'my dinner in some other place.'[3] The renderings agree precisely in a gross inaccuracy, and the Latin—*nec me cum asino vel equo meo compascuus cœtus attinere potuit adhuc insolitum alioquin prandere fœnum*—is involved enough to explain Adlington's reliance upon the French. Another passage[4] is even more convincing. *Ad quandam villam possessoris beati perveniunt*, writes Apuleius, whom Adlington translates: 'we fortuned to come to one Britunis house'[4]; nor would it appear who this Britunis might be, unless you turned to Michel's French and read, *en aucun village chiez ung riche laboureur nomme Brulinus*. This strange correspondence in error might be enforced by countless examples. But by this it is evident that, although Adlington did not, like Angell Day, Sir Thomas North, George Nichols

[1] P. 28. [2] P. 49. [3] P. 83. [4] P. 114.

THE GOLDEN ASSE

INTRO-
DUCTION
(translator of Thucydides), render his author from the French openly and without shame, he consulted the French as well as the Latin, and fared rather the worse therefor.

Adlington the Man
If for a judgment of Adlington the writer there is ample material, of Adlington the man we know nothing more than he vouchsafes himself. That six editions appeared in some seventy years is proof of the book's popularity. But its only mention is in the Register of the Stationers' Company, where it figures 'In the enterynge of Coopyes' between the 22nd July 1565 and the 22nd July 1566—something earlier than the date of the dedication. 'Wekes. Recevyd of henry 'wekes,' thus it runs, 'for his lycense for pryntinge of a 'boke intituled the hole boke of lucious apelious of ye golden 'asse, viijd.' The epistle dedicatory to Thomas, Earle of Sussex, is dated 'from University College in Oxenford, the 'xviii. of September, 1566.'[1] But whether or no he was a graduate of that seat of learning is still uncertain. His name does not appear in the Register of the University, and in vain you consult the common sources of information. He presents his book to his patron in the customary terms of extravagant eulogy: 'The which if your honourable Lordship 'shall accept,' writes he of his Apuleius, 'and take in good 'part, I shall not only thinke my small travell and labour 'well employed, but shall also receive a further comfort to 'attempt some more serious matter.' If the serious matter were ever attempted, its very gravity has sunk it out of know-

---

[1] The first edition was 'imprinted at London in Fleet streate at the signe 'of the Oliphante by Henry Wykes, Anno 1566.' Other editions appeared in 1571, 1582 (the rarest), 1596, 1600, 1639.

OF LUCIUS APULEIUS

ledge: unless, indeed, he be the author of that very rare and exceeding obvious tract in verse, entitled, *A Speciall Remedie against the force of lawlesse Love*.[1] This was published in 1579, and ascribed upon the title-page to W. A. As the agreement of name and date is perfect, so also the tone of the preface corresponds precisely with Adlington's admonition to the reader of *The Golden Asse*. When the 'friendly Reader' of the *Speciall Remedie* is warned how 'like unto a beast love transformeth a man, during the which 'nothing can be exercised in minde, nothing by reason or 'study of minde can be done,' you are forthwith reminded of Adlington and of Lucius changed to an ass. The verses are properly forgotten, but by his own confession we know him subject to an invincible morality which, ill according with his century, drove him perchance to undertake this enterprise gloomy enough for oblivion. *Lector intende: lætaberis* —such is the bidding of Apuleius. And Adlington apologises that 'although the matter seeme very light and merry, 'yet the effect thereof tendeth to a good and vertuous moral,'[2] just as the author of the *Speciall Remedie* remarks with Plinie, 'there is no book so simple, but that therein is some-'what worthy the noating.' As though the Milesian Tale were judged, not by its pleasantry and delight, but by the quality of its moral sustenance! But Adlington was of

INTRO-
DUCTION

His Morality

His Love of Allegory

---

[1] The full title runs thus :—'A Speciall Remedie against the furious force 'of lawlesse Love. And also, a true description of the same. With other 'delightfull devices of daintie delightes to passe away idle time, with plea-'sure and profit. Newly compiled in English verse by W. A. Imprinted 'by Richard Ihones, and are to be sold at his shop over against S. 'Sepulchres Church without Newgate. 1579.' The tract, which is unique, was found in the Evidence Room in Northumberland House, and reprinted in 1844 by the Roxburghe Society. [2] P. 4.

THE GOLDEN ASSE

INTRO- those who would allegorise both mythology and romance.
DUCTION 'The fall of Icarus is an example to proud and arrogant
'persons, that weeneth to climbe up to the heavens'; and
further, he holds that 'by Mydas is carped the foul sin of
'Avarice.'[1] And, as if to excuse the translation of a 'meere
'jeast and fable,' he addresses to the reader a most solemn
homily, setting forth the example of Nebuchadnezzar and
upholding the efficacy of prayer. 'Verily under the wrap of
'this transformation is taxed the life of mortall men,' thus
he writes in the proper spirit of the divine; concluding that
'we can never bee restored to the right figure of our selves,
'except we taste and eat the sweet Rose of reason and vertue,
'which the rather by mediation of praier we may assuredly
'attaine.'[2] Nor is this the mere perversion of ingenuity.
His prudery is perfectly sincere. In many places he is inclined, by a modest suppression, to mitigate the gaiety of
the Apuleian narrative. But only once does he completely
sacrifice his author's effect to his own scruples; and the
restrained nobility of his prose more than atones for lack of
scholarship and a prudish habit of mind. The lapse of
three centuries has left his book as fresh and living as its
original, and withal as brave a piece of narrative as the
literature of his century has to show.

CHARLES WHIBLEY.

[1] P. 5.   [2] P. 9.

NOTE

This text is reprinted verbatim and literatim from the edition of 1639

THE XI. BOOKES OF
THE GOLDEN ASSE

CONTAINING

THE METAMORPHOSIE OF
LUCIUS APULEIUS

INTERLACED WITH SUNDRY PLEASANT AND
DELECTABLE TALES: WITH AN EXCELLENT
NARRATION OF THE MARRIAGE OF

CUPID AND PSYCHES

SET OUT IN THE FOURTH, FIFTH, AND
THE SIXTH BOOKES

TRANSLATED

OUT OF LATINE INTO ENGLISH, BY

WILLIAM ADLINGTON

To the Right Honourable and Mighty Lord,
THOMAS EARLE OF SUSSEX,
Viscount Fitzwalter, Lord of Egremont and of
Burnell, Knight of the most noble Order of the Garter,
Iustice of the forrests and Chases from Trent Southward;
Captain of the Gentlemen Pensioners of the House
of the QUEENE our Soveraigne Lady.

AFTER that I had taken upon me (right Honourable) in manner of that unlearned and foolish Poet Cherillus, who rashly and unadvisedly wrought a big volume in verses, of the valiant prowesse of Alexander the Great, to translate this present booke, contayning the Metamorphosis of Lucius Apuleius; being mooved thereunto by the right pleasant pastime and delectable matter therein: I eftsoones consulted with my selfe, to whome I might best offer so pleasant and worthy a work, devised by the Author, it being now barbarously

THE GOLDEN ASSE

THE EPISTLE DEDICATORY

and simply framed in our English tongue. And after long deliberation had, your honorable Lordship came to my remembrance, a man much more worthy, than to whom so homely and rude a translation should be presented. But when I again remembred the jesting and sportfull matter of the booké, unfit to be offered to any man of gravity and wisdome, I was wholly determined to make no Epistle Dedicatory at all: till as now of late perswaded thereunto by my friends, I have boldly enterprised to offer the same to your Lordship, who as I trust wil accept the same, than if it did entreat of some serious and lofty matter, considering that although the matter therein seeme very light and merry, yet the effect thereof tendeth to a good and vertuous moral, as in the following Epistle to the Reader may be declared. For so have all writers in times past employed their travell and labours, that their posterity might receive some fruitfull profit by the same. And therfore the Poets feined not their fables in vain, considering that children in time of their first studies, are very much allured thereby to proceed to more grave and deepe studies and disciplines, whereas otherwise their mindes would quickly loath the wise and prudent workes of learned men, wherein in such unripe years they take no sparke

OF LUCIUS APULEIUS

of delectation at all. And not only that profit ariseth to children by such feined fables, but also the vertues of men are covertly thereby commended, and their vices discommended and abhorred. For by the Fable of Actæon, where it is feigned that when he saw Diana washing her selfe in a Well, hee was immediately turned into an Hart, and so was slain of his owne Dogs; may bee meant, That when a man casteth his eyes on the vaine and soone fading beauty of the world, consenting thereto in his minde, hee seemeth to bee turned into a brute beast, and so to be slaine through the inordinate desire of his owne affects. By Tantalus that standeth in the midst of the floud Eridan, having before him a tree laden with pleasant apples, he beeing neverthelesse alwayes thirsty and hungry, betokeneth the insatiable desires of covetous persons. The fables of Atreus, Thiestes, Tereus and Progne signifieth the wicked and abhominable facts wrought and attempted by mortall men. The fall of Icarus is an example to proud and arrogant persons, that weeneth to climbe up to the heavens. By Mydas, who obtained of Bacchus, that all things which he touched might be gold, is carped the foul sin of Avarice. By Phaeton, that unskilfully took in hand to rule the Chariot of the Sunne, are repre-

THE GOLDEN ASSE

<small>THE EPISTLE DEDICATORY</small> sented those persons which attempt things passing their power and capacity. By Castor and Pollux, turned into a signe in heaven called Gemini, is signified, that vertuous and godly persons shall be rewarded after life with perpetuall blisse. And in this feined jest of Lucius Apuleius is comprehended a figure of mans life, ministring most sweet and delectable matter, to such as shall be desirous to reade the same. The which if your honourable Lordship shall accept and take in good part, I shall not onely thinke my small travell and labour well employed, but also receive a further comfort to attempt some more serious matter, which may be more acceptable to your Lordship: desiring the same to excuse my rash and bold enterprise at this time, as I nothing doubt of your Lordships goodnesse. To whome I beseech Almighty God to impart long life, with encrease of much honour.

From Vniversity Colledge in Oxenford, the xviij. of September, 1566.

Your Honours most bounden,

WIL. ADLINGTON.

OF LUCIUS APULEIUS

TO THE READER

HEN that I had (gentle Reader) slightly here and there runne over the pleasant and delectable jeasts of Lucius Apuleius (a man of antient descent, and endued with singular learning) written in such a franke and flourishing stile, as he seemed to have the Muses at his will, to feed and maintaine his pen. And when againe I perceived the matter to minister such exceeding plenty of mirth, as never in my judgement the like hath been shewed by any other, I purposed according to my slender knowledge (though it were rudely, and farre disagreeing from the fine and excellent doings now adayes) to translate the same into our vulgar tongue, to the end that amongst so many sage and serious works (as every man well nigh endeavour daily to encrease) there might bee some fresh and pleasant matter to recreate the mindes of the Readers withall. Howbeit I was eftsoones driven from my purpose by two causes: First, perceiving that the Author had written his work in so darke and high a stile, in so strange and absurd words, and in such new invented phrases, as hee seemed rather to set it forth to shew his magnificencie of prose, than to participate his doings to other. Secondly, fearing least the translation of this present Booke (which seemeth a meere jeast and fable, and a Worke worthy to be laughed at, by reason of the vanity of the Author) might be contemned and despised of all men, and so consequently I to be had in derision, to occupie my selfe in such frivolous and trifling toyes. But on the other side, when I had throughly learned the intent of the Author, and the pur-

THE GOLDEN ASSE

TO THE READER
pose why hee invented so sportfull a jest, I was verily perswaded that my small travell should not onely be accepted by many, but the matter it selfe allowed and praised of all. Wherefore I intend, God willing, as nigh as I can, to utter and open the meaning thereof, to the simple and ignorant, whereby they may not take the same, as a thing only to jest and laugh at (for the fables of Æsop and the feigning of Poets were never written for that purpose) but by the pleasantnesse thereof bee rather induced to the knowledge of their present estate, and thereby transforme themselves into the right and perfect shape of men. The argument of the book is, how Lucius Apuleius the Author himselfe travelled into Thessaly, being a region in Greece, where all the women for the most part bee such wonderfull Witches, that they can transforme men into the figure of brute beasts: Where after he had continued a few dayes, by the mighty force of a violent confection hee was changed into a miserable Asse, and nothing might reduce him to his wonted shape but the eating of a Rose, which after the indurance of infinite sorrow, at length he obtained by prayer. Verily under the wrap of this transformation is taxed the life of mortall men, when as we suffer our mindes so to bee drowned in the sensuall lusts of the flesh, and the beastly pleasure thereof (which aptly may be called the violent confection of Witches) that wee lose wholly the use of reason and vertue, which properly should be in man, and play the parts of brute and savage beasts. By like occasion we reade, how divers of the companions of Vlysses were turned by the marvellous power of Circe into swine. And finde we not in Scripture, that Nabuchadnezzar the ninth King of Babylon, by reason of his great dominions and realmes, fell into such exceeding pride, that he was suddenly transformed of Almighty God into an horrible monster, having the head of an Oxe, the feet of a Beare, and the taile of Lion, and did eat hay as a Beast. But as Lucius Apuleius was changed into his humane shape by a Rose, the companions of Vlysses by great intercession, and Nabuchadnezzar by the continual prayers of Daniel, wherby they knew themselves, and lived after a good and

OF LUCIUS APULEIUS

TO THE READER

vertuous life: so can we never bee restored to the right figure of our selves, except we taste and eat the sweet Rose of reason and vertue, which the rather by mediation of praier we may assuredly attaine. Againe, may not the meaning of this worke be altered and turned in this sort: A man desirous to apply his minde to some excellent art, or given to the study of any of the sciences, at the first appeareth to himselfe an asse without wit, without knowledge, and not much unlike a brute beast, till such time as by much paine and travell he hath atchieved to the perfectnesse of the same, and tasting the sweet floure and fruit of his studies, doth thinke himselfe well brought to the right and very shape of a man.

Finally, the metamorphosie of Lucius Apuleius may be resembled to youth without discretion, and his reduction to age possessed with wisedome and vertue.

Now since this booke of Lucius is a figure of mans life, and toucheth the nature and manners of mortall men, egging them forward from their Asinall forme, to their humane and perfect shape, beside the pleasant and delectable jests therein contained, I trust if my simple translation be nothing accepted, yet the matter it selfe shall be esteemed by such as not onely delight to please their fancies in reading the same, but also take a patterne thereby to regenerate their minds from brutish and beastly custome. Howbeit I have not so exactly passed through the Author, as to point every sentence according as it is in Latine, or so absolutely translated every word as it lieth in the prose, (for so the French and Spanish translators have not done) considering the same in our vulgar tongue would have appeared very obscure and darke, and thereby consequently loathsome to the Reader, but nothing erring as I trust from the true and naturall meaning of the Author, have used more common and familiar words, yet not so much as I might doe, for the plainer setting forth of the same.

But howsoever it be, gentle Reader, I pray thee take it in good part, considering that for thee I have taken this paine, to the intent that thou mayst read the same with pleasure.

LUCIUS APULEIUS

THE LIFE OF LUCIUS APULEIUS
BRIEFELY DESCRIBED

UCIUS APULEIUS *African, an excellent follower of Plato his sect, born in Madaura, a Countrey sometime inhabited by the Romans, and under the jurisdiction of Syphax, scituate and lying upon the borders of Numidia and Getulia, whereby he calleth himselfe halfe a Numidian and halfe a Getulian : and Sidonius named him the Platonian Madaurence : his father called Theseus had passed all offices of dignity in his countrey with much honour. His mother named Salvia was of such excellent vertue, that she passed all the Dames of her time, borne of an antient house, and descended from the noble Philosopher Plutarch, and Sextus his Nephew. His wife called Prudentila was endowed with as much vertue and riches as any woman might be. Hee himselfe was of an high and comely stature, gray eyed, his haire yellow, and a beautifull personage. He flourished in Carthage in the time of Iolianus Avitus and Cl. Maximus Proconsuls, where he spent his youth in learning the liberall Sciences, and much profited under his masters there, whereby not without cause hee calleth himselfe the Nource of Carthage, and the celestiall Muse and venerable mistresse of Africke. Soone after, at Athens (where in times past the well of all doctrine flourished) he tasted many of the cups of the Muses, he learned Poetry, Geometry, Musicke, Logicke, and the universall knowledge of Philosophy, and studied not in*

THE GOLDEN ASSE

THE LIFE OF LUCIUS APULEIUS

vaine the nine Muses, that is to say, the nine noble and royall disciplines.

Immediatly after he went to Rome, and studied there the Latine tongue, with such labour and continuall study, that he atchieved to great eloquence, and was knowne and approved to be excellently learned, whereby he might worthily be called Polyhistor, that is to say, one that knoweth much or many things.

And being thus no lesse endued with eloquence, than with singular learning, he wrote many books for them that should come after: whereof part by negligence of times be intercepted, and part now extant, doe sufficiently declare, with how much wisedome and doctrine hee flourished, and with how much vertue hee excelled amongst the rude and barbarous people. The like was Anacharsis amongst the most luskish Scythes. But amongst the Bookes of Lucius Apuleius, which are perished and prevented, howbeit greatly desired as now adayes, one was intituled Banquetting questions, another entreating of the nature of fish, another of the generation of beasts, another containing his Epigrams, and another called 'Hermagoras': but such as are now extant are the foure bookes named 'Floridorum,' wherein is contained a flourishing stile, and a savory kind of learning, which delighteth, holdeth, and rejoiceth the Reader marvellously; wherein you shall finde a great variety of things, as leaping one from another: One excellent and copious Oration, containing all the grace and vertue of the art Oratory, wherby he cleareth himselfe of the crime of art Magick, which was slanderously objected against him by his Adversaries, wherein is contained such force of eloquence and doctrine, as he seemeth to passe and excell himselfe. There is another booke of the god of the spirit of Socrates, whereof S. Augustine maketh mention in his booke of the definition of spirits, and description of men. Two other books of the opinion of Plato, wherein is briefely contained that which before was largely expressed. One booke of Cosmography, comprising many things of Aristotles Meteors. The Dialogue of Trismegistus, translated by him out of Greeke into Latine, so fine, that it rather seemeth with more eloquence turned into Latine, than it was before written in Greeke. But

OF LUCIUS APULEIUS

principally these eleven Bookes of the 'Golden Asse,' are enriched with such pleasant matter, with such excellency and variety of flourishing tales, that nothing may be more sweet and delectable, whereby worthily they may be intituled, The Bookes of the 'Golden Asse,' for the passing stile and matter therein. For what can be more acceptable than this Asse of Gold indeed. Howbeit there be many which would rather intitle it 'Metamorphosis,' that is to say, A transfiguration or transformation, by reason of the argument and matter therein.

THE LIFE OF LUCIUS APULEIUS

LUCIUS APULEIUS

THE PREFACE OF THE AUTHOR
TO HIS SONNE, FAUSTINUS
And unto the Readers of this Book

> *THAT I to thee some joyous jests*
>   *may shew in gentle glose,*
> *And frankly feed thy bended eares*
>   *with passing pleasant prose:*
> *So that thou daine in seemely sort*
>   *this wanton booke to view,*
> *That is set out and garnisht fine,*
>   *with written phrases new.*
> *I will declare how one by hap*
>   *his humane figure lost,*
> *And how in brutish formed shape*
>   *his loathed life he tost.*
> *And how he was in course of time*
>   *from such estate unfold,*
> *Who eftsoone turn'd to pristine shape,*
>   *his lot unlucky told.*

HAT and who he was attend a while, and you shall understand that it was even I, the writer of myne owne Metamorphosie and strange alteration of figure. Hymettus, Athens, Isthmia, Ephire, Tenaros, and Sparta, being fat and fertile soiles (as I pray you give credit to the bookes of more everlasting fame) be places where myne antient progeny and linage did sometime flourish : there I say, in Athens, when I was yong, I went first to schoole.

THE GOLDEN ASSE

THE PREFACE

Soone after (as a stranger) I arrived at Rome, whereas by great industry, and without instruction of any schoolemaster, I attained to the full perfection of the Latine tongue. Behold, I first crave and beg your pardon, lest I should happen to displease or offend any of you by the rude and rustick utterance of this strange and forrein language. And verily this new alteration of speech doth correspond to the enterprised matter wherof I purpose to entreat, I will set forth unto you a pleasant Grecian jeast. Whereunto gentle Reader if thou wilt give attendant care, it will minister unto thee such delectable matter as thou shalt be contented withall.

THE
FIRST BOOKE
of LUCIUS APULEIUS of
THE GOLDEN ASSE

THE FIRST BOOKE

THE FIRST CHAPTER

How Apuleius riding in Thessaly, fortuned to fall into company with two strangers, that reasoned together of the mighty power of Witches.

S I fortuned to take my voyage into Thessaly, about certaine affaires which I had to doe (for there myne auncestry by my mothers side inhabiteth, descended of the line of that most excellent person Plutarch, and of Sextus the Philosopher his Nephew, which is to us a great honour) and after that by much travell and great paine I had passed over the high mountaines and slipperie vallies, and had ridden through the cloggy fallowed fields ; perceiving that my horse did waxe somwhat slow, and to the intent likewise I might repose and strengthen my self (being weary with riding) I lighted off my horse, and wiping away the sweat from every part of his body, I unbrideled him, and walked him softly in my hand, to the end he might pisse, and ease himselfe of his wearinesse and travell : and while hee went grazing freshly in the field (casting his head sometimes aside, as a token of rejoycing and gladnesse) I perceived a little before me two companions riding, and so I overtaking them made the third. And while I listned to heare their communication, the one of them laughed and mocked his fellow, saying, Leave off I pray thee and speake no more, for

THE FIRST BOOKE

CHAPTER I
How Apuleius riding in Thessaly, fortuned to fall into company with two strangers, that reasoned together of the mighty power of Witches

I cannot abide to heare thee tell such absurd and incredible lies; which when I heard, I desired to heare some newes, and said, I pray you masters make me partaker of your talk, that am not so curious as desirous to know all your communication: so shall we shorten our journey, and easily passe this high hill before us, by merry and pleasant talke.

But he that laughed before at his fellow, said againe, Verily this tale is as true, as if a man would say that by sorcery and inchantment the floods might be inforced to run against their course, the seas to be immovable, the aire to lacke the blowing of windes, the Sunne to be restrayned from his naturall race, the Moone to purge his skimme upon herbes and trees to serve for sorceries: the starres to be pulled from heaven, the day to be darkned, and the darke night to continue still. Then I being more desirous to heare his talke than his companions, sayd, I pray you, that began to tell your tale even now, leave not off so, but tell the residue. And turning to the other I sayd, You perhappes that are of an obstinate minde and grosse eares, mocke and contemne those things which are reported for truth, know you not that it is accounted untrue by the depraved opinion of men, which either is rarely seene, seldome heard, or that passeth the capacitie of mans reason, which if it be more narrowly scanned, you shall not onely finde it evident and plaine, but also very easie to be brought to passe.

OF LUCIUS APULEIUS

THE SECOND CHAPTER
How Apuleius told to the strangers, what he saw a Iugler do in Athens.

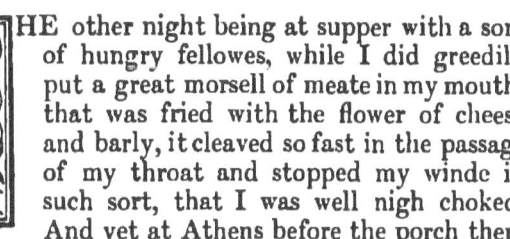HE other night being at supper with a sort of hungry fellowes, while I did greedily put a great morsell of meate in my mouth, that was fried with the flower of cheese and barly, it cleaved so fast in the passage of my throat and stopped my winde in such sort, that I was well nigh choked. And yet at Athens before the porch there called Peale, I saw with these eyes a Iugler that swallowed up a two hand sword, with a very keene edge, and by and by for a little money that we that looked on gave him, hee devoured a chasing speare with the point downeward. And after that hee had conveyed the whole speare within the closure of his body, and brought it out againe behind, there appeared on the top therof (which caused us all to marvell) a faire boy pleasant and nimble, winding and turning himselfe in such sort, that you would suppose he had neither bone nor gristle, and verily thinke that he were the naturall Serpent, creeping and sliding on the knotted staffe, which the god of Medicine is feigned to beare. But turning me to him that began his tale, I pray you (quoth I) follow your purpose, and I alone will give credit unto you, and for your paynes will pay your charges at the next Inne we come unto. To whom he answered, Certes sir I thanke you for your gentle offer, and at your request I wil proceed in my tale; but first I will sweare unto you by the light of this Sunne that shineth here, that those things that I shall tell be true, lest when you come to the next city called Thessaly, you should doubt any thing of that which is rife in the mouthes of every person, and done before the face of all men. And that I may first make relation unto you, what and who I am, and whither I go, and for what purpose, know ye that I am of Egin, travel-

THE FIRST BOOKE

CHAPTER II
How Apuleius told to the strangers, what he saw a Iugler do in Athens

ling these countries about from Thessaly to Etolia, and from Etolia to Boetia, to provide for honey, cheese, and other victuals to sell againe: and understanding that at Hippata (which is the principall city of all Thessaly) is accustomed to be sould new cheeses of exceeding good taste and relish, I fortuned on a day to goe thither, to make my market there: but as it often happeneth, I came in an evill houre; for one Lupus a Purveyor had bought and ingrossed up all the day before, and so I was deceived.

Wherefore towards night being very weary, I went to the Baines to refresh my selfe, and behold, I fortuned to espy my companion Socrates sitting upon the ground, covered with a torne and course mantle; who was so meigre and of so sallow and miserable a countenance, that I scantly knew him: for fortune had brought him into such estate and calamity, that he verily seemed as a common begger that standeth in the streets to crave the benevolence of the passers by. Towards whom (howbeit he was my singular friend and familiar acquaintance, yet halfe in despaire) I drew nigh and said, Alas my Socrates, what meaneth this? how fareth it with thee? What crime hast thou committed? verily there is great lamentation and weeping made for thee at home: Thy children are in ward by the decree of the Provinciall Iudge: Thy wife (having ended her mourning time in lamentable wise, with face and visage blubbered with teares, in such sort that she hath well nigh wept out both her eyes) is constrained by her parents to put out of remembrance the unfortunate losse and lacke of thee at home, and against her will to take a new husband. And dost thou live here as a ghost or hogge, to our great shame and ignominy?

Then answered he to me and said, O my friend Aristomenus, now perceive I well that you are ignorant of the whirling changes, the unstable forces, and slippery inconstancy of Fortune: and therewithall he covered his face (even then blushing for very shame) with his rugged mantle, insomuch that from his navel downwards he appeared all naked.

But I not willing to see him any longer in such great miserie and calamitie, took him by the hand and lifted him

OF LUCIUS APULEIUS

up from the ground: who having his face covered in such sort, Let Fortune (quoth he) triumph yet more, let her have her sway, and finish that which shee hath begun. And therewithall I put off one of my garments and covered him, and immediatly I brought him to the Baine, and caused him to be anointed, wiped, and the filthy scurfe of his body to be rubbed away; which done, although I were very weary my selfe, yet I led the poore miser to my Inne, where he reposed his body upon a bed, and then I brought him meat and drinke, and so wee talked together: for there we might be merry and laugh at our pleasure, and so we were, untill such time as he (fetching a pittifull sigh from the bottome of his heart, and beating his face in miserable sort) began to say.

CHAPTER II
How Apuleius told to the strangers, what he saw a Iugler do in Athens

THE THIRD CHAPTER

How Socrates in his returne from Macedony to Larissa, was spoyled and robbed, and how he fell acquainted with one Meroe a Witch.

LAS poore miser that I am, that for the onely desire to see a game of triall of weapons, am fallen into these miseries and wretched snares of misfortune. For in my returne from Macedonie, wheras I sould all my wares, and played the Merchant by the space of ten months, a little before that I came to Larissa, I turned out of the way, to view the scituation of the countrey there, and behold in the bottome of a deep valley I was suddenly environed with a company of theeves, who robbed and spoiled me of such things as I had, and yet would hardly suffer me to escape. But I beeing in such extremity, in the end was happily delivered from their hands, and so I fortuned to come to the house of an old woman that sold wine, called Meroe, who had her tongue sufficiently instructed to flattery: unto whom I opened the causes of my long peregrination

THE FIRST BOOKE

CHAPTER III

How Socrates in his returne from Macedony to Larissa, was spoyled and robbed, etc.

and carefull travell, and of myne unlucky adventure: and after that I had declared unto her such things as then presently came to my remembrance, shee gently entertained mee and made mee good cheere: and by and by beeing pricked by carnall desire, shee brought mee to her own bed chamber; whereas I poore miser the very first night of our lying together did purchase to my selfe this miserable face, and for her lodging I gave her such apparel as the theeves left to cover me withall.

Then I understanding the cause of his miserable estate, sayd unto him, In faith thou art worthy to sustaine the most extreame misery and calamity, which hast defiled and maculated thyne owne body, forsaken thy wife traiterously, and dishonoured thy children, parents, and friends, for the love of a vile harlot and old strumpet. When Socrates heard mee raile against Meroe in such sort, he held up his finger to mee, and as halfe abashed sayd, Peace peace I pray you, and looking about lest any body should heare, I pray you (quoth hee) take heed what you say against so venerable a woman as shee is, lest by your intemperate tongue you catch some harm. Then with resemblance of admiration, What (quoth I) is she so excellent a person as you name her to be? I pray you tell mee. Then answered hee, Verily shee is a Magitian, which hath power to rule the heavens, to bring downe the sky, to beare up the earth, to turne the waters into hills, and the hills into running waters, to lift up the terrestrial spirits into the aire, and to pull the gods out of the heavens, to extinguish the planets, and to lighten the deepe darkenesse of hell. Then sayd I unto Socrates, I pray thee leave off this high and mysticall kinde of talke, and tell the matter in a more plaine and simple fashion. Then answered he, Will you heare one or two, or moe of her facts which she hath done, for whereas she inforceth not onely the inhabitants of the countrey here, but also the Indians and the Ethiopians the one and the other, and also the Antictons, to love her in most raging sort, such are but trifles and chips of her occupation, but I pray you give eare, and I will declare of more greater matters, which shee hath done openly and before the face of all men.

OF LUCIUS APULEIUS

THE FOURTH CHAPTER
How Meroe the Witch turned divers persons into miserable beasts.

IN faith Aristomenus to tell you the truth, this woman had a certaine Lover, whom by the utterance of one only word she turned into a Bever, because he loved another woman beside her: and the reason why she transformed him into such a beast is, for that it is his nature, when hee perceiveth the hunters and hounds to draw after him, to bite off his members, and lay them in the way, that the hounds may be at a stop when they finde them, and to the intent it might so happen unto him (because he fancied another woman) she turned him into that kinde of shape.

Semblably she changed one of her neighbours, being an old man and one that sold wine, into a Frog, in that he was one of her occupation, and therefore she bare him a grudge, and now the poore miser swimming in one of his pipes of wine, and well nigh drowned in the dregs, doth cry and call with an hoarse voice, for his old guests and acquaintance that pass by. Likewise she turned one of the Advocates of the Court (because he pleaded and spake against her in a rightful cause) into a horned Ram, and now the poore Ram is become an Advocate. Moreover she caused, that the wife of a certain lover that she had should never be delivered of her childe, but according to the computation of all men, it is eight yeares past since the poore woman began first to swell, and now shee is encreased so big, that shee seemeth as though she would bring forth some great Elephant: which when it was knowne abroad, and published throughout all the towne, they tooke indignation against her, and ordayned that the next day shee should most cruelly be stoned to death. Which purpose of theirs she prevented by the

THE FIRST BOOKE

CHAPTER IV

How Meroe the Witch turned divers persons into miserable beasts

vertue of her inchantments, and as Medea (who obtained of King Creon but one days respit before her departure) did burne all his house, him, and his daughter: so she, by her conjurations and invocations of spirits (which she useth in a certaine hole in her house, as shee her selfe declared unto me the next day following) closed all the persons in the towne so sure in their houses, and with such violence of power, that for the space of two dayes they could not get forth, nor open their gates nor doore, nor break downe their walls, whereby they were inforced by mutuall consent to cry unto her, and to binde themselves strictly by oaths, that they would never afterwards molest or hurt her: and moreover, if any did offer her any injury they would be ready to defend her. Whereupon shee, mooved by their promises, and stirred by pitty, released all the towne. But shee conveyed the principal Author of this ordinance about midnight, with all his house, the walls, the ground, and the foundation, into another towne, distant from thence an hundred miles, scituate and beeing on the top of an high hill, and by reason thereof destitute of water, and because the edifices and houses were so nigh built together, that it was not possible for the house to stand there, she threw it downe before the gate of the towne. Then spake I and said, O my friend Socrates, you have declared unto me many marvellous things and strange chances, and moreover stricken me with no small trouble of minde, yea rather with great feare, lest the same old woman using the like practise, should fortune to heare all our communication. Wherefore let us now sleepe, and after that we have taken our rest, let us rise betimes in the morning, and ride away hence before day, as far as we can possible.

OF LUCIUS APULEIUS

THE FIFTH CHAPTER

How Socrates and Aristomenus slept together in one Chamber, and how they were handled by Witches.

IN speaking these words, and devising with my selfe of our departing the next morrow, lest Meroe the Witch should play by us as she had done by divers other persons, it fortuned that Socrates did fall asleepe, and slept very soundly, by reason of his travell, and plenty of meat and wine wherewithall hee had filled himselfe. Wherefore I closed and barred fast the doores of the chamber, and put my bed behinde the doore, and so layed mee downe to rest. But I could in no wise sleepe, for the great feare which was in my heart, untill it was about midnight, and then I began to slumber. But alas, behold suddenly the chamber doores brake open, and lockes, bolts, and posts fell downe, that you would verily have thought that some Theeves had beene presently come to have spoyled and robbed us. And my bed whereon I lay being a truckle bed, fashioned in forme of a Cradle, and one of the feet broken and rotten, by violence was turned upside downe, and I likewise was overwhelmed and covered lying in the same. Then perceived I in my selfe, that certaine affects of the minde by nature doth chance contrary. For as tears oftentimes trickle down the cheekes of him that seeth or heareth some joyfull newes, so I being in this fearefull perplexity, could not forbeare laughing, to see how of Aristomenus I was made like unto a snaile in his shell. And while I lay on the ground covered in this sort, I peeped under the bed to see what would happen. And behold there entred in two old women, the one bearing a burning torch, and the other a sponge and a naked sword: and so in this habit they stood about Socrates being fast asleepe. Then shee which

Feare and care keepe men waking.

THE FIRST BOOKE

CHAPTER V

How Socrates and Aristomenus slept together in one Chamber, and how they were handled by Witches

bare the sword sayd unto the other, Behold sister Panthia, this is my deare and sweet heart, which both day and night hath abused my wanton youthfulnesse. This is he, who little regarding my love, doth not onely defame me with reproachfull words, but also intendeth to run away. And I shall be forsaken by like craft as Vlysses did use, and shall continually bewaile my solitarinesse as Calipso. Which said, shee pointed towards mee that lay under the bed, and shewed me to Panthia. This is hee, quoth she, which is his Counsellor, and perswadeth him to forsake me, and now being at the point of death he lieth prostrate on the ground covered with his bed, and hath seene all our doings, and hopeth to escape scot-free from my hands, but I will cause that hee shall repent himselfe too late, nay rather forthwith, of his former untemperate language, and his present curiosity. Which words when I heard I fell into a cold sweat, and my heart trembled with feare, insomuch that the bed over me did likewise rattle and shake. Then spake Panthia unto Meroe and said, Sister let us by and by teare him in pieces, or tye him by the members, and so cut them off. Then Meroe (being so named because she was a Taverner, and loved wel good wines) answered, Nay rather let him live, and bury the corps of this poore wretch in some hole of the earth; and therewithall shee turned the head of Socrates on the other side, and thrust her sword up to the hilts into the left part of his necke, and received the bloud that gushed out, into a pot, that no drop thereof fell beside: which things I saw with myne owne eyes, and as I thinke to the intent she might alter nathing that pertained to sacrifice, which she accustomed to make, she thrust her hand downe into the intrals of his body, and searching about, at length brought forth the heart of my miserable companion Socrates, who having his throat cut in such sort, yeelded out a dolefull cry and gave up the ghost. Then Panthia stopped the wide wound of his throat with the Sponge, and said, O Sponge sprung and made of the sea, beware that thou passe not by running River. This being sayd, the one of them moved and turned up my bed, and then they strid over mee, and clapped their buttocks upon

Meroe, so called of Merum, which in English is strong wine untempered.

OF LUCIUS APULEIUS

my face, and all bepissed mee till I was wringing wet. When this was ended they went their wayes, and the doores closed fast, the posts stood in their old places, and the lockes and bolts were shut againe. But I that lay upon the ground like one without soule, naked and cold, and wringing wet with pisse, like to one that were more than halfe dead, and yet reviving my selfe, and appointed as I thought for the Gallowes, began to say, Alasse what shall become of me to morrow, when my companion shall be found murthered here in the chamber? To whom shall I seeme to tell any similitude of truth, when as I shall tell the trueth in deed? They will say, If thou wert unable to resist the violence of the women, yet shouldest thou have cried for helpe; Wouldst thou suffer the man to be slaine before thy face and say nothing? Or why did they not slay thee likewise? Why did they spare thee that stood by and saw them commit that horrible fact? Wherefore although thou hast escaped their hands, yet thou shalt not escape ours. While I pondered these things with my selfe the night passed on, and so I resolved to take my horse before day, and goe forward on my journy.

_{CHAPTER V}
_{How Socrates and Aristomenus slept together in one Chamber, and how they were handled by Witches}

Howbeit the wayes were unknowne unto me, and thereupon I tooke up my packet, unlocked and unberred the doors, but those good and faithfull doores which in the night did open of their owne accord, could then scantly be opened with their keyes. And when I was out I cried, O sirrah Hostler where art thou? open the stable doore, for I will ride away by and by. The Hostler lying behinde the stable doore upon a pallet, and halfe asleepe, What (quoth hee) doe you not know that the wayes be very dangerous? What meane you to rise at this time of night? If you perhaps guilty of some heynous crime, be weary of your life, yet thinke you not that wee are such Sots that we will die for you. Then said I, It is well nigh day, and moreover, what can Theeves take from him that hath nothing? Doest thou not know (Foole as thou art) if thou be naked, if ten Gyants should assaile thee, they could not spoyle or rob thee? Whereunto the drowsie Hostler halfe asleepe, and turning on the other side, answered, What know I whether you have murthered

_{The wayfaring man that hath no money may sing merrily before a theefe.}

THE FIRST BOOKE

CHAPTER V

How Socrates and Aristomenus slept together in one Chamber, and how they were handled by Witches

your Companion whom you brought in yesternight, or no, and now seeke the meanes to escape away ? O Lord, at that time I remember the earth seemed to open, and me thought I saw at hell gate the Dog Cerberus ready to devour mee ; and then I verily beleeved, that Meroe did not spare my throat, mooved with pitty, but rather cruelly pardoned mee to bring mee to the Gallowes. Wherefore I returned to my chamber, and there devised with my selfe in what sort I should finish my life. But when I saw that fortune would minister unto mee no other instrument, than that which my bed profered mee, I sayd, O bed, O bed, most dear unto me at this present, which hast abode and suffered with me so many miseries, judge and arbiter of such things as were done here this night, whome onely I may call to witnesse for my innocency, render (I say) unto me some wholsome weapon to end my life, that am most willing to dye. And therewithal I pulled out a piece of the rope wherewith the bed was corded, and tyed one end therof about a rafter by the window, and with the other end I made a sliding knot, and stood upon my bed, and so put my neck into it, and when I leaped from the bed, thinking verily to strangle my selfe and so dye, behold the rope beeing old and rotten burst in the middle, and I fell downe tumbling upon Socrates that lay under: And even at that same very time the Hostler came in crying with a loud voyce, and sayd, Where are you that made such hast at midnight, and now lies wallowing abed ? Whereupon (I know not whether it was by my fall, or by the great cry of the Hostler) Socrates as waking out of a sleepe, did rise up first and sayd, It is not without cause that strangers do speake evill of all such Hostlers, for this Caitife in his comming in, and with his crying out, I thinke under a colour to steale away somthing, hath waked me out of a sound sleepe. Then I rose up joyfull with a merry countenance, saying, Behold good Hostler, my friend, my companion and my brother, whom thou didst falsly affirme to be slaine by mee this night. And therewithall I embraced my friend Socrates and kissed him : but hee smelling the stinke of the pisse wherewith those Hagges had embrued me, thrust me away and sayd, Clense thy selfe from this

OF LUCIUS APULEIUS

CHAPTER V

How Socrates and Aristomenus slept together in one Chamber, and how they were handled by Witches

filthy odour, and then he began gently to enquire, how that noysome sent hapned unto mee. But I finely feigning and colouring the matter for the time, did breake off his talk, and tooke him by the hand and sayd, Why tarry we? Why lose wee the pleasure of this faire morning? Let us goe, and so I tooke up my packet, and payed the charges of the house and departed: and we had not gone a mile out of the Towne but it was broad day, and then I diligently looked upon Socrates throat, to see if I could espy the place where Meroe thrust in her sword: but when I could not perceive any such thing, I thought with my selfe, What a mad man am I, that being overcome with wine yester night, have dreamed such terrible things? Behold, I see Socrates is sound, safe, and in health. Where is his wound? where is the Sponge? Where is his great and new cut? And then I spake to him and sayd, Verily it is not without occasion, that Physitians of experience do affirme, That such as fill their gorges abundantly with meat and drinke, shall dreame of dire and horrible sights: for I my selfe, not tempering my appetite yester night from the pots of wine, did seeme to see this night strange and cruel visions, that even yet I think my self sprinkled and wet with human blood: whereunto Socrates laughing made answer and said, Nay, thou art not wet with the blood of men, but thou art imbrued with stinking pisse; and verily I my self dreamed this night that my throat was cut, and that I felt the paine of the wound, and that my heart was pulled out of my belly, and the remembrance thereof makes me now to feare, for my knees do so tremble that I can scarse goe any further, and therefore I would faine eat somewhat to strengthen and revive my spirits. Then said I, Behold here thy breakefast, and therwithall I opened my scrip that hanged upon my shoulder, and gave him bread and cheese, and we sate downe under a great Plane tree, and I eat part with him; and while I beheld him eating greedily, I perceived that he waxed meigre and pale, and that his lively colour faded away, insomuch that beeing in great fear, and remembring those terrible furies of whom I lately dreamed, the first morsell of bread that I put in my mouth (which was but very small) did so sticke in my jawes, that I

THE FIRST BOOKE

CHAPTER V

How Socrates and Aristomenus slept together in one Chamber, and how they were handled by Witches

could neither swallow it downe, nor yet yeeld it up, and moreover the small time of our being together increased my feare, and what is hee that seeing his companion die in the high-way before his face, would not greatly lament and bee sorry? But when that Socrates had eaten sufficiently hee waxed very thirsty, for indeed he had well nigh devoured all a whole Cheese: and behold evill fortune! there was behinde the Plane tree a pleasant running water as cleere as Crystal, and I sayd unto him, Come hither Socrates to this water and drinke thy fill. And then he rose and came to the River, and kneeled downe upon the side of the banke to drinke, but he had scarce touched the water with his lips, when as behold the wound of his throat opened wide, and the Sponge suddenly fell into the water, and after issued out a little remnant of bloud, and his body being then without life, had fallen into the river, had not I caught him by the leg and so pulled him up. And after that I had lamented a good space the death of my wretched companion, I buried him in the Sands there by the river.

Which done, in great feare I rode through many Outwayes and desart places, and as culpable of the death of Socrates, I forsooke my countrey, my wife, and my children, and came to Etolia where I married another Wife.

This tale told Aristomenus, and his fellow which before obstinatly would give no credit unto him, began to say, Verily there was never so foolish a tale, nor a more absurd lie told than this. And then he spake unto me saying, Ho sir, what you are I know not, but your habit and countenance declareth that you should be some honest Gentleman, (speaking to Apuleius) doe you beleeve this tale? Yea verily (quoth I) why not? For whatsoever the fates have appointed to men, that I beleeve shall happen. For many things chance unto me and unto you, and to divers others, which beeing declared unto the ignorant bee accounted as lies. But verily I give credit unto his tale, and render entire thankes unto him, in that by the pleasant relation thereof we have quickly passed and shortned our journey, and I thinke that my horse also

OF LUCIUS APULEIUS

was delighted with the same, and hath brought me to the gate of this city without any paine at all. Thus ended both our talke and journey, for they two turned on the left hand to the next villages, and I rode into the City.

CHAPTER V
How Socrates and Aristomenus slept together in one Chamber, and how they were handled by Witches

THE SIXTH CHAPTER

How Apuleius came to a city named Hipate, and was lodged in one Milos house, and brought him letters from Demea of Corinth.

AFTER that those two Companions were departed I entred into the City: where I espied an old woman, of whom I enquired whether that City were called Hipata, or no: Who answered, Yes. Then I demaunded, whether she knew one Milo an Alderman of the city: Wherat she laughed and sayd, Verily it is not without cause that Milo is called an Elderman, and accounted as chiefe of those which dwel without the walls of the City. To whom I sayd againe, I pray thee good mother doe not mocke, but tell me what manner of man he is, and where he dwelleth. Mary (quoth shee) doe you see those Bay windowes, which on the one side abut to the gates of the city, and on the other side to the next lane? There Milo dwelleth, very rich both in mony and substance, but by reason of his great avarice and insatiable covetousnes, he is evill spoken of, and he is a man that liveth all by usurie, and lending his money upon pledges. Moreover he dwelleth in a small house, and is ever counting his money, and hath a wife that is a companion of his extreame misery, neither keepeth he any more in his house than onely one maid, who goeth apparelled like unto a beggar. Which when I heard, I laughed in my selfe and thought, In faith my friend Demeas hath served me well, which hath sent me being a stranger, unto such a man, in whose house I shall not bee

THE FIRST BOOKE

CHAPTER VI

How Apuleius came to a city named Hipate, and was lodged in one Milos house, and brought him letters from Demea of Corinth

afeard either of smoke or of the sent of meat; and therewithall I rode to the doore, which was fast barred, and knocked aloud. Then there came forth a maid which sayd, Ho sirrah that knocks so fast, in what kinde of sort will you borrow money? Know you not that we use to take no gage, unlesse it be either plate or Jewels? To whom I answered, I pray thee maid speake more gently, and tel me whether thy master be within or no? Yes (quoth shee) that he is, why doe you aske? Mary (said I) I am come from Corinth, and have brought him letters from Demeas his friend. Then sayd the Maid, I pray you tarry here till I tell him so, and therewithall she closed fast the doore, and went in, and after a while she returned againe and sayd, My master desireth you to alight and come in. And so I did, whereas I found him sitting upon a little bed, going to supper, and his wife sate at his feet, but there was no meat upon the table, and so by appointment of the maid he came to him and saluted him, and delivered the letters which I had brought from Demeas. Which when hee had read hee sayd, Verily I thanke my friend Demeas much, in that hee hath sent unto mee so worthy a guest as you are. And therewithall he commanded his wife to sit away and bid mee sit in her place; which when I refused by reason of courtesie, hee pulled me by the garment and willed me to sit downe; for wee have (quoth he) no other stool here, nor no other great store of houshold stuffe, for fear of robbing. Then I according to his commandement, sate downe; and he fell in further communication with me and sayd, Verily I doe conjecture by the comly feature of your body, and by the maidenly shamefastnesse of your face, that you are a Gentleman borne, as my Friend Demeas hath no lesse declared the same in his letters. Wherfore I pray you take in good part our poore lodging, and behold yonder chamber is at your commaundement, use it as your owne, and if you be contented therewithall, you shal resemble and follow the vertuous qualities of your good father Theseus, who disdained not the slender and poore Cottage of Hecades.

And then he called his maid which was named Fotis, and said, Carry this gentlemans packet into the chamber, and

OF LUCIUS APULEIUS

lay it up safely, and bring water quickly to wash him, and a towel to rub him, and other things necessary, and then bring him to the next Baines, for I know that he is very weary of travell.

These things when I heard, I partly perceived the manners of Milo, and endeavoring to bring my selfe further into his favour, I sayd, Sir there is no need of any of these things, for they have been every where ministred unto mee by the way, howbeit I will go into the Baines, but my chiefest care is that my horse be well looked to, for hee brought mee hither roundly, and therefore I pray thee Fotis take this money and buy some hay and oats for him.

CHAPTER VI
How Apuleius came to a city named Hipate, and was lodged in one Milos house, and brought him letters from Demea of Corinth

THE SEVENTH CHAPTER

How Apuleius going to buy fish, met with his companion Pythias.

WHEN this was done, and all my things brought into the Chamber, I walked towards the Baines; but first I went to the market to buy some victuals for my supper, whereas I saw great plenty of fish set out to be sould: and so I cheapened part therof, and that which they first held at an hundred pence, I bought at length for twenty. Which when I had done, and was departing away, one of myne old acquaintance, and fellow at Athens, named Pithias, fortuned to passe by, and viewing me a good space, in the end brought me to his remembrance, and gently came and kissed mee, saying, O my deare friend Lucius, it is a great while past since we two saw each other, and moreover, from the time that wee departed from our Master Vestius, I never heard any newes from you. I pray you Lucius tell mee the cause of your peregrination hither. Then I answered and sayd, I will make relation therof unto you to morrow: But I pray you tell me, what

THE FIRST BOOKE

CHAPTER VII

How Apuleius going to buy fish, met with his companion Pythias

So used Magistrats to go somtimes in Rome.

meaneth these Servitors that follow you, and these rods or verges which they beare, and this habit which you wear like unto a Magistrate, verily I thinke you have obtained your own desire, whereof I am right glad. Then answered Pithias, I beare the office of the Clerke of the market, and therfore if you will have any pittance for your supper speake and I will purvey it for you. Then I thanked him heartily, and sayd I had bought meat sufficient already. But Pithias when hee espied my basket wherein my fish was, tooke it and shaked it, and demanded of me what I payd for all my Sprots. In faith (quoth I) I could scarse inforce the fishmonger to sell them for twenty pence. Which when he heard, he brought me backe again into the market, and enquired of me of whom I bought them. I shewed him the old man which sate in a corner, whome by and by, by reason of his office hee did greatly blame, and sayd, Is it thus that you serve and handle strangers, and specially our friends? Wherefore sell you this fish so deare, which is not worth a halfepenny? Now perceive I well, that you are an occasion to make this place, which is the principall city of all Thessaly, to be forsaken of all men, and to reduce it into an unhabitable Desart, by reason of your excessive prices of victuals, but assure your selfe that you shall not escape without punishment, and you shall know what myne office is, and how I ought to punish such as offend. Then he tooke my basket and cast the fish on the ground, and commaunded one of his Sergeants to tread them under his feet. This done he perswaded mee to depart, and sayd that that onely shame and reproach done unto the old Caitife did suffice him. So I went away all amazed and astonied, towards the Baines, considering with my selfe and devising of the grace of my companion Pithias. Where when I had well washed and refreshed my body, I returned againe to Milos house, both without money and meat, and so got into my chamber. Then came Fotis immediately unto mee, and said that her master desired me to come to supper. But I not ignorant of Milos abstinence, prayed that I might be pardoned, since as I thought best to ease my wearied bones rather with sleepe and quietnesse, than with meat. When

OF LUCIUS APULEIUS

Fotis had told this to Milo, he came himselfe and tooke mee by the hand, and while I did modestly excuse my selfe, I will not (quoth he) depart from this place, untill such time as you shall goe with me: and to confirme the same, hee bound his words with an oath, whereby he enforced me to follow him, and so he brought me into his chamber, where hee sate him downe upon the bed, and demaunded of mee how his friend Demeas did, his wife, and children, and all his family: and I made him answer to every question, specially hee enquired the causes of my peregrination and travell, which when I had declared, he yet busily demanded of the state of my Countrey, and of the chiefe magistrates there, and principally of our Lievtenant and Viceroy; who when he perceived that I was not only wearied by travell, but also with talke, and that I fell asleep in the midst of my tale, and further that I spake nothing directly or advisedly, he suffered me to depart to my chamber. So scaped I at length from the pratling and hungry supper of this rank old man, and beeing compelled by sleepe, and not by meat, and having supped only with talke, I returned into my chamber, and there betooke me to my quiet and long desired rest.

CHAPTER VII
How Apuleius going to buy fish, met with his companion Pythias

THE
SECOND BOOKE
of LUCIUS APULEIUS of
THE GOLDEN ASSE

THE SECOND BOOKE

THE EIGHTH CHAPTER
How Apuleius fortuned to meet with his Cousin Byrrhena.

AS soone as night was passed, and the day began to spring, I fortuned to awake, and rose out of my bed as halfe amazed, and very desirous to know and see some marvellous and strange things, remembring with my selfe that I was in the middle part of all Thessaly, whereas by the common report of all the World, the Sorceries and Inchauntments are most used, I oftentimes repeated with my self the tale of my companion Aristomenus touching the manner of this City, and being mooved by great desire, I viewed the whole scituation thereof, neither was there any thing which I saw there, that I did beleeve to be the same which it was indeed, but every thing seemed unto me to be transformed and altered into other shapes, by the wicked power of Sorcerie and Inchantment, insomuch that I thought the stones which I found were indurate, and turned from men into that figure, and that the birds which I heard chirping, and the trees without the walls of the city, and the running waters, were changed from men into such kinde of likenesses. And further I thought the Statues, Images, and Walls could goe, and the Oxen and other brute beasts, could speake and tell strange newes, and that immediately I should see and heare some Oracles from the heavens, and from the

THE SECOND BOOKE

CHAPTER VIII
How Apuleius fortuned to meet with his Cousin Byrrhena

gleed of the Sun. Thus being astonied or rather dismayed and vexed with desire, knowing no certaine place whither I intended to go, I went from street to street, and at length (as I curiously gazed on every thing) I fortuned unwares to come into the market place, whereas I espied a certaine woman, accompanied with a great many servants, towards whom I drew nigh, and viewed her garments beset with gold and pretious stone, in such sort that she seemed to be some noble matron. And there was an old man which followed her, who as soon as he had espied me, said to himselfe, Verily this is Lucius, and then he came and embraced me, and by and by he went unto his mistresse and whispered in her eare, and came to mee againe saying, How is it Lucius that you will not salute your deere Cousin and singular friend? To whom I answered, Sir I dare not be so bold as to take acquaintance of an unknowne woman.

Howbeit as halfe ashamed I drew towards her, and shee returned her selfe, and sayd, Behold how he resembleth the very same grace as his mother Salvia doth, behold his countenance and stature, agreeing thereto in each poynt, behold his comely state, his fine slendernesse, his Vermilion colour, his haire yellow by nature, his gray and quicke eyes like to the Eagle, and his trim and comely gate, which do sufficiently prove him to be the naturall childe of Salvia. And moreover she sayd, O Lucius, I have nourished thee with myne owne proper hand: and why not? For I am not onely of kindred unto thy mother by blood, but also by nourice, for wee both descended of the line of Plutarch, lay in one belly, sucked the same paps, and were brought up together in one house. And further there is no other difference beetweene us two, but that she is married more honourably than I: I am the same Byrrhena whom you have often heard named amongst your friends at home: wherfore I pray you to take so much pains as to come with me to my house, and use it as your owne. At whose words I was partly abashed and sayd, God forbid Cosin that I should forsake myne Host Milo without any reasonable cause; but verily I will, as often as I have occasion to passe by your house, come and see how you doe. And while we went talking thus together, by little and little wee

OF LUCIUS APULEIUS

CHAPTER VIII

How Apuleius fortuned to meet with his Cousin Byrrhena

came to her house, and behold the gates of the same were very beautifully set with pillars quadrangle wise, on the top wherof were placed carved statues and images, but principally the Goddesse of Victory was so lively and with such excellencie portrayed and set forth, that you would verily have thought that she had flyed, and hovered with her wings hither and thither. On the contrary part, the Image of the goddesse Diana was wrought in white marble, which was a marvellous sight to see, for shee seemed as though the winde did blow up her garments, and that she did encounter with them that came into the house. On each side of her were Dogs made of stone, that seemed to menace with their fiery eyes, their pricked eares, their bended nosethrils, and their grinning teeth, in such sort that you would have thought they had bayed and barked. And moreover (which was a greater marvel to behold) the excellent carver and deviser of this worke had fashioned the Dogs to stand up fiercely with their former feet, and their hinder feet on the ground ready to fight. Behinde the backe of the goddesse was carved a stone in manner of a Caverne, environed with mosse, hearbes, leaves, sprigs, green branches and bowes, growing in and about the same, insomuch that within the stone it glistered and shone marvellously, under the brim of the stone hanged apples and grapes carved finely, wherein Art envying Nature, shewed her great cunning. For they were so lively set out, that you would have thought if Summer had been come, they might have bin pulled and eaten; and while I beheld the running water, which seemed to spring and leap under the feet of the goddesse, I marked the grapes which hanged in the water, which were like in every point to the grapes of the vine, and seemed to move and stirre by the violence of the streame. Moreover, amongst the branches of the stone appeared the image of Acteon : and how that Diana (which was carved within the same stone, standing in the water) because he did see her naked, did turne him into an Hart, and so he was torne and slaine of his owne hounds. And while I was greatly delighted with the view of these things, Byrrhena spake to me and sayd, Cousin all things here be at your commandement. And therewithall she willed secretly

THE SECOND BOOKE

CHAPTER VIII

How Apuleius fortuned to meet with his Cousin Byrrhena

the residue to depart: who being gone she sayd, My most deare Cousin Lucius, I swear by this goddesse Diana, that I doe greatly tender your safety, and am as carefull for you as if you were myne owne naturall childe, beware I say, beware of the evil arts and wicked allurements of that Pamphiles who is the wife of Milo, whom you call your Host, for she is accounted the most chiefe and principall Magitian and Enchantresse living, who by breathing out certain words and charmes over bowes, stones, and other frivolous things, can throw down all the powers of the heavens into the deepe bottome of hell, and reduce all the whole world againe to the old Chaos. For as soone as shee espieth any comely yong man, shee is forthwith stricken with his love, and presently setteth her whole minde and affection on him. She soweth her seed of flattery, she invades his spirit and intangleth him with continuall snares of unmeasurable love.

And then if any accord not to her filthy desire, or if they seeme loathsome in her eye, by and by in the moment of an houre she either turneth them into stones, sheep, or some other beast, as her selfe pleaseth, and some she presently slayeth and murthereth, of whom I would you should earnestly beware. For she burneth continually, and you by reason of your tender age and comely beauty are capable of her fire and love.

This with great care Byrrhena gave me in charge, but I (that always coveted and desired, after that I had heard talk of such Sorceries and Witchcrafts, to be experienced in the same) little esteemed to beware of Pamphiles, but willingly determined to bestow my money in learning of that art, and now wholly to become a Witch. And so I waxed joyful, and wringing my selfe out of her company, as out of linkes or chaines, I bade her farewell, and departed toward the house of myne host Milo, by the way reasoning thus with my selfe: O Lucius now take heed, be vigilant, have a good care, for now thou hast time and place to satisfie thy desire, now shake off thy childishnesse, and shew thy selfe a man, but especially temper thy selfe from the love of thyne hostesse, and abstain from violation of the bed of Milo, but hardly

OF LUCIUS APULEIUS

attempt to winne the maiden Fotis, for she is beautifull, wanton, and pleasant in talke. And soone when thou goest to sleepe, and when shee bringeth thee gently into thy chamber, and tenderly layeth thee downe in thy bed, and lovingly covereth thee, and kisseth thee sweetly, and departeth unwillingly, and casteth her eyes oftentimes backe, and stands still, then hast thou a good occasion ministred unto thee to prove and try the minde of Fotis. Thus while I reasoned with my selfe I came to Milos doore, persevering still in my purpose, but I found neither Milo nor his wife at home.

CHAPTER VIII
How Apuleius fortuned to meet with his Cousin Byrrhena

THE NINTH CHAPTER

How Apuleius fell in love with Fotis.

HEN I was within the house I found my deare and sweet love Fotis mincing of meat and making pottage for her master and mistresse, the Cupboord was all set with wines, and I thought I smelled the savor of some dainty meats: she had about her middle a white and clean apron, and shee was girded about her body under the paps with a swathell of red silke, and she stirred the pot and turned the meat with her faire and white hands, in such sort that with stirring and turning the same, her loynes and hips did likewise move and shake, which was in my mind a comely sight to see.

These things when I saw I was halfe amazed, and stood musing with my selfe, and my courage came then upon mee, which before was scant. And I spake unto Fotis merrily and sayd, O Fotis how trimmely you can stirre the pot, and how finely, with shaking your buttockes, you can make pottage. O happy and twice happy is hee to whom you give leave and licence but to touch you there. Then shee beeing likewise merrily disposed, made answer, Depart I say, Miser from me, depart from my fire, for if the flame thereof doe

45

THE SECOND BOOKE

CHAPTER IX
How Apuleius fell in love with Fotis

never so little blaze forth it will burne thee extreamely, and none can extinguish the heate thereof but I alone, who in stirring the pot and making the bed can so finely shake my selfe. When she had sayd these words she cast her eyes upon mee and laughed, but I did not depart from thence until such time as I had viewed her in every point. But what should I speake of others, when as I doe accustome abroad to marke and view the face and haire of every dame, and afterwards delight my selfe therewith privately at home, and thereby judge the residue of their shape, because the face is the principall part of all the body, and is first open to our eyes. And whatsoever flourishing and gorgeous apparell doth worke and set forth in the corporal parts of a woman, the same doth the naturall and comely beauty set out in the face. Moreover there be divers, that to the intent to shew their grace and feature, wil cast off their partlets, collars, habiliments, fronts, cornets and krippins, and doe more delight to shew the fairenesse of their skinne, than to decke themselves up in gold and pretious stones. But because it is a crime unto me to say so, and to give no example thereof, know yee, that if you spoyle and cut off the haire of any woman, or deprive her of the colour of her face, though shee were never so excellent in beauty, though shee were throwne downe from heaven, sprung of the Seas, nourished of the flouds, though she were Venus her selfe, though shee were accompanied with the Graces, though shee were waited upon of all the Court of Cupid, though shee were girded with her beautifull skarfe of Love, and though shee smelled of perfumes and musks, yet if shee appeared bald, shee could in no wise please, no not her owne Vulcanus.

O how well doth a faire colour and a shining face agree with glittering hair! Behold, it encountreth with the beams of the Sunne, and pleaseth the eye marvellously. Sometimes the beauty of the haire resembleth the colour of gold and honey, sometimes the blew plumes and azured feathers about the neckes of Doves, especially when it is either anointed with the gumme of Arabia, or trimmely tuft out with the teeth of a fine combe, which if it be tyed up in the pole of the necke, it seemeth to the lover that beholdeth the same, as a

OF LUCIUS APULEIUS

CHAPTER IX
How Apuleius fell in love with Fotis

glasse that yeeldeth forth a more pleasant and gracious comelinesse than if it should be sparsed abroad on the shoulders of the woman, or hang downe scattering behind. Finally there is such a dignity in the haire, that whatsoever shee be, though she be never so bravely attyred with gold, silkes, pretious stones, and other rich and gorgeous ornaments, yet if her hair be not curiously set forth shee cannot seeme faire. But in my Fotis, her garments unbrast and unlaste increased her beauty, her haire hanged about her shoulders, and was dispersed abroad upon her partlet, and in every part of her necke, howbeit the greater part was trussed upon her pole with a lace. Then I unable to sustaine the broiling heate that I was in, ran upon her and kissed the place where she had thus laid her haire. Wherat she turned her face, and cast her rolling eyes upon me, saying, O Scholler, thou hast tasted now both hony and gall, take heed that thy pleasure do not turne into repentance. Tush (quoth I) my sweet heart, I am contented for such another kisse to be broiled here upon this fire, wherwithall I embraced and kissed her more often, and shee embraced and kissed me likewise, and moreover her breath smelled like Cinnamom, and the liquor of her tongue was like unto sweet Nectar, wherewith when my mind was greatly delighted I sayd, Behold Fotis I am yours, and shall presently dye unlesse you take pitty upon me. Which when I had said she eftsoone kissed me, and bid me be of good courage, and I will (quoth shee) satisfie your whole desire, and it shall be no longer delayed than until night, when as assure your selfe I will come and lie with you: wherfore go your wayes and prepare your selfe, for I intend valiantly and couragiously to encounter with you this night.
Thus when we had lovingly talked and reasoned together, we departed for that time.

THE SECOND BOOKE

THE TENTH CHAPTER

How Byrrhena sent victuals unto Apuleius, and how hee talked with Milo of Diophanes, and how he lay with Fotis.

HEN noone was come, Byrrhena sent unto me a fat Pigge, five hennes, and a flagon of old wine. Then I called Fotis and sayd, Behold how Bacchus the egger and stirrer of Venery, doth offer himself of his owne accord, let us therefore drink up this wine, that we may prepare our selves and get us courage against soone, for Venus wanteth no other provision than this, that the Lampe may be all the night replenished with oyle, and the cups with wine. The residue of the day I passed away at the Bains and in banquetting, and towards evening I went to supper, for I was bid by Milo, and so I sate downe at the table, out of Pamphiles sight as much as I could, being mindfull of the commandement of Byrrhena, and sometimes I would cast myne eyes upon her as upon the furies of hell, but I eftsoones turning my face behinde me, and beholding my Fotis ministring at the table, was again refreshed and made merry. And behold when Pamphiles did see the candle standing on the table, she said, Verily wee shall have much raine to morrow. Which when her husband did heare, he demanded of her by what reason she knew it? Mary (quoth shee) the light on the table sheweth the same. Then Milo laughed and said, Verily we nourish a Sybel prophesier, which by the view of a candle doth divine of Celestiall things, and of the Sunne it selfe. Then I mused in my minde and sayd unto Milo, Of truth it is a good experience and proofe of divination. Neither is it any marvell, for although this light is but a small light, and made by the hands of men, yet hath it a remembrance of that great and heavenly light, as of his parent, and doth shew unto us what

OF LUCIUS APULEIUS

will happen in the Skies above. For I knew at Corinth a certaine man of Assyria, who would give answers in every part of the City, and for the gaine of money would tell every man his fortune, to some he would tel the dayes of their marriages, to others hee would tell when they should build, that their edifices should continue. To others, when they should best goe about their affaires. To others, when they should go by sea or land: to me, purposing to take my journay hither, he declared many things strange and variable. For sometimes hee sayd that I should winne glory enough, sometimes he sayd I should write a great Historie: sometimes againe hee sayd that I should devise an incredible Tale: and sometimes that I should make Bookes. Whereat Milo laughed againe, and enquired of me, of what stature this man of Assyria was, and what he was named. In faith (quoth I) he is a tall man and somewhat blacke, and hee is called Diophanes. Then sayd Milo, the same is he and no other, who semblably hath declared many things here unto us, whereby hee got and obtained great substance and Treasure.

CHAPTER X

How Byrrhena sent victuals unto Apuleius, and how hee talked with Milo of Diophanes, etc.

But the poore miser fell at length into the hands of unpittifull and cruell fortune: For beeing on a day amongst a great assembly of people, to tell the simple sort their fortune, a certaine Cobler came unto him, and desired him to tel when it should be best for him to take his voyage, the which hee promised to do: the Cobler opened his purse and told a hundred pence to pay him for his paines. Whereupon came a certaine young gentleman and tooke Diophanes by the Garment. Then he turning himselfe, embraced and kissed him, and desired the Gentleman, who was one of his acquaintance, to sit downe by him: and Diophanes being astonied with this sudden chance, forgot what he was doing, and sayd, O deare friend you are heartily welcome, I pray you when arrived you into these parts? Then answered he, I will tell you soone, but brother I pray you tell mee of your comming from the Isle of Euboea, and how you sped by the way? Whereunto Diophanes this notable Assyrian (not yet come unto his minde, but halfe amased) soone answered and sayd, I would to God that all our enemies and

THE SECOND BOOKE

CHAPTER X

How Byrrhena sent victuals unto Apuleius, and how hee talked with Milo of Diophanes, etc.

evill willers might fall into the like dangerous peregrination and trouble. For the ship where we were in, after it was by the waves of the seas and by the great tempests tossed hither and thither, in great peril, and after that the mast and stern brake likewise in pieces, could in no wise be brought to shore, but sunk into the water, and so we did swim, and hardly escaped to land. And after that, whatsoever was given unto us in recompence of our losses, either by the pitty of strangers, or by the benevolence of our friends, was taken away from us by theeves, whose violence when my brother Arisuatus did assay to resist, hee was cruelly murthered by them before my face. These things when he had sadly declared, the Cobler tooke up his money againe which he had told out to pay for the telling of his fortune, and ran away. Then Diophanes comming to himselfe perceived what he had done, and we all that stood by laughed greatly. But that (quoth Milo) which Diophanes did tell unto you Lucius, that you should be happy and have a prosperous journey, was only true. Thus Milo reasoned with me. But I was not a little sorry that I had traind him into such a vaine of talke, that I lost a good part of the night, and the sweete pleasure thereof: but at length I boldly said to Milo, Let Diophanes fare well with his evill fortune, and get againe that which he lost by sea and land, for I verily do yet feel the wearinesse of my travell, wherefore I pray you pardon mee, and give me licence to depart to bed : wherewithall I rose up and went unto my chamber, where I found all things finely prepared, and the childrens bed (because they should not heare what we did in the night) was removed far off without the chamber doore. The table was all covered with those meats that were left at supper, the cups were filled halfe full with water, to temper and delay the wines, the flaggon stood ready prepared, and there lacked nothing that was necessary for the preparation of Venus. And when I was entring into the bed, behold my Fotis (who had brought her mistresse to bed) came in and gave me roses and floures which she had in her apron, and some she threw about the bed, and kissed mee sweetly, and tied a garland about my head, and bespred the chamber with the residue. Which

OF LUCIUS APULEIUS

CHAPTER X
How Byrrhena sent victuals unto Apuleius, and how hee talked with Milo of Diophanes, etc.

when shee had done, shee tooke a cup of wine and delaied it with hot water, and profered it me to drinke; and before I had drunk off all she pulled it from my mouth, and then gave it me againe, and in this manner we emptied the pot twice or thrice together. Thus when I had wel replenished my self with wine, and was now ready unto Venery not onely in minde but also in body, I removed my cloathes, and shewing to Fotis my great impatiencie I sayd, O my sweet heart take pitty upon me and helpe me, for as you see I am now prepared unto the battell, which you your selfe did appoint: for after that I felt the first Arrow of cruell Cupid within my breast, I bent my bow very strong, and now feare (because it is bended so hard) lest my string should breake: but that thou mayst the better please me, undresse thy haire and come and embrace mee lovingly: whereupon she made no long delay, but set aside all the meat and wine, and then she unapparelled her selfe, and unattyred her haire, presenting her amiable body unto me in manner of faire Venus, when shee goeth under the waves of the sea. Now (quoth shee) is come the houre of justing, now is come the time of warre, wherefore shew thy selfe like unto a man, for I will not retyre, I will not fly the field, see then thou bee valiant, see thou be couragious, since there is no time appointed when our skirmish shall cease. In saying these words she came to me to bed, and embraced me sweetly, and so wee passed all the night in pastime and pleasure, and never slept until it was day: but wee would eftsoones refresh our wearinesse, and provoke our pleasure, and renew our venery by drinking of wine. In which sort we pleasantly passed away many other nights following.

THE SECOND BOOKE

THE ELEVENTH CHAPTER

How Apuleius supped with Byrrhena, and what a strange tale Bellephoron told at the table.

IT fortuned on a day, that Byrrhena desired me earnestly to suppe with her; and shee would in no wise take any excusation. Whereupon I went unto Fotis, to aske counsell of her as some Divine, who although she was unwilling that I should depart one foot from her company, yet at length shee gave me license to bee absent for a while, saying, Beware that you tarry not long at supper there, for there is a rabblement of common Barrettors and disturbers of the publique peace, that rove about in the streets and murther all such as they may take, neither can law nor justice redresse them in any case. And they will the sooner set upon you, by reason of your comelinesse and audacity, in that you are not afeard at any time to walke in the streets.

Then I answered and sayd, Have no care of me Fotis, for I esteeme the pleasure which I have with thee, above the dainty meates that I eat abroad, and therefore I will returne againe quickly. Neverthelesse I minde not to come without company, for I have here my sword, wherby I hope to defend my selfe.

And so in this sort I went to supper, and behold I found at Byrrhena's house a great company of strangers, and of the chiefe and principall of the city: the beds made of Citron and Ivory, were richly adorned and spred with cloath of gold, the Cups were garnished pretiously, and there were divers other things of sundry fashion, but of like estimation and price: here stood a glasse gorgeously wrought, there stood another of Christall finely painted. There stood a cup of glittering silver, and here stood another of shining gold, and here was another of amber artificially carved and

OF LUCIUS APULEIUS

made with pretious stones. Finally, there was all things that might be desired : the Servitors waited orderly at the table in rich apparell, the pages arayed in silke robes, did fill great gemmes and pearles made in forme of Cups, with excellent wine. Then one brought in Candles and Torches, and when we were set downe and placed in order we began to talke, to laugh, and to be merry. And Byrrhena spake unto me and sayd, I pray you Cousine how like you our countrey? Verily I thinke there is no other City which hath the like Temples, Baynes, and other commodities which we have here. Further we have abundance of houshold stuffe, we have pleasure, we have ease, and when the Roman merchants arrive in this City they are gently and quietly entertained, and all that dwell within this province (when they purpose to solace and repose themselves) do come to this city. Whereunto I answered, Verily (quoth I) you tell truth, for I can finde no place in all the world which I like better than this, but · I greatly feare the blind inevitable trenches of witches, for they say that the dead bodies are digged out of their graves, and the bones of them that are burnt be stollen away, and the toes and fingers of such as are slaine be cut off, and afflict and torment such as live. And the old Witches as soone as they heare of the death of any person, do forthwith goe and uncover the hearse and spoyle the corpse, to worke their inchantments. Then another sitting at the table spake and sayd, In faith you say true, neither yet do they spare or favor the living. For I know one not farre hence that was cruelly handled by them, who being not contented with cutting off his nose, did likewise cut off his ears, whereat all the people laughed heartily, and looked upon one that sate at the boords end, who being amased at their gazing, and somewhat angry withall, would have risen from the Table, had not Byrrhena spake unto him and sayd, I pray thee friend Bellepheron sit still, and according to thy accustomed curtesie declare unto us the losse of thy nose and eares, to the end that my cousin Lucius may be delighted with the pleasantnes of the tale. To whom he answered, Madam you in the office of your bounty shall prevaile heerein, but the insolencie of some is not to be

CHAPTER XI

How Apuleius supped with Byrrhena, and what a strange tale Bellepheron told at the table

THE SECOND BOOKE

CHAPTER XI

How Apuleius supped with Byrrhena, and what a strange tale Bellephoron told at the table

supported. This hee spake very angerly: But Byrrhena was earnest upon him, and assured him hee should have no wrong at any mans hand. Whereby he was inforced to declare the same, and so lapping up the end of the Table cloath and carpet together, hee leaned with his elbow thereon, and held out the three forefingers of his right hand in manner of an Orator, and sayd, When I was a young man I went unto a certaine city called Milet, to see the games and triumphs there named Olympia, and being desirous to come into this famous province, after that I had travelled over all Thessaly, I fortuned in an evill houre to come to the City Larissa, where while I went up and down to view the streets to seeke some reliefe for my poore estate (for I had spent all my money) I espied a tall old man standing upon a stone in the middest of the market place, crying with a loud voice and saying, That if any man would watch a dead corps that night hee should bee reasonably rewarded for his paines. Which when I heard, I sayd to one that passed by, What is here to doe? Doe dead men use to run away in this Countrey? Then answered he, Hold your peace, for you are but a Babe and a stranger here, and not without cause you are ignorant how you are in Thessaly, where the women Witches do bite off by morsels the flesh of the faces of dead men, and thereby worke their sorceries and inchantments. Then quoth I, In good fellowship tell me the order of this custody, and how it is. Marry (quoth he) first you must watch all the night, with your eyes bent continually upon the Corps, never looking off, nor moving aside. For these Witches doe turn themselves into sundry kindes of beasts, whereby they deceive the eyes of all men, sometimes they are transformed into birds, somtimes into Dogs and Mice, and sometimes into flies. Moreover, they will charme the keepers of the corps asleepe, neither can it be declared what meanes and shifts these wicked women do use, to bring their purpose to passe: and the reward for such dangerous watching is no more than foure or sixe shillings. But hearken further (which I had well nigh forgotten) if the keeper of the dead body doe not render on the morning following, the corps whole and sound as he received the same, he shall be

OF LUCIUS APULEIUS

CHAPTER XI

How Apuleius supped with Byrrhena, and what a strange tale Bellephoron told at the table

punished in this sort: That is, if the corps bee diminished or spoyled in any part of his face, hands or toes, the same shall be diminished and spoyled in the keeper. Which when I heard I tooke a good heart, and went unto the Crier and bid him cease, for I would take the matter in hand, and so I demanded what I should have. Marry (quoth he) a thousand pence: but beware I say young man, that you do wel defend the dead corps from the wicked witches, for hee was the son of one of the chiefest of the city. Tush (sayd I) you speake you cannot tell what, behold I am a man made all of iron, and have never desire to sleepe, and am more quicke of sight than Lynx or Argus. I had scarse spoken these words, when he tooke me by the hand and brought mee to a certaine house, the gate whereof was closed fast, so that I went through the wicket, then he brought me into a chamber somewhat darke, and shewed me a Matron cloathed in mourning vesture, and weeping in lamentable wise. And he spake unto her and said, Behold here is one that will enterprise to watch the corpes of your husband this night. Which when she heard she turned her blubbered face covered with haire unto me, saying, I pray you young man take good heed, and see well to your office. Have no care (quoth I) so you will give mee any thing above that which is due to be given. Wherewith shee was contented, and then she arose and brought me into a chamber whereas the corps lay covered with white sheets, and shee called seven witnesses, before whom she shewed the dead body, and every part and parcell thereof, and with weeping eyes desired them all to testifie the matter. Which done, shee sayd these words of course as follow: Behold, his nose is whole, his eyes safe, his eares without scarre, his lips untouched, and his chin sound: All which was written and noted in tables, and subscribed with the hands of witnesses to confirme the same. Which done I sayd unto the Matron, Madam I pray you that I may have all things here necessary. What is that? (quoth she). Marry (quoth I) a great lampe with oyle, pots of wine, and water to delay the same, and some other drinke and dainty dish that was left at supper. Then she shaked her head and sayd, Away foole as thou art, thinkest

THE SECOND BOOKE

CHAPTER XI
How Apuleius supped with Byrrhena, and what a strange tale Bellephoron told at the table

thou to play the glutton here, and to looke for dainty meats where so long time hath not been seene any smoke at all? Commest thou hither to eat, where we should weepe and lament? And therewithall she turned backe, and commanded her maiden Myrrhena to deliver me a lampe with oyle, which when shee had done they closed the chamber doore and departed. Now when I was alone, I rubbed myne eyes, and armed my selfe to keep the corpes, and to the intent I would not sleepe, I began to sing, and so I passed the time till it was midnight, when as behold there crept in a Wesel into the chamber, and she came against me and put me in very great feare, insomuch that I marvelled greatly at the audacity of so little a beast. To whom I sayd, Get thee hence thou whore and high thee to thy fellowes, lest thou feele my fingers. Why wilt thou not go? Then incontinently she ranne away, and when she was gon, I fell on the ground so fast asleepe, that Apollo himself could not discerne whether of us two was the dead corps, for I lay prostrat as one without life, and needed a keeper likewise. At length the cockes began to crow, declaring that it was day: wherewithall I awaked, and being greatly afeard, ran to the dead body with the lamp in my hand, and I viewed him round about: and immediatly came in the Matron weeping with her Witnesses, and ran to the corps, and eftsoons kissing him, turned his body and found no part diminished. Then she willed Philodespotus her steward to pay me my wages forthwith. Which when he had done he sayd, We thanke you gentle young man for your paines, and verily for your diligence herein wee wil account you as one of the family. Whereunto I (being joyous of my unhoped gaine, and ratling my money in my hand) did answer, I pray you Madam esteeme me as one of your Servants, and if you want my service at any time, I am at your commandement. I had not fully declared these words, when as behold all the servants of the house were assembled with weapons to drive me away, one buffeted me about the face, another about the shoulders, some strook me in the sides, some kicked me, and some tare my garments, and so I was handled amongst them and driven from the house, as the proud young man Adonis who was torne by

OF LUCIUS APULEIUS

a Bore. And when I was come into the next street, I mused with my selfe, and remembred myne unwise and unadvised words which I had spoken, whereby I considered that I had deserved much more punishment, and that I was worthily beaten for my folly. And by and by the corps came forth, which because it was the body of one of the chiefe of the city, was carried in funeral pompe round about the market place, according to the right of the Countrey there. And forthwith stepped out an old man weeping and lamenting, and ranne unto the Biere and embraced it, and with deepe sighes and sobs cried out in this sort, O masters, I pray you by the faith which you professe, and by the duty which you owe unto the weale publique, take pitty and mercy upon this dead corps, who is miserably murdered, and doe vengeance on this wicked and cursed woman his wife which hath committed this fact: for it is shee and no other which hath poysoned her husband my sisters sonne, to the intent to maintaine her whoredome, and to get his heritage. In this sort the old man complained before the face of all people. Then they (astonied at these sayings, and because the thing seemed to be true) cried out, Burne her, burne her, and they sought for stones to throw at her, and willed the boyes in the street to doe the same. But shee weeping in lamentable wise, did sweare by all the gods, that shee was not culpable of this crime. No quoth the old man, here is one sent by the providence of God to try out the matter, even Zachlas an Egyptian, who is the most principall Prophecier in all this countrey, and who was hired of me for money to reduce the soule of this man from hell, and to revive his body for the triall hereof. And therewithall he brought forth a certain young man cloathed in linnen rayment, having on his feet a paire of pantofiles, and his crowne shaven, who kissed his hands and knees, saying, O priest have mercy, have mercy I pray thee by the Celestiall Planets, by the Powers infernall, by the vertue of the naturall clements, by the silences of the night, by the buildings of Swallows nigh unto the towne Copton, by the increase of the floud Nilus, by the secret mysteries of Memphis, and by the instruments and trumpets of the Isle Pharos, have mercy I say, and call againe to life this dead

CHAPTER XI

How Apuleius supped with Byrrhena, and what a strange tale Bellepheron told at the table

THE SECOND BOOKE

CHAPTER XI

How Apuleius supped with Byrrhena, and what a strange tale Bellephoron told at the table

body, and make that his eyes which be closed and shut, may be open and see. Howbeit we meane not to strive against the law of death, neither intend wee to deprive the earth of his right, but to the end this fact may be knowne, we crave but a small time and space of life. Whereat this Prophet was mooved, and tooke a certaine herbe and layd it three times upon the mouth of the dead, and he took another and laid it upon his breast in like sort. Thus when hee had done hee turned himselfe into the East, and made certaine Orisons unto the Sunne, which caused all the people to marvell greatly, and to looke for this strange miracle that should happen. Then I pressed in amongst them nigh unto the biere, and got upon a stone to see this mysterie, and behold incontinently the dead body began to receive spirit, his principall veines did moove, his life came again, and he held up his head and spake in this sort: Why doe you call mee backe againe to this transitorie life, that have already tasted of the water of Lethe, and likewise beene in the deadly den of Styx? Leave off I pray, leave off, and let me lie in quiet rest. When these words were uttered by the dead corps, the Prophet drew nigh unto the Biere and sayd, I charge thee to tell before the face of all the people here, the occasion of thy death: What, dost thou thinke that I cannot by my conjurations call up the dead, and by my puissance torment thy body? Then the corps moved his head again, and made reverence unto the people, and sayd, Verily I was poysoned by the meanes of my wicked wife, and so thereby yeelded my bed unto an adulterer. Whereat his wife taking present audacity, and reproving his sayings, with a cursed minde did deny it. The people were bent against her sundry wayes, some thought best that shee should bee buried alive with her husband: but some said that there ought no credit to be given to the dead body. Which opinion was cleane taken away, by the words which the corps spake againe and sayd, Behold, I will give you some evident token, which never yet any other man knew, whereby you shall perceive that I declare the truth: and by and by he pointed towards me that stood on the stone, and sayd, When this the good Gardian of my body watched me diligently in the night, and that the wicked

OF LUCIUS APULEIUS

Witches and Enchantresses came into the chamber to spoyle mee of my limbes, and to bring such their purpose to passe did transforme themselves into the shape of beasts; and when as they could in no wise deceive or beguile his vigilant eyes, they cast him into so dead and sound a sleepe, that by their witchcraft he seemed without spirit or life. After this they called me by my name, and did never cease til as the cold members of my body began by little and little and little to revive. Then he being of more lively soule, howbeit buried in sleep, in that he and I were named by one name, and because he knew not that they called me, rose up first, and as one without sence or perseverance passed by the dore fast closed, unto a certain hole, whereas the Witches cut off first his nose, and then his ears, and so that was done to him which was appointed to be done to me. And that such their subtilty might not be perceived, they made him a like paire of eares and nose of wax: wherfore you may see that the poore miser for lucre of a little mony sustained losse of his members. Which when he had sayd I was greatly astonied, and minding to prove whether his words were true or no, put my hand to my nose, and my nose fell off, and put my hand to my ears and my ears fell off. Wherat all the people wondred greatly, and laughed me to scorne: but I beeing strucken in a cold sweat, crept between their legs for shame and escaped away. So I disfigured returned home againe, and covered the losse of myne ears with my long hair, and glewed this clout to my face to hide my shame. As soon as Telephoron had tolde his tale, they which sate at the table replenished with wine, laughed heartily. And while they drank one to another, Birrhena spake to me and said, From the first foundation of this city we have a custome to celebrate the festivall day of the god Risus, and to-morrow is the feast, when as I pray you to bee present, to set out the same more honourably, and I would with all my heart that you could find or devise somewhat of your selfe, that might be in honor of so great a god. To whom I answered, Verily cousin I will do as you command me, and right glad would I be, if I might invent any laughing or merry matter to please or satisfie Risus withall. Then I rose from the table

CHAPTER XI

How Apuleius supped with Byrrhena, and what a strange tale Bellephoron told at the table

THE SECOND BOOKE

CHAPTER XI

How Apuleius supped with Byrrhena, and what a strange tale Bellepheron told at the table

and took leave of Byrrhena and departed. And when I came into the first street my torch went out, that with great pain I could scarse get home, by reason it was so dark, for fear of stumbling: and when I was wel nigh come unto the dore, behold I saw three men of great stature, heaving and lifting at Milo's gates to get in: and when they saw me they were nothing afeard, but assaied with more force to breake down the dores, whereby they gave me occasion, and not without cause, to thinke that they were strong theeves. Whereupon I by and by drew out my sword, which I carried for that purpose under my cloak, and ran in amongst them, and wounded them in such sort that they fell downe dead before my face. Thus when I had slaine them all, I knocked sweating and breathing at the doore til Fotis let me in. And then full weary with the slaughter of those Theeves, like Hercules when he fought against the king Gerion, I went to my chamber and layd me down to sleep.

THE
THIRD BOOKE
of LUCIUS APULEIUS of
THE GOLDEN ASSE

THE THIRD BOOKE

THE TWELFTH CHAPTER
How Apuleius was taken and put in prison for murther.

WHEN morning was come, and that I was awaked from sleep, my heart burned sore with remembrance of the murther which I had committed the night before: and I rose and sate downe on the side of the bed with my legges acrosse, and wringing my hands, I weeped in most miserable sort. For I imagined with my selfe, that I was brought before the Judge in the Judgment place, and that he awarded sentence against me, and that the hangman was ready to leade me to the gallows. And further I imagined and sayd, Alasse what Judge is he that is so gentle or benigne, that will thinke that I am unguilty of the slaughter and murther of these three men. Howbeit the Assyrian Diophanes did firmely assure unto me, that my peregrination and voyage hither should be prosperous. But while I did thus unfold my sorrowes, and greatly bewail my fortune, behold I heard a great noyse and cry at the dore, and in came the magistrates and Officers, who commanded two Sergeants to binde and leade me to prison. Whereunto I was willingly obedient, and as they led me through the street, all the City gathered together and followed me, and although I looked alwayes on the ground for very shame, yet sometimes I cast my head aside, and marvelled greatly, that among so many

THE THIRD BOOKE

CHAPTER XII
How Apuleius was taken and put in prison for murther

thousand people there was not one but laughed exceedingly. Finally, when they had brought me through all the streets of the city, in manner of those that go in procession, and do sacrifice to mitigate the ire of the gods, they placed mee in the Judgement hall, before the seat of the Judges: and after that the Crier had commanded all men to keepe silence, the people desired the Judges to give sentence in the great Theatre, by reason of the great multitude that was there, whereby they were in danger of stifling. And behold the prease of people increased stil, some climed to the top of the house, some got upon the beames, some upon the Images, and some thrust their heads through the windowes, little regarding the dangers they were in, so they might see me.

Then the officers brought mee forth openly into the middle of the hall, that every man might behold me. And after that the Crier had made a noyse, and willed all such as would bring any evidence against me, should come forth, there stept out an old man with a glasse of water in his hand, dropping out softly, who desired that hee might have liberty to speake during the time of the continuance of the water. Which when it was granted, he began his oration in this sort.

THE THIRTEENTH CHAPTER

How Apuleius was accused by an old man, and how hee answered for himselfe.

MOST reverend and just Judges, the thing which I purpose to declare unto you is no small matter, but toucheth the estate and tranquility of this whole City, and the punishment thereof may be a right good example to others. Wherefore I pray you most venerable Fathers, to whom and to every of whom it doth appertain, to provide for the dignity and safety of the Commonweale, that

OF LUCIUS APULEIUS

you would in no wise suffer this wicked Homicide, embrued with the bloud of so many murthered citisens, to escape unpunished. And thinke you not that I am moved hereunto by envy or hatred, but by reason of my office, in that I am captain of the night Watch, and because no man alive should accuse mee to bee remisse in the same, I wil declare all the whole matter, orderly as it was done this last night.

CHAPTER XIII
How Apuleius was accused by an old man, and how hee answered for himselfe

This night past, when as at our accustomed houre I diligently searched every part of the city, Behold, I fortuned to espy this cruell young man drawing out his sword against three Citisens, and after a long combat foughten betweene them, he murthered one after another miserably: which when he had done, moved in his conscience at so great a crime hee ran away, and aided by reason of darknes, slipt into a house, and there lay hidden all night, but by the providence of the Gods, which suffereth no heynous offence to passe unpunished, hee was taken by us this morning before he escaped any further, and so brought hither to your honourable presence to receive his desert accordingly.

So have you here a guilty person, a culpable homicide, and an accused stranger, wherefore pronounce yee judgement against this man beeing an alien, when as you would most severely and sharply revenge such an offence found in a known Citisen. In this sort the cruell accuser finished and ended his terrible tale. Then the Crier commanded me to speake, if I had any thing to say for my selfe, but I could in no wise utter any word at all for weeping. And on the other side I esteemed not so much his rigorous accusation, as I did consider myne owne miserable conscience. Howbeit, beeing inspired by divine audacity, at length I gan say, Verily I know that it is an hard thing for him that is accused to have slaine three persons, to perswade you that he is not innocent, although he should declare the whole truth, and confesse the matter how it was indeed, but if your honours will vouchsafe to give me audience, I will shew you, that if I bee condemned to die, I have not deserved it as myne owne desert, but that I was mooved by fortune and reasonable cause to doe that fact. For returning somewhat late from supper yester night (beeing well tipled with wine, which I will not deny) and

I 65

THE THIRD BOOKE

CHAPTER XIII
How Apuleius was accused by an old man, and how hee answered for himselfe

approching nigh to my common lodging, which was in the house of one Milo a Citisen of this city, I fortuned to espy three great theeves attempting to break down his walls and gates, and to open the locks to enter in. And when they had removed the dores out of the hookes, they consulted amongst themselves, how they would handle such as they found in the house. And one of them being of more courage, and of greater stature than the rest, spake unto his fellows and sayd, Tush you are but boyes, take mens hearts unto you, and let us enter into every part of the house, and such as we finde asleep let us kill, and so by that meanes we shall escape without danger. Verily ye Judges, I confesse that I drew out my sword against those three Citizens, but I thought it was the office and duty of one that beareth good will to this weale publique, so to doe, especially since they put me in great fear, and assayed to rob and spoyl my friend Milo. But when those cruell and terrible men would in no case run away, nor feare my naked sword, but boldly resist against me, I ran upon them and fought valiantly. One of them which was the Captaine invaded me strongly, and drew me by the haire with both his hands, and began to beat me with a great stone: but in the end I proved the hardier man, and threw him downe at my feet and killed him. I tooke likewise the second that clasped about my legs and bit me, and slew him also. And the third that came running violently against me, after that I had strucken him under the stomacke fell downe dead. Thus when I had delivered my selfe, the house, myne Hoste, and all his family from this present danger, I thought that I should not onely escape unpunished, but also have some great reward of the city for my paines.

Moreover, I that have alwayes beene cleare and unspotted of crime, and that have esteemed myne innocency above all the treasure of the world, can finde no reasonable cause why upon myne accusation I should be condemned to die, since first I was mooved to set upon the theeves by just occasion. Secondly, because there is none that can affirme, that there hath been at any time either grudge or hatred between us. Thirdly, we were men meere strangers, and of no acquaint-

OF LUCIUS APULEIUS

ance. Last of all, no man can proove that I committed that fact for lucre or gaine.

When I had ended my words in this sort, behold, I weeped againe pitteously, and holding up my hands I prayed all the people by the mercy of the Commonweale, and for the love of my poore infants and children, to shew me some pitty and favour. And when their hearts were somewhat relented and mooved by my lamentable teares, I called all the gods to witnesse that I was unguilty of the crime, and so to their divine providence I committed my present estate, but turning my selfe againe, I perceived that all the people laughed exceedingly, and especially my good friend and host Milo. Then thought I with my selfe, Alasse where is faith? Where is remorse of conscience? Behold, I am condemned to die as a murtherer, for the safegard of myne Host Milo and his Family. Yet is he not contented with that, but likewise laugheth me to scorne, when otherwise he should comfort and helpe mee.

CHAPTER XIII
How Apuleius was accused by an old man, and how hee answered for himselfe

THE FOURTEENTH CHAPTER

How Apuleius was accused by two women, and how the slaine bodies were found blowne bladders.

WHEN this was done, out came a woman weeping in the middle of the Theatre arrayed in mourning vesture, and bearing a childe in her armes. And after her came an old woman in ragged robes, crying and howling likewise: and they brought with them the Olive boughs wherewith the three slain bodies were covered on the Beere, and cried out on this manner: O right Judges, we pray you by the justice and humanity which is in you, to have mercy upon these slaine persons, and succour our Widowhood and losse of our deare husbands, and especially this poore Infant, who is now an

THE THIRD BOOKE

CHAPTER XIV

How Apuleius was accused by two women, and how the slaine bodies were found blowne bladders

Orphan, and deprived of all good fortune: and execute your justice by order and law, upon the bloud of this Theefe, who is the occasion of all our sorrowes. When they had spoken these words, one of the most antient Judges did rise and say, Touching this murther, which deserveth great punishment, this malefactor himselfe cannot deny, but our duty is to enquire and try out, whether he had no Coadjutors to helpe him. For it is not likely that one man alone could kill three such great and valiant persons, wherefore the truth must be tried out by the racke, and so wee shall learne what other companions he hath, and root out the nest of these mischievous murtherers. And there was no long delay, for according unto the custome of Grecia, the fire, the wheele, and many other torments were brought in. Then my sorrow encreased or rather doubled, in that I could not end my life with whole and unperished members. And by and by the old woman, who troubled all the Court with her howling, desired the Judges, that before I should be tormented on the racke, I might uncover the bodies which I had slaine, that every man might see their comely shape and youthfull beauty, and that I might receive condigne and worthy punishment, according to the quality of my offence: and therewithall shee made a signe of joy. Then the Judge commanded me forthwith to discover the bodies of the slain, lying upon the beere, with myne owne hands: but when I refused a good space, by reason I would not make my fact apparant to the eies of all men, the Sergeants charged me by commandement of the Judges, and thrust me forward to do the same. I then being forced by necessity, though it were against my wil, uncovered their bodies: but O good Lord what a strange sight did I see, what a monster? What sudden change of all my sorrows? I seemed as though I were one of the house of Proserpina and of the family of death, insomuch that I could not sufficiently expresse the forme of this new sight, so far was I amased and astonied therat: for why, the bodies of the three slain men were no bodies, but three blown bladders mangled in divers places, and they seemed to be wounded in those parts where I remembred I wounded the theeves the night before. Wherat the people laughed exceedingly: some

OF LUCIUS APULEIUS

rejoyced marvellously at the remembrance thereof, some held their stomacks that aked with joy, but every man delighted at this passing sport, so passed out of the theatre. But I from the time that I uncovered the bodies stood stil as cold as ice, no otherwise than as the other Statues and images there, neither came I into my right sences, until such time as Milo my Host came and tooke mee by the hand, and with civil violence lead me away weeping and sobbing, whether I would or no. And because that I might be seene, he brought mee through many blinde wayes and lanes to his house, where he went about to comfort me, beeing sad and yet fearefull, with gentle entreaty of talke. But he could in no wise mitigate my impatiency of the injury which I conceived within my minde. And behold, by and by the Magistrates and Judges with their ensignes entred into the house, and endeavoured to pacifie mee in this sort, saying, O Lucius, we are advertised of your dignity, and know the genealogie of your antient linage, for the nobility of your Kinne doe possesse the greatest part of all this Province: and thinke not that you have suffered the thing wherfore you weepe, to any your reproach and ignominy, but put away all care and sorrow out of your minde. For this day, which we celebrate once a yeare in honour of the god Risus, is alwaies renowned with some solemne novel, and the god doth continually accompany with the inventor therof, and wil not suffer that he should be sorrowfull, but pleasantly beare a joyfull face. And verily all the City for the grace that is in you, intend to reward you with great honours, and to make you a Patron. And further, that your statue or image may be set up for a perpetuall remembrance.

To whom I answered, As for such benefits as I have received of the famous City of Thessaly, I yeeld and render most entire thanks, but as touching the setting up of any statues or Images, I would wish that they should bee reserved for myne Auntients, and such as are more worthy than I.

And when I had spoken these words somewhat gravely, and shewed my selfe more merry than I was before, the Judges and magistrates departed, and I reverendly tooke my leave of them, and bid them farewell. And behold, by and

CHAPTER XIV

How Apuleius was accused by two women, and how the slaine bodies were found blowne bladders

THE THIRD BOOKE

CHAPTER XIV
How Apuleius was accused by two women, and how the slaine bodies were found, blowne bladders

by there came one running unto me in haste and sayd, Sir, your cousin Byrrhena desireth you to take the paines according to your promise yester night, to come to supper, for it is ready. But I greatly fearing to goe any more to her house in the night, said unto the messenger, My friend I pray you tell to my cousine your mistresse, that I would willingly be at her commandement, but for breaking my troth and credit. For myne host Milo enforced me to assure him, and compelled me by the feast of this present day, that I should not depart from his company, wherefore I pray you to excuse me, and to defer my promise to another time.

And while I was speaking these words, Milo tooke me by the hand, and lead me towards the next Baine: but by the way I went couching under him, to hide my selfe from the sight of men, because I had ministred such an occasion of laughter. And when I had washed and wiped my selfe, and returned home againe, I never remembred any such thing, so greatly was I abashed at the nodding and poynting of every person. Then I went to supper with Milo, where God wot we fared but meanly. Wherefore feigning that my head did ake by reason of my sobbing and weeping all the day, I desired license to depart to my Chamber, and so I went to bed.

THE FIFTEENTH CHAPTER
How Fotis told to Apuleius, what witchcraft her mistresse did use.

WHEN I was a bed I began to call to minde all the sorrowes and griefes that I was in the day before, untill such time as my love Fotis, having brought her mistresse to sleepe, came into the chamber, not as shee was wont to do, for she seemed nothing pleasant neither in countenance nor talke, but with sowre face and frowning looke, gan speake in this sort, Verily I confesse that I

OF LUCIUS APULEIUS

have been the occasion of all thy trouble this day, and therewith shee pulled out a whippe from under her apron, and delivered it unto mee saying, Revenge thy selfe of me mischievous harlot, or rather slay me.

And thinke you not that I did willingly procure this anguish and sorrow unto you, I call the gods to witnesse. For I had rather myne owne body to perish, than that you should receive or sustaine any harme by my meanes, but that which I did was by the commandement of another, and wrought as I thought for some other, but behold the unlucky chance fortuned on you by my evill occasion.

Then I, very curious and desirous to know the matter, answered, In faith (quoth I) this most pestilent and evill favoured whip which thou hast brought to scourge thee withal, shal first be broken in a thousand pieces, than it should touch or hurt thy delicate and dainty skin. But I pray you tell me, how have you been the cause and mean of my trouble and sorow? For I dare sweare by the love that I beare unto you, and I will not be perswaded, though you your selfe should endeavor the same, that ever you went to trouble or harm me: perhaps sometimes you imagined an evil thought in your mind, which afterwards you revoked, but that is not to bee deemed as a crime.

When I had spoken these words, I perceived by Fotis eys being wet with tears, and well nigh closed up, that shee had a desire unto pleasure, and specially because shee embraced and kissed me sweetly. And when she was somewhat restored unto joy, she desired mee that shee might first shut the chamber doore, least by the untemperance of her tongue, in uttering any unfitting words, there might grow further inconvenience. Wherewithall she barred and propped the doore, and came to me againe, and embracing me lovingly about the necke with both her armes, spake with a soft voice and said, I doe greatly feare to discover the privities of this house, and to utter the secret mysteries of my dame. But I have such a confidence in you and in your wisedome, by reason that you are come of so noble a line, and endowed with so profound sapience, and further instructed in so many holy and divine things, that you will faithfully keepe silence,

CHAPTER XV
How Fotis told to Apuleius, what witchcraft her mistresse did use

THE THIRD BOOKE

CHAPTER XV

How Fotis told to Apuleius, what witchcraft her mistresse did use

and that whatsoever I shall reveale or declare unto you, you would close them within the bottome of your heart, and never discover the same: for I ensure you, the love that I beare unto you, enforceth mee to utter it. Now shal you know all the estate of our house, now shal you know the hidden secrets of my mistres, unto whome the powers of hel do obey, and by whom the celestial planets are troubled, the gods made weake, and the elements subdued, neither is the violence of her art in more strength and force, than when she espieth some comly yong man that pleaseth her fancie, as oftentimes it hapneth, for now she loveth one Boetian a fair and beautiful person, on whom she employes al her sorcery and enchantment, and I heard her say with mine own ears yesternight, that if the Sun had not then presently gon downe, and the night come to minister convenient time to worke her magicall enticements, shee would have brought perpetuall darkenes over all the world her selfe. And you shall know, That when she saw yester night, this Beotian sitting at the Barbers a polling, when she came from the Baines shee secretly commanded me to gather some of the haire of his head which lay dispersed upon the ground, and to bring it home. Which when I had thought to have done the Barber espied me, and by reason it was bruted throughout all the City that we were Witches and Enchantresses, he cried out and said, Wil you never leave off stealing of young mens haires? In faith I assure you, unlesse you cease your wicked Sorceries, I will complaine to the Justices. Wherewithall he came angerly towards me, and tooke away the haire which I had gathered, out of my apron: which grieved me very much; for I knew my Mistresses manners, that she would not be contented but beat me cruelly.

Wherefore I intended to runne away, but the remembrance of you put alwayes that thought out of my minde, and so I came homeward very sorrowfull: but because I would not seeme to come to my mistresse sight with empty hands, I saw a man shearing of blowne goat skinnes, and the hayre which he had shorne off was yellow, and much resembled the haire of the Beotian, and I tooke a good deale therof, and colouring the matter, brought it to my mistresse. And so

OF LUCIUS APULEIUS

when night came, before your returne from supper, she to bring her purpose to passe, went up to a high Gallery of her house, opening to the East part of the world, and preparing her selfe according to her accustomed practise, shee gathered together all substance for fumigations, she brought forth plates of mettal carved with strange characters, she prepared the bones of such as were drowned by tempest in the seas, she made ready the members of dead men, as the nosethrils and fingers, shee set out the lumps of flesh of such as were hanged, the blood which she had reserved of such as were slaine, and the jaw bones and teeth of wilde beasts, then she said certaine charmes over the haire, and dipped it in divers waters, as in Wel water, Cow milke, mountaine honey, and other liquor. Which when she had done, she tied and lapped it up together, and with many perfumes and smells threw it into an hot fire to burn. Then by the great force of this Sorcerie, and the violence of so many confections, those bodies whose haire was burning in the fire, received humane shape, and felt, heard, and walked: And smelling the sent of their owne haire, came and rapped at our doores in stead of Boetius. Then you being well tipled, and deceived by the obscurity of the night, drew out your sword couragiously like furious Ajax, and killd not as he did, whole heard of beasts, but three blowne skinnes, to the intent that I after the slaughter of so many enemies, without effusion of bloud might embrace and kisse not an homicide, but an Utricide.

CHAPTER XV

How Fotis told to Apuleius, what witchcraft her mistresse did use

Thus when I was pleasantly mocked and taunted by Fotis, I sayd unto her, Verily now may I for this atchieved enterprise be numbered as Hercules, who by his valiant prowesse performed the twelve notable Labors, as Gerion with three bodies, and as Cerberus with three heads, for I have slaine three blown Goats skinnes. But to the end I may pardon thee of that which thou hast committed, performe the thing which I shall most earnestly desire of thee, that is, bring me that I may see and behold when thy mistresse goeth about any Sorcery or enchantment, and when she prayeth unto the gods: For I am very desirous to learne that art, and as it seemeth unto mee, thou thy selfe hath some experience in

THE THIRD BOOKE

CHAPTER XV
How Fotis told to Apuleius, what witchcraft her mistresse did use

the same. For this I know and plainely feele, That whereas I have alwayes yrked and loathed the embracings and love of Matrones, I am so stricken and subdued with thy shining eyes, ruddy cheekes, glittering haire, sweet cosses, and lilly white paps, that I neither have minde to goe home, nor to depart hence, but esteeme the pleasure which I shall have with thee this night, above all the joyes of the world. Then (quoth shee) O my Lucius, how willing would I be to fulfil your desire, but by reason shee is so hated, she getteth her selfe into solitary places, and out of the presence of every person, when she mindeth to work her enchantments. Howbeit I regard more to gratifie your request, than I doe esteeme the danger of my life: and when I see opportunitie and time I wil assuredly bring you word, so that you shal see all her enchantments, but alwayes upon this condition, that you secretly keepe close such things as are done.

Thus as we reasoned together the courage of Venus assailed, as well our desires as our members, and so shee unrayed her selfe and came to bed, and we passed the night in pastime and dalliance, till as by drowsie and unlusty sleep I was constrained to lie still.

THE SIXTEENTH CHAPTER
How Fotis brought Apuleius to see her Mistresse enchant.

ON a day Fotis came running to me in great feare, and said that her mistresse, to worke her sorceries on such as shee loved, intended the night following to transforme her selfe into a bird, and to fly whither she pleased. Wherefore she willed me privily to prepare my self to see the same. And when midnight came she led me softly into a high chamber, and bid me look thorow the chink of a doore: where first I saw how shee put of all her garments,

OF LUCIUS APULEIUS

and took out of a certain coffer sundry kindes of Boxes, of the which she opened one, and tempered the ointment therein with her fingers, and then rubbed her body therewith from the sole of the foot to the crowne of the head, and when she had spoken privily with her selfe, having the candle in her hand, she shaked the parts of her body, and behold, I perceived a plume of feathers did burgen out, her nose waxed crooked and hard, her nailes turned into clawes, and so she became an Owle. Then she cried and screeched like a Bird of that kinde, and willing to proove her force, mooved her selfe from the ground by little and little, til at last she flew quite away.

<small>CHAPTER XVI

How Fotis brought Apuleius to see her Mistresse enchant</small>

Thus by her sorcery shee transformed her body into what shape she would. Which when I saw I was greatly astonied; and although I was inchanted by no kind of charme, yet I thought that I seemed not to have the likenesse of Lucius, for so was I banished from my sences, amazed in madnesse, and so I dreamed waking, that I felt myne eyes, whether I were asleepe or no. But when I was come againe to my selfe, I tooke Fotis by the hand, and moved it to my face and said, I pray thee while occasion doth serve, that I may have the fruition of the fruits of my desire, and grant me some of this oyntment. O Fotis I pray thee by thy sweet paps, to make that in the great flames of my love I may bee turned into a bird, so wil I ever hereafter be bound unto you, and obedient to your commandement. Then said Fotis, Wil you go about to deceive me now, and inforce me to work my own sorow? Are you in the mind that you wil not tarry in Thessaly? if you be a bird, where shal I seek you, and when shal I see you? Then answered I, God forbid that I should commit such a crime, for though I could fly in the aire as an Eagle, or though I were the messenger of Jupiter, yet would I have recourse to nest with thee: and I swear by the knot of thy amiable hair, that since the time I first loved thee, I never fancied any other person: moreover, this commeth to my minde, that if by vertue of the oyntment I shall become an Owle, I will take heed that I come nigh no mans house: for I am not to learn, how these matrons would handle their lovers, if they knew that they

THE THIRD BOOKE

CHAPTER XVI
How Fotis brought Apuleius to see her Mistresse enchant

were transformed into Owles: Moreover, when they are taken in any place they are nayled upon posts, and so they are worthily rewarded, because it is thought that they bring evill fortune to the house. But I pray you (which I had almost forgotten) tell me by what meanes when I am an Owle, I shall returne to my pristine shape, and become Lucius againe. Feare not (quoth she) for my mistres hath taught me the way to bring that to passe, neither thinke you that she did it for any good will and favour, but to the end I might helpe her, and minister some remedy when she returneth home.

Consider I pray you with your selfe, with what frivolous trifles so marvellous a thing is wrought: For by Hercules I sweare I give her nothing else save a little Dill and Lawrell leaves, in Well water, the which she drinketh, and washeth her selfe withall. Which when she had spoken shee went into the chamber and tooke a box out of the coffer, which I first kissed and embraced, and prayed that I might [have] good successe in my purpose. And then I put off all my garments, and greedily thrust my hand into the box, and took out a good deale of oyntment and rubbed my selfe withall.

THE SEVENTEENTH CHAPTER

How Apuleius thinking to be turned into a Bird, was turned into an Asse, and how hee was led away by Theeves.

AFTER that I had well rubbed every part and member of my body, I hovered with myne armes, and moved my selfe, looking still when I should bee changed into a Bird as Pamphiles was, and behold neither feathers nor appearance of feathers did burgen out, but verily my haire did turne in ruggednesse, and my tender skin waxed tough and hard, my fingers and toes losing the number of five, changed into hoofes, and out of myne arse grew a great taile, now my face became monstrous, my nosthrils wide, my lips hanging downe, and myne eares rugged with haire: neither could I see any comfort of my transformation, for my members encreased likewise, and so without all helpe (viewing every part of my poore body) I perceived that I was no bird, but a plaine Asse.

Then I thought to blame Fotis, but being deprived as wel of language as humane shape, I looked upon her with my hanging lips and watery eyes. Who as soone as shee espied me in such sort, cried out, Alas poore wretch that I am, I am utterly cast away. The feare I was in, and my haste hath beguiled me, but especially the mistaking of the boxe hath deceived me. But it forceth not much, in regard a sooner medicine may be gotten for this than for any other thing. For if thou couldst get a Rose and eat it, thou shouldst be delivered from the shape of an Asse, and become my Lucius againe. And would to God I had gathered some garlands this evening past, according to my custome, then thou shouldst not continue an Asse one nights space, but in the morning I will seeke some remedy. Thus Fotis lamented in pittifull sort, but I that was now a perfect asse, and for Lucius a brute beast, did yet retaine the sence and understanding of a man. And did devise a good space with my selfe, whether it were best for me to teare this mischievous and wicked harlot with my mouth, or to kicke and kill her with my heels. But a better thought reduced me from so rash a purpose: for I feared lest by the death of Fotis I should be deprived of all remedy and help. Then shaking myne head, and dissembling myne ire, and taking my adversity in good part, I went into the stable to my own horse, where I found another Asse of Miloes, somtime my host, and I did verily think that mine owne horse (if there were any natural conscience or knowledge in brute beasts) would take pitty upon me, and profer me lodging for that night: but it chanced far otherwise. For see, my horse and the asse as it were consented together to work my harm, and fearing lest I should eat up their provender, would in no wise suffer me to come nigh the manger, but kicked me with their

CHAPTER XVII

How Apuleius thinking to be turned into a Bird, was turned into an Asse, and how hee was led away by Theeves

THE THIRD BOOKE

CHAPTER XVII
How Apuleius thinking to be turned into a Bird, was turned into an Asse, and how hee was led away by Theeves

heeles from their meat, which I my selfe gave them the night before. Then I being thus handled by them, and driven away, got me into a corner of the stable, where while I remembred their uncurtesie, and how on the morrow I should returne to Lucius by the help of a Rose, when as I thought to revenge my self of myne owne horse, I fortuned to espy in the middle of a pillar sustaining the rafters of the stable the image of the goddesse Hippone, which was garnished and decked round about with faire and fresh roses: then in hope of present remedy, I leaped up with my fore feet as high as I could, stretching out my neck, and with my lips coveting to snatch some roses. But in an evill hour I did go about that enterprise, for behold the boy to whom I gave charge of my horse came presently in, and finding mee climbing upon the pillar, ranne fretting towards me and said, How long shall wee suffer this wild Asse, that doth not onely eat up his fellowes meat, but also would spoyle the images of the gods? Why doe not I kill this lame theefe and weake wretch? And therewithall looking about for some cudgel, hee espied where lay a fagot of wood, and chusing out a crabbed truncheon of the biggest hee could finde, did never cease beating of me poore wretch, untill such time as by great noyse and rumbling hee heard the doores of the house burst open, and the neighbours crying in most lamentable sort, which inforced him being stricken in feare, to fly his way. And by and by a troup of theeves entred in, and kept every part and corner of the house with weapons. And as men resorted to aid and help them which were within the doores, the theeves resisted and kept them back, for every man was armed with a sword and target in his hand, the glimpses whereof did yeeld out such light as if it had bin day. Then they brake open a great chest with double locks and bolts, wherin was layd all the treasure of Milo, and ransackt the same: which when they had done they packed it up and gave every one a portion to carry: but when they had more than they could beare away, yet were they loth to leave any behind, but came into the stable, and took us two poore asses and my horse, and laded us with greater trusses than wee were able to beare. And when we were out of the house

OF LUCIUS APULEIUS

CHAPTER XVII

How Apuleius thinking to be turned into a Bird, was turned into an Asse, and how hee was led away by Theeves

they followed us with great staves, and willed one of their fellows to tarry behind, and bring them tydings what was done concerning the robbery: and so they beat us forward over great hils out of the way. But I, what with my heavy burden and long journy, did nothing differ from a dead asse: wherfore I determined with my self to seek some civil remedy, and by invocation of the name of the prince of the country to be delivered from so many miseries: and on a time I passed through a great faire, I came among a multitude of Greeks, and I thought to call upon the renowned name of the Emperor, and to say, O Cesar, and cried out aloud, O, but Cesar I could in no wise pronounce. The Theeves little regarding my crying, did lay mee on and beate my wretched skinne in such sort, that after it was neither apt nor meet to make Sives or Sarces. Howbeit at last Jupiter administred unto me an unhoped remedy. For when we had passed through many townes and villages, I fortuned to espy a pleasant garden, wherein beside many other flowers of delectable hiew, were new and fresh roses: and being very joyful, and desirous to catch some as I passed by, I drew neerer and neerer: and while my lips watered upon them, I thought of a better advice more profitable for me, lest if from an Asse I should become a man, I might fall into the hands of the theeves, and either by suspition that I were some witch, or for feare that I should utter their theft, I should be slaine, wherefore I abstained for that time from eating of Roses, and enduring my present adversity, I eat hay as other Asses did.

THE
FOURTH FIFTH
AND SIXTH BOOKES
of LUCIUS APULEIUS of
THE GOLDEN ASSE

THE FOURTH BOOKE

THE EIGHTEENTH CHAPTER

How Apuleius thinking to eat Roses, was cruelly beaten by a Gardener, and chased by dogs.

WHEN noone was come, that the broyling heate of the sunne had most power, we turned into a village to certaine of the theeves acquaintance and friends, for verily their meeting and embracing together did give me, poore asse, cause to deeme the same, and they tooke the trusse from my backe, and gave them part of the Treasure which was in it, and they seemed to whisper and tell them that it was stollen goods, and after that we were unladen of our burthens, they let us loose into a medow to pasture, but myne own horse and Milocs Asse would not suffer me to feed there with them, but I must seeke my dinner in some other place.

Wherefore I leaped into a garden which was behinde the stable, and being well nigh perished with hunger, although I could finde nothing there but raw and green fallets, yet I filled my hungry guts therwithall abundantly, and praying unto all the gods, I looked about in every place if I could espy any red roses in the gardens by, and my solitary being alone did put me in good hope, that if I could find any remedy, I should presently of an Asse be changed into Lucius out of every mans sight. And while I considered these things, I looked about, and behold I saw

THE FOURTH BOOKE

CHAPTER XVIII

How Apuleius thinking to eat Roses, was cruelly beaten by a Gardener, and chased by dogs

a farre off a shadowed valley adjoyning nigh unto a wood, where amongst divers other hearbes and pleasant verdures, me thought I saw divers flourishing Roses of bright damaske colour; and said within my beastiall mind, Verily that place is the place of Venus and the Graces, where secretly glistereth the royall hew, of so lively and delectable a floure. Then I desiring the help of the guide of my good fortune, ranne lustily towards the wood, insomuch that I felt my self that I was no more an Asse, but a swift coursing horse: but my agility and quicknes could not prevent the cruelty of my fortune; for when I came to the place I perceived that they were no roses, neither tender nor pleasant, neither moystned with the heavenly drops of dew, nor celestiall liquor, which grew out of the thicket and thornes there. Neither did I perceive that there was any valley at all, but onely the bank of the river, environed with great thick trees, which had long branches like unto lawrell and bearing a flour without any manner of sent, and the common people call them by the name of Lawrel roses, which be very poyson to all manner of beasts. Then was I so intangled with unhappy fortune that I little esteemed mine own danger, and went willingly to eat of those roses, though I knew them to be present poyson: and as I drew neere I saw a yong man that seemed to be the gardener, come upon mee, and when he perceived that I had devoured all his hearbs in the garden, he came swearing with a great staffe in his hand, and laid upon me in such sort, that I was well nigh dead, but I speedily devised some remedy my self, for I lift up my legs and kicked me with my hinder heels, that I left him lying at the hill foot wel nigh slain, and so I ran away. Incontinently came out his wife, who seeing her husband halfe dead, cried and howled in pittifull sort, and went toward her husband, to the intent that by her lowd cries shee might purchase to me present destruction. Then all the persons of the town, moved by her noise came forth, and cried for dogs to tear me down. Out came a great company of Bandogs and mastifes, more fit to pul down bears and lions than me, whom when I beheld I thought verily I should presently die: but I turned my self about, and ranne as fast as ever I might to the stable from

OF LUCIUS APULEIUS

whence I came. Then the men of the towne called in their dogs, and took me and bound mee to the staple of a post, and scourged mee with a great knotted whip till I was well nigh dead, and they would undoubtedly have slaine me, had it not come to passe, that what with the paine of their beating, and the greene hearbes that lay in my guts, I caught such a laske that I all besprinkled their faces with my liquid dung, and enforced them to leave off.

CHAPTER XVIII
How Apuleius thinking to eat Roses, was cruelly beaten by a Gardener, and chased by dogs

THE NINETEENTH CHAPTER

How Apuleius was prevented of his purpose, and how the Theeves came to their den.

NOT long after, the theeves laded us againe, but especially me, and brought us forth of the stable, and when wee had gone a good part of our journey, what with the long way, my great burthen, the beating of staves, and my worne hooves, I was so weary that I could scantly go. Then I saw a little before mee a river running with faire water, and I said to my selfe, Behold, now I have found a good occasion: for I will fall downe when I come yonder, and surely I will not rise againe, neither with scourging nor beating, for I had rather be slaine there presently, than goe any further.

And the cause why I determined so to doe was this, I thought that the theeves when they did see me so feeble and weake that I could not travell, to the intent they would not stay in their journey, they would take the burthen from my backe and put it upon my fellowes, and so for my further punishment to leave me as a prey to the wolves and ravening beasts. But evill fortune prevented so good a consideration; for the other Asse being of the same purpose that I was of, by feigned and coloured wearinesse fell downe first, with all his burthen upon the ground as though hee were dead, and

THE FOURTH BOOKE

CHAPTER XIX
How Apuleius was prevented of his purpose, and how the Theeves came to their den

hee would not rise neither with beating nor pricking, nor stand upon his feet, though they pulled him by the tayl, by his legs, and by his eares: which when the theeves beheld, as without all hope they said one unto another, What should we stand here so long about a dead, or rather a stony asse? let us bee gone: and so they tooke his burthen, and divided some to mee, and some to my horse. And then they drew out their swords and cut off his legs, and threw his body from the point of an hill downe into a great valley. Then I considering with my selfe of the evill fortune of my poore companion, and purposed now to forget all subtilty and deceit, and to play the good Asse to get my masters favour, for I perceived by their talke that we were come home well nigh at our journies end. And after that wee had passed over a little hill, wee came to our appointed place, where when we were unladen of our burthens, and all things carried in, I tumbled and wallowed in the dust, to refresh my selfe in stead of water. The thing and the time compelleth me to make description of the places, and especially of the den where the theeves did inhabit, I will prove my wit what I can doe, and then consider you whether I was an asse in judgement and sence, or no. For first there was an exceeding great hill compassed about with big trees very high, with many turning bottoms full of sharpe stones, whereby it was inaccessible. There was many winding and hollow vallies, environed with thickets and thornes, and naturally fortressed round about. From the top of the hill ranne a running water as cleare as silver, and watered all the valleyes below, that it seemed like unto a sea inclosed, or a standing floud. Before the denne where was no hill stood an high tower, and at the foot thereof were sheepe-coats fenced and walled with clay. Before the gate of the house were pathes made in stead of wals, in such sort that you would easily judge it to be a very den for theeves, and there was nothing else save a little coat covered with thatch, wherein the Theeves did nightly accustome to watch by order, as I after perceived. And when they were all crept into the house, and we fast tied with halters at the dore, they began to chide with an old woman there, crooked with age, who had

OF LUCIUS APULEIUS

the government and rule of all the house, and said, How is it old witch, old trot, and strumpet, that thou sittest idley all day at home, and having no regard to our perillous labors, hast provided nothing for our suppers, but sittest eating and swilling thy selfe from morning till night? Then the old woman trembled, and scantly able to speak gan say, Behold my puissant and faithfull masters, you shall have meat and pottage enough by and by: here is first store of bread, wine plenty, filled in cleane rinsed pots, likewise here is hot water prepared to bathe you.

CHAPTER XIX
How Apuleius was prevented of his purpose, and how the Theeves came to their den

Which when she had said, they put off all their garments and refreshed themselves by the fire. And after they were washed and nointed with oyle, they sate downe at the table garnished with all kind of dainty meats. They were no sooner sate downe, but in came another company of yong men more in number than was before, who seemed likewise to bee Theeves, for they brought in their preyes of gold and silver, Plate, Jewels, and rich robes, and when they had likewise washed, they sate amongst the rest, and served one another by order. Then they drank and eat exceedingly, crying, laughing and making such noyse, that I thought I was amongst the tyrannous and wilde Lapithes, Thebans, and Centaures. At length one of them more valiant than the rest, spake in this sort, We verily have manfully conquered the house of Milo of Hippata, and beside all the riches and treasure which by force we have brought away, we are all come home safe, and are increased the more by this horse and this Asse. But you that have roved about in the country of Beotia, have lost your valiant captaine Lamathus, whose life I more regarded than all the treasure which you have brought: and therfore the memory of him shall bee renowned for ever amongst the most noble kings and valiant captains: but you accustome when you goe abroad, like men with ganders hearts to creepe through every corner and hole for every trifle. Then one of them that came last answered, Why are you only ignorant, that the greater the number is, the sooner they may rob and spoile the house? And although the family be dispersed in divers lodgings, yet every man had rather to defend his own life, than to save

THE FOURTH BOOKE

CHAPTER XIX
How Apuleius was prevented of his purpose, and how the Theeves came to their den

the riches of his master: but when there be but a few theeves, then will they rather not only regard themselves, but also their substance, how little or great soever it be. And to the intent you may beleeve me I will shew you an example: wee were come nothing nigh to Thebes, where is the fountain of our art and science, but we learned where a rich Chuffe called Chriseros did dwell, who for fear of offices in the publique weal dissembled his estate, and lived sole and solitary in a small coat, howbeit replenished with aboundance of treasure, and went daily in ragged and torn apparel. Wherefore wee devised with our selves to go to his house and spoyl him of all his riches. And when night came we drew towards the dore, which was so strongly closed, that we could neither move it, nor lift it out of the hooks, and we thought it not best to break it open, lest by the noyse we should raise up to our harm the neighbors by. Then our strong and valiant captain Lamathus trusting in his own strength and force, thrust in his hand through a hole of the dore, and thought to pull back the bolt: but the covetous caitif Chriseros being awake, and making no noise came softly to the dore and caught his hand and with a great naile nailed it fast to the post: which when he had done, he ran up unto a high chamber and called every one of his neighbors by name, desiring them to succor him with all possible speed, for his house was on fire. Then every one for fear of their owne danger came running out to aid him, wherewith we fearing our present peril, knew not what was best to be don, whether wee should leave our companion there, or yeeld our selves to die with him: but we by his consent devised a better way, for we cut off his arm by the elbow and so let it hang there: then wee bound his wound with clouts, lest we should be traced by the drops of blood: which don we took Lamathus and led him away, for fear we would be taken: but being so nigh pursued that wee were in present danger, and that Lamathus could not keepe our company by reason of faintnesse; and on the other side perceiving that it was not for his profit to linger behinde, he spake unto us as a man of singular courage and vertue, desiring us by much entreaty and prayer and by the

OF LUCIUS APULEIUS

CHAPTER XIX

How Apuleius was prevented of his purpose, and how the Theeves came to their den

puissance of the god Mars, and the faith of our confederacy, to deliver his body from torment and miserable captivity: and further he said, How is it possible that so couragious a Captaine can live without his hand, wherewith he could somtime rob and slay so many people? I would thinke my selfe sufficiently happy if I might be slaine by one of you. But when he saw that we all refused to commit any such fact, he drew out his sword with his other hand, and after that he had often kissed it, he thrust it clean through his body. Then we honoured the corps of so puissant a man, and wrapped it in linnen cloathes and threw him into the sea. So lieth our master Lamathus, buried and hid in the grave of water, and ended his life as I have declared. But Alcinus, though he were a man of great enterprise, yet could he not beware by Lamathus, nor void himselfe from evill fortune: for on a day when he had entred into an old womans house to rob her, he went up into a high chamber, where hee should first have strangled her: but he had more regard to throw down the bags of mony and gold out at a window, to us that stood under; and when he was so greedy that he would leave nothing behinde, he went unto the old womans bed where she lay asleep, and would have taken off the coverlet to have thrown downe likewise, but shee awaked, and kneeling on her knees, desired him in this manner: O sir I pray you cast not away such torne and ragged clouts into my neighbours houses, for they are rich enough, and need no such things. Then Alcinus thinking her words to be true, was brought in beleefe, that such things as he had throwne out already, and such things as hee should throw out after, was not fallen downe to his fellowes, but into other mens houses: wherefore hee went to the window to see, and as hee thought to behold the places round about, thrusting his body out of the window, the old woman marked him wel, and came behind him softly, and though shee had but small strength, yet with a sudden force she tooke him by the heeles and thrust him out headlong, and so he fell upon a marvellous great stone and burst his ribs, wherby he vomited and spewed flakes of blood and presently died. Then wee threw him into the river likewise, as we had done Lamathus before.

THE FOURTH BOOKE

CHAPTER XIX

How Apuleius was prevented of his purpose, and how the Theeves came to their den

When we had thus lost two of our companions, wee liked not Thebes, but marched towards the next city called Platea, where we found a man of great fame named Demochares, that purposed to set forth a great game, where should be a triall of all kind of weapons: hee was come of a good house, marvellous rich, liberall, and wel deserved that which he had, and had prepared many showes and pleasures for the Common people, insomuch that there is no man can either by wit or eloquence shew in words his worthy preparations: for first he had provided all sorts of armes, hee greatly delighted in hunting and chasing, he ordained great towers and Tables to move hither and thither, hee made many places to chase and encounter in: he had ready a great number of men and wilde beasts, and many condemned persons were brought from the Judgement place, to try and fight with those beasts. But amongst so great preparations of noble price, he bestowed the most part of his patrimony in buying of Beares, which he nourished to his great cost, and esteemed more than all the other beasts, which either by chasing hee caught himselfe, or which he dearely bought, or which were given him from divers of his friends.

Howbeit for all his sumptuous cost, hee could not be free from the malitious eyes of envy, for some of them were well nigh dead with too long tying up, some meagre with the broyling heate of the sun, some languished with lying, but all having sundry diseases, were so afflicted that they died one after another, and there was well nigh none left, in such sort that you might see them lying in the streets pittiously dead. And the common people having no other meat to feed on, little regarding any curiosity, would come forth and fill their bellies with the flesh of the beares. Then by and by Babulus and I devised a pretty sport, wee drew one of the greatest of the Beares to our lodging, as though wee would prepare to eat thereof, where wee flayed of his skinne, and kept his ungles whole, but we medled not with the head, but cut it off by the necke, and so let it hang to the skinne. Then we rased off the flesh from the necke, and cast dust thereon, and set it in the sun to dry.

OF LUCIUS APULEIUS

THE TWENTIETH CHAPTER
How Trasileon was disguised in a Beares skin, and how he was handled.

HEN the skinne was a drying we made merry with the flesh, and then we devised with our selves, that one of us being more valiant than the rest both in body and courage (so that he would consent thereto) should put on the skin, and feigning that hee were a Beare, should be led to Demochares house in the night, by which means we thought to be received and let in. Many were desirous to play the Beare, but especially one Thrasileon of a couragious minde would take this enterprise in hand. Then wee put him into the Beares skin, which fitted him finely in every point, wee buckled it fast under his belly, and covered the seam with the haire, that it might not be seen. After this we made little holes through the bears head, and through his nosthrils and eyes, for Thrasileon to see out and take wind at, in such sort that he seemed a very lively and natural beast: when this was don we went into a cave which we hired for the purpose, and he crept in after like a bear with a good courage. Thus we began our subtilty, and then wee imagined thus, wee feigned letters as though they came from one Nicanor which dwelt in the Country of Thracia, which was of great acquaintance with this Demochares, wherein we wrote, that hee had sent him beeing his friend, the first fruits of his coursing and hunting. When night was come, which was a meet time for our purpose, we brought Thrasileon and our forged letters and presented them to Demochares. When Demochares beheld this mighty Beare, and saw the liberality of Nicanor his friend, hee commanded his servants to deliver unto us x. crowns, having great store in his coffers. Then (as the novelty of a thing doth accustom to stir mens minds to behold the same) many persons

THE FOURTH BOOKE

CHAPTER XX
How Trasileon was disguised in a Beares skin, and how he was handled

came on every side to see this bear: but Thrasileon, lest they should by curious viewing and prying perceive the truth, ran upon them to put them in feare that they durst not come nigh. The people said, Verily Demochares is right happy, in that after the death of so many beasts, hee hath gotten maugre fortunes head, so goodly a bear. Then Demochares commanded him with all care to be put into the park among the other beasts: but immediatly I spake unto him and said, Sir I pray you take heed how you put a beast tired with the heat of the sun and with long travell, among others which as I hear say have divers maladies and diseases, let him rather ly in some open place of your house nie some water, where he may take air and ease himself, for doe not you know that such kind of beasts do greatly delight to couch under the shadow of trees and hillocks neer pleasant wels and waters? Hereby Demochares admonished, and remembring how many he had before that perished, was contented we should put the bear where we would. Moreover we said unto him, that we our selves were determined to lie all night neer the Bear, to looke unto him, and to give him meat and drinke at his due houre.

Then he answered, Verily masters you need not put your selves to such paines, for I have men that serve for nothing but for that purpose. So wee tooke leave of him and departed: and when we were come without the gates of the town, we perceived before us a great sepulchre standing out of the highway in a privy and secret place, and thither we went and opened the mouth thereof, whereas we found the sides covered with the corruption of man, and the ashes and dust of his long buried body, wherin we got our selves to bring our purpose to passe, and having respect to the dark time of night, according to our custome, when we thought that every one was asleepe, we went with our weapons and besieged the house of Demochares round about. Then Thrasileon was ready at hand, and leaped out of the caverne, and went to kill all such as he found asleepe: but when he came to the Porter, he opened the gates and let us all in, and then he shewed us a large Counter, wherein we saw put the night before a great aboundance of treasure: which when

OF LUCIUS APULEIUS

by violence we had broke open, I bid every one of my fellowes take as much gold and silver as they could carry away, and beare it to the Sepulchre, and still as they carried I stood at the gate, watching diligently when they would returne. The Beare running about the house, to make such of the family afeard as fortuned to wake and come out. For who is he that is so puissant and couragious, that at the ougly sight of so great a monster will not quayle and keepe his chamber especially in the night? But when wee had brought this matter to so good a point, there chanced a pittifull case, for as I looked for my companions that should come from the sepulchre, behold there was a Boy of the house that fortuned to looke out of a window, and espied the Bear running about, and he went and told all the servants of the house. Whereupon incontinently they came forth with Torches, Lanthornes, and other lights, that they might see all the yard over: they came with clubs, speares, naked swords, Greyhounds, and Mastifes to slay the poore beast. Then I during this broyle thought to run away, but because I would see Thrasileon fight with the Dogs, I lay behinde the gate to behold him. And although I might perceive that he was well nigh dead, yet remembred he his owne faithfulnes and ours, and valiantly resisted the gaping and ravenous mouths of the hell hounds, so tooke hee in gree the pagiant which willingly he tooke in hand himselfe, and with much adoe tumbled at length out of the house: but when hee was at liberty abroad yet could he not save himselfe, for all the dogs of the Streete joyned themselves to the greyhounds and mastifes of the house, and came upon him.

Alas what a pittifull sight it was to see our poore Thrasileon thus environed and compassed with so many dogs that tare and rent him miserably. Then I impatient of so great a misery, ranne in amongst the prease of the people, and ayding him with my words as much as I might, exhorted them all in this manner: O great and extreame mischance, what a pretious and excellent beast have we lost. But my words did nothing prevaile, for there came out a tall man with a spear in his hand, that thrust him cleane through, and afterwards many that stood by drew out their swords, and so

CHAPTER XX

How Trasileon was disguised in a Beares skin, and how he was handled

THE FOURTH BOOKE

CHAPTER XX
How Trasileon was disguised in a Beares skin, and how he was handled

they killed him. But verily our good Captaine Thrasileon, the honour of our comfort, received his death so patiently, that he would not bewray the league betweene us, either by crying, howling or any other meanes, but being torne with dogs and wounded with weapons, did yeeld forth a dolefull cry, more like unto a beast than a man. And taking his present fortune in good part, with courage and glory enough did finish his life, with such a terror unto the assembly, that no person was so hardy untill it was day, as to touch him, though hee were starke dead: but at last there came a Butcher more valiant than the rest, who opening the panch of the beast, slit out an hardy and ventrous theefe.

In this manner we lost our Captain Thrasileon, but hee left not his fame and honour.

When this was done wee packed up our treasure, which we committed to the sepulchre to keepe, and got us out of the bounds of Platea, thus thinking with our selves, that there was more fidelity amongst the dead than amongst the living, by reason that our preyes were so surely kept in the sepulchre. So being wearied with the weight of our burthens, and well nigh tyred with long travell, having lost three of our soldiers, we are come home with these present cheats.

Thus when they had spoken in memory of their slaine companions, they tooke cups of gold, and sung hymnes unto the god Mars, and layd them downe to sleep. Then the old woman gave us fresh barley without measure, insomuch that my horse fed so abundantly that he might well thinke hee was at some banquet that day. But I that was accustomed to eate bran and flower, thought that but a sower kinde of meate. Wherfore espying a corner where lay loaves of bread for all the house, I got me thither and filled my hungry guts therewith.

OF LUCIUS APULEIUS

THE TWENTY-FIRST CHAPTER
How the Theeves stole away a Gentlewoman, and brought her to their den.

HEN night was come the Theeves awaked and rose up, and when they had buckled on their weapons, and disguised their faces with visards, they departed. And yet for all the great sleep that came upon me, I could in no wise leave eating: and whereas when I was man I could be contented with one or two loaves at the most, now my guts were so greedy that three panniers full would scantly serve me, and while I considered all these things the morning came, and being led to a river, notwithstanding myne Assie shamefastnesse I quencht my thirst. And suddenly after, the Theeves returned home carefull and heavy, bringing no burthens with them, no not so much as traffe or baggage, save only a maiden, that seemed by her habit to be some gentlewoman borne, and the daughter of some worthy matron of that country, who was so fair and beautifull, that though I were an Asse, yet had I a great affection to her. The virgin lamented and tare her hair, and rent her garments, for the great sorrow she was in; but the theeves brought her within the cave, and assaied to comfort her in this sort, Weep not fair gentlewoman we pray you, for be you assured we wil do no outrage nor violence to your person: but take patience a while for our profit, for necessity and poore estate hath compelled us to do this enterprise: we warrant you that your parents, although they bee covetous, will be contented to give us a great quantity of mony to redeeme and ransome you from our hands.

With such and like flattering words they endeavoured to appease the gentlewoman, howbeit she would in no case bee comforted, but put her head betwixt her knees, and cried pittiously. Then they called the old woman, and commaunded her to sit by the maiden, and pacifie her dolor as much as

THE FOURTH BOOKE

CHAPTER XXI

How the Theeves stole away a Gentlewoman, and brought her to their den

shee might. And they departed awey to rob, as they accustomed to doe, but the virgin would not asswage her griefes, nor mitigate her sorrow by any entreaty of the old woman, but howled and sobbed in such sort, that she made me poore Asse likewise to weepe, and thus she said, Alasse can I poore wench live any longer, that am come of so good a house, forsaken of all my parents, friends, and family, made a rapine and prey, closed servilely in this stony prison, deprived of all pleasure, wherein I have beene brought up, throwne in danger, ready to be rent in pieces among so many sturdy theeves and dreadful robbers, can I (I say) cease from weeping, and live any longer? Thus she cried and lamented, and after she had wearied her selfe with sorrow and blubbered her face with teares, she closed the windowes of her hollow eyes and laid her down to sleepe. And after that she had slept, she rose againe like a furious and mad woman, and beat her breast and comely face more than she did before.

Then the old woman enquired the causes of her new and sudden lamentation. To whom sighing in pittifull sort shee answered, Alas now am I utterly undone, now am I out of all hope, O give me a knife to kill me, or a halter to hang me. Whereat the old [woman] was more angry, and severely commanded her to tell her the cause of her sorrow, and why after her sleep she should renew her dolour and miserable weeping. What, thinke you (quoth she) to deceive our yong men of the price of your ransome? No, no, therefore cease your crying, for the Theeves doe little esteeme your howling, and if you will not, I will surely burn you alive. Hereat the Maiden was greatly feared, and kissed her hand and said, O mother take pitty upon me and my wretched fortune, and give me license a while to speake, for I thinke I shall not long live, let there be mercy ripe and franke in your venerable hoare head, and hear the sum of my calamity.

There was a comely young man, who for his bounty and grace was beloved entirely of all the towne, my cousine Germane, and but three yeares older than I; we two were nourished and brought up in one house, lay under one roofe, and in one chamber, and at length by promise of mariage, and by consent of our parents we were contracted together.

OF LUCIUS APULEIUS

CHAPTER XXI
How the Theeves stole away a Gentlewoman, and brought her to their den

The marriage day was come, the house was garnished with lawrel, and torches were set in every place in the honour of Hymeneus, my espouse was accompanied with his parents, kinsfolke and friends, and made sacrifice in the temples and publique places. And when my unhappy mother pampered me in her lap, and decked me like a bride, kissing me sweetly, and making me a parent for Children, behold there came in a great multitude of theeves armed like men of warre, with naked swords in their hands, who went not about to doe any harme, neither to take any thing away, but brake into the chamber where I was, and violently tooke me out of my mothers armes, when none of our family would resist for feare.

In this sort was our marriage disturbed, like the mariage of Hyppodame and Perithous. But behold my good mother, now my unhappy fortune is renewed and encreased: For I dreamed in my sleepe, that I was pulled out of our house, out of our chamber, and out of my bed, and that I removed about in solitary and unknowne places, calling upon the name of my unfortunate husband, and how that he, as soone as he perceived that I was taken away, even smelling with perfumes and crowned with garlands, did trace me by the steppes, desiring the aid of the people to assist him, in that his wife was violently stollen away. And as he went crying up and down, one of the theeves mooved with indignation, by reason of his pursuit, took up a stone that lay at his feet, and threw it at my husband and killed him. By the terror of which sight, and the feare of so dreadfull a dreame, I awaked.

Then the old woman rendring out like sighes, beganne to speake in this sort: My daughter take a good heart unto you, and bee not afeard at feigned and strange visions and dreams, for as the visions of the day are accounted false and untrue, so the visions of the night doe often chance contrary. And to dreame of weeping, beating, and killing, is a token of good lucke and prosperous change. Whereas contrary to dreame of laughing, carnall dalliance, and good cheere, is a signe of sadnesse, sickenesse, losse of substance, and displeasure. But I will tell thee a pleasant Tale, to put away all thy sorrow, and to revive thy spirits. And so she began in this manner.

THE MARRIAGE OF

THE TWENTY-SECOND CHAPTER

The most pleasant and delectable tale of the marriage of Cupid and Psyches.

HERE was sometimes a certaine King, inhabiting in the West parts, who had to wife a noble Dame, by whom he had three daughters exceeding fair: of whom the two elder were of such comly shape and beauty, as they did excell and passe all other women living, whereby they were thought worthily to deserve the praise and commendation of every person, and deservedly to be preferred above the residue of the common sort. Yet the singular passing beauty and maidenly majesty of the yongest daughter did so farre surmount and excell them two, as no earthly creature could by any meanes sufficiently expresse or set out the same.

By reason wherof, after the fame of this excellent maiden was spread abroad in every part of the City, the Citisens and strangers there beeing inwardly pricked by the zealous affection to behold her famous person, came daily by thousands, hundreths, and scores, to her fathers palace, who was astonied with admiration of her incomparable beauty, did no lesse worship and reverence her with crosses, signes and tokens, and other divine adorations, according to the custome of the old used rites and ceremonies, than if she were Lady Venus indeed: and shortly after the fame was spread into the next cities and bordering regions, that the goddesse whom the deep seas had born and brought forth, and the froth of the waves had nourished, to the intent to shew her high magnificencie and divine power on earth, to such as erst did honour and worship her, was now conversant amongst mortall men, or else that the earth and not the sea, by a new concourse and influence of the Celestiall planets, had budded and yeelded forth a new Venus, endued with the floure of virginity.

CUPID AND PSYCHES

CHAPTER XXII
The most pleasant and delectable tale of the marriage of Cupid and Psyches

So daily more and more encreased this opinion, and now is her flying fame dispersed into the next Island, and well nigh into every part and province of the whole world. Whereupon innumerable strangers resorted from farre Countries, adventuring themselves by long journies on land and by great perils on water, to behold this glorious virgin. By occasion whereof such a contempt grew towards the goddesse Venus, that no person travelled unto the Towne Paphos, nor to the Isle Gyndos, nor to Cythera to worship her. Her ornaments were throwne out, her temples defaced, her pillowes and cushions torne, her ceremonies neglected, her images and Statues uncrowned, and her bare altars unswept, and fowl with the ashes of old burnt sacrifice. For why, every person honoured and worshipped this maiden in stead of Venus, and in the morning at her first comming abroad offered unto her oblations, provided banquets, called her by the name of Venus, which was not Venus indeed, and in her honour presented floures and garlands in most reverend fashion.

This sudden change and alteration of celestiall honour, did greatly inflame and kindle the love of very Venus, who unable to temper her selfe from indignation, shaking her head in raging sort, reasoned with her selfe in this manner, Behold the originall parent of all these elements, behold the Lady Venus renowned throughout all the world, with whome a mortall maiden is joyned now partaker of honour: my name registred in the city of heaven, is prophaned and made vile by terrene absurdities. If I shall suffer any mortall creature to present my Majesty on earth, or that any shall beare about a false surmised shape of my person, then in vain did Paris the sheepheard (in whose just judgement and confidence the great Jupiter had affiance) preferre me above the residue of the goddesses, for the excellency of my beauty: but she, whatsoever she be that hath usurped myne honour, shal shortly repent her of her unlawfull estate. And by and by she called her winged sonne Cupid, rash enough and hardy, who by his evil manners contemning all publique justice and law, armed with fire and arrowes, running up and downe in the nights from house to house, and corrupting the lawfull

THE MARRIAGE OF

CHAPTER XXII

The most pleasant and delectable tale of the marriage of Cupid and Psyches

marriages of every person, doth nothing but that which is evill, who although that hee were of his owne proper nature sufficiently prone to worke mischiefe, yet she egged him forward with words, and brought him to the city, and shewed him Psyches (for so the maid was called), and having told the cause of her anger, not without great rage, I pray thee (quoth she) my dear childe, by motherly bond of love, by the sweet wounds of thy piercing darts, by the pleasant heate of thy fire, revenge the injury which is done to thy mother by the false and disobedient beauty of a mortall maiden, and I pray thee, that without delay shee may fall in love with the most miserablest creature living, the most poore, the most crooked, and the most vile, that there may bee none found in all the world of like wretchednesse. When she had spoken these words she embraced and kissed her sonne, and took her voyage towards the sea.

When she came upon the sea she began to cal the gods and goddesses, who were obedient at her voyce. For incontinent came the daughters of Nereus, singing with tunes melodiously: Portunus with his bristled and rough beard, Salita with her bosome full of fish, Palemon the driver of the Dolphine, the Trumpetters of Tryton, leaping hither and thither, and blowing with heavenly noyse: such was the company which followed Venus, marching towards the ocean sea.

In the meane season Psyches with all her beauty received no fruit of honor. She was wondred at of all, she was praised of all, but she perceived that no King nor Prince, nor any of the superiour sort did repaire to wooe her. Every one marvelled at her divine beauty, as it were some Image well painted and set out. Her other two sisters which were nothing so greatly exalted by the people, were royally married to two Kings: but the virgin Psyches sitting at home alone, lamented her solitary life, and being disquieted both in mind and body, although she pleased all the world, yet hated shee in her selfe her owne beauty. Whereupon the miserable father of this unfortunate daughter, suspecting that the gods and powers of heaven did envy her estate, went to the town called Milet to receive the Oracle of

CUPID AND PSYCHES

Apollo, where he made his prayers and offered sacrifice, and desired a husband for his daughter: but Apollo though he were a Grecian, and of the country of Ionia, because of the foundation of Milet, yet hee gave answer in Latine verse, the sence wherof was this:

CHAPTER XXII
The most pleasant and delectable tale of the marriage of Cupid and Psyches

> Let Psyches corps be clad in mourning weed,
> And set on rocke of yonder hill aloft :
> Her husband is no wight of humane seed,
> But Serpent dire and fierce as might be thought.
> Who flies with wings above in starry skies,
> And doth subdue each thing with firie flight.
> The gods themselves, and powers that seem so wise,
> With mighty Jove, be subject to his might,
> The rivers blacke, and deadly flouds of paine,
> And darknesse eke, as thrall to him remaine.

The King, sometimes happy when hee heard the prophesie of Apollo, returned home sad and sorrowfull, and declared to his wife the miserable and unhappy fate of his daughter. Then they began to lament and weep, and passed over many dayes in great sorrow. But now the time approached of Psyches marriage, preparation was made, blacke torches were lighted, the pleasant songs were turned into pittifull cries, the melody of Hymeneus was ended with deadly howling, the maid that should be married did wipe her eyes with her vaile. All the family and people of the city weeped likewise, and with great lamentation was ordained a remisse time for that day, but necessity compelled that Psyches should be brought to her appointed place, according to the divine appointment.

And when the solemnity was ended, they went to bring this sorrowfull spowse, not to her marriage, but to her finall end and buriall. And while the father and mother of Psyches did go forward weeping and crying to do this enterprise, Psyches spake unto them in this sort: Why torment you your unhappy age with continuall dolour? Why trouble you your spirits, which are more rather myne than yours? Why soyle ye your faces with teares, which I ought to adore and worship? Why teare you my eyes in yours? why pull you your hory haires? Why knocke ye your breasts for me? Now you see the reward of my excellent beauty: now, now

THE MARRIAGE OF

CHAPTER XXII

The most pleasant and delectable tale of the marriage of Cupid and Psyches

you perceive, but too late, the plague of envy. When the people did honour me, and call me new Venus, then yee should have wept, then you should have sorrowed as though I had been dead: for now I see and perceive that I am come to this misery by the only name of Venus, bring mee, and as fortune hath appointed, place me on the top of the rocke, I greatly desire to end my marriage, I greatly covet to see my husband. Why doe I delay? why should I refuse him that is appointed to destroy all the world?

Thus ended she her words, and thrust her selfe amongst the people that followed. Then they brought her to the appointed rocke of the high hill, and set [her] hereon, and so departed. The Torches and lights were put out with the tears of the people, and every man gone home, the miserable Parents well nigh consumed with sorrow, gave themselves to everlasting darknes.

Thus poore Psyches being left alone, weeping and trembling on the toppe of the rocke, was blowne by the gentle aire and of shrilling Zephyrus, and caried from the hill with a meek winde, which retained her garments up, and by little and little brought her downe into a deepe valley, where she was laid in a bed of most sweet and fragrant flowers.

Thus faire Psyches beeing sweetly couched among the soft and tender hearbs, as in a bed of sweet and fragrant floures, and having qualified the thoughts and troubles of her restlesse minde, was now well reposed. And when she had refreshed her selfe sufficiently with sleepe, she rose with a more quiet and pacified minde, and fortuned to espy a pleasant wood invironed with great and mighty trees. Shee espied likewise a running river as cleare as crystall: in the midst of the wood well nigh at the fall of the river was a princely Edifice, wrought and builded not by the art or hand of man, but by the mighty power of God: and you would judge at the first entry therin, that it were some pleasant and worthy mansion for the powers of heaven. For the embowings above were of Citron and Ivory, propped and undermined with pillars of gold, the walls covered and seeled with silver, divers sorts of beasts were graven and carved, that seemed to encounter with such as entered in. All things

CUPID AND PSYCHES

were so curiously and finely wrought, that it seemed either to be the worke of some Demy god, or God himselfe. The pavement was all of pretious stones, divided and cut one from another, whereon was carved divers kindes of pictures, in such sort that blessed and thrice blessed were they which might goe upon such a pavement: Every part and angle of the house was so well adorned, that by reason of the pretious stones and inestimable treasure there, it glittered and shone in such sort, that the chambers, porches, and doores gave light as it had beene the Sunne. Neither otherwise did the other treasure of the house disagree unto so great a majesty, that verily it seemed in every point an heavenly Palace, fabricate and built for Jupiter himselfe.

CHAPTER XXII
The most pleasant and delectable tale of the marriage of Cupid and Psyches

Then Psyches moved with delectation approched nigh, and taking a bold heart entred into the house, and beheld every thing there with great affection, she saw storehouses wrought exceeding fine, and replenished with aboundance of riches. Finally, there could nothing be devised which lacked there: but amongst such great store of Treasure this was most marvellous, that there was no closure, bolt, nor locke to keepe the same. And when with great pleasure she had viewed all these things, she heard a voyce without any body, that sayd, Why doe you marvell Madame at so great riches? behold, all that you see is at your commandement, wherefore goe you into the chamber, and repose your selfe upon the bed, and desire what bath you will have, and we whose voyces you heare bee your servants, and ready to minister unto you according to your desire. In the meane season, royall meats and dainty dishes shall be prepared for you.

Then Psyches perceived the felicity of divine providence, and according to the advertisement of the incorporeall voyces she first reposed her selfe upon the bed, and then refreshed her body in the baines. This done, shee saw the table garnished with meats, and a chaire to sit downe.

When Psyches was set downe, all sorts of divine meates and wines were brought in, not by any body, but as it were with a winde, for she saw no person before her, but only heard voyces on every side. After that all the services were brought to the table, one came in and sung invisibly,

THE MARRIAGE OF

CHAPTER XXII

The most pleasant and delectable tale of the marriage of Cupid and Psyches

another played on the harpe, but she saw no man. The harmony of the Instruments did so greatly shrill in her ears, that though there were no maner of person, yet seemed she in the midst of a multitude of people.

All these pleasures finished, when night aproched Psyches went to bed, and when she was layd, that the sweet sleep came upon her, she greatly feared her virginity, because shee was alone. Then came her unknowne husband and lay with her: and after that hee had made a perfect consummation of the marriage, he rose in the morning before day, and departed. Soone after came her invisible servants, and presented to her such things as were necessary for her defloration. And thus she passed forth a great while, and as it happeneth, the novelty of things by continuall custome did encrease her pleasure, but specially the sound of the instruments was a comfort unto her being alone.

During this time that Psyches was in this place of pleasures, her father and mother did nothing but weepe and lament, and her two sisters hearing of her most miserable fortune, came with great dolour and sorrow to comfort and speake with their parents.

The night following, Psyches husband spake unto her (for she might feele his eyes, his hands, and his ears) and sayd, O my sweet Spowse and dear wife, fortune doth menace unto thee imminent danger, wherof I wish thee greatly to beware: for know that thy sisters, thinking that thou art dead, bee greatly troubled, and are come to the mountain by thy steps. Whose lamentations if thou fortune to heare, beware that thou doe in no wise either make answer, or looke up towards them, for if thou doe thou shalt purchase to mee great sorrow, and to thy selfe utter destruction. Psyches hearing her Husband, was contented to doe all things as hee had commanded.

After that hee was departed and the night passed away, Psyches lamented and lamented all the day following, thinking that now shee was past all hopes of comfort, in that shee was closed within the walls of a prison, deprived of humane conversation, and commaunded not to aid her sorrowfull Sisters, no nor once to see them. Thus she passed all the

CUPID AND PSYCHES

day in weeping, and went to bed at night, without any refection of meat or baine.

Incontinently after came her husband, who when hee had embraced her sweetly, began to say, Is it thus that you performe your promise, my sweet wife? What do I finde heere? Passe you all the day and the night in weeping? And wil you not cease in your husbands armes? Goe too, doe what ye will, purchase your owne destruction, and when you finde it so, then remember my words, and repent, but too late. Then she desired her husband more and more, assuring him that shee should die, unlesse he would grant that she might see her sisters, wherby she might speake with them and comfort them, whereat at length he was contented, and moreover hee willed that shee should give them as much gold and jewels as she would. But he gave her a further charge saying, Beware that ye covet not (being mooved by the pernicious counsell of your sisters) to see the shape of my person, lest by your curiosity you deprive your selfe of so great and worthy estate. Psyches being glad herewith, rendred unto him most entire thankes, and said, Sweet husband, I had rather die than to bee separated from you, for whosoever you be, I love and retaine you within my heart as if you were myne owne spirit or Cupid himselfe : but I pray you grant this likewise, that you would commaund your servant Zephyrus to bring my sisters downe into the valley as he brought mee.

Wherewithall shee kissed him sweetly, and desired him gently to grant her request, calling him her spowse, her sweetheart, her Joy, and her Solace. Wherby she enforced him to agree to her mind, and when morning came he departed away.

After long search made, the sisters of Psyches came unto the hill where she was set on the rocke, and cried with a loud voyce in such sort that the stones answered againe. And when they called their sister by her name, that their lamentable cries came unto her eares, shee came forth and said, Behold, heere is shee for whom you weepe, I pray you torment your selves no more, cease your weeping. And by and by shee commaunded Zephyrus by the appointment

O

THE MARRIAGE OF

CHAPTER XXII
The most pleasant and delectable tale of the marriage of Cupid and Psyches

of her husband to bring them downe. Neither did hee delay, for with gentle blasts he retained them up and layd them softly in the valley. I am not able to expresse the often embracing, kissing and greeting which was betweene them three, all sorrows and tears were then layd apart.

Come in (quoth Psyches) into our house, and refresh your afflicted mindes with your sister.

After this she shewed them the storehouses of treasure, shee caused them to hear the voices which served her, the bain was ready, the meats were brought in, and when they had filled themselves with divine delecates, they conceived great envy within their hearts, and one of them being curious, did demand what her husband was, of what estate, and who was Lord of so pretious a house? But Psyches remembring the promise which she had made to her husband, feigned that hee was a young man, of comely stature, with a flaxen beard, and had great delight in hunting in the hills and dales by. And lest by her long talke she should be found to trip or faile in her words, she filled their laps with gold, silver, and Jewels, and commanded Zephyrus to carry them away.

When they were brought up to the mountain, they tooke their wayes homeward to their owne houses, and murmured with envy that they bare against Psyches, saying, Behold cruell and contrary fortune, behold how we, borne all of one Parent, have divers destinies: but especially we that are the elder two bee married to strange husbands, made as Handmaidens, and as it were banished from our Countrey and friends. Whereas our younger sister hath great abundance of treasure, and hath gotten a god to her husband, although shee hath no skill how to use so great plenty of riches. Saw you not sister what was in the house, what great store of jewels, what glittering robes, what Gemmes, what gold we trod on? That if shee have a husband according as shee affirmeth, there is none that liveth this day more happy in all the world than she. And so it may come to passe, that at length for the great affection which hee may beare unto her hee may make her a goddesse: for by Hercules, such was her countenance, so she behaved her self, that as a

CUPID AND PSYCHES

goddesse she had voices to serve her, and the winds did obey her.

But I poore wretch have first maried an husband elder than my father, more bald than a Coot, more weake than a child, and that locketh me up all day in the house.

Then said the other sister, And in faith I am maried to a husband that hath the gout, twyfold, crooked, not couragious in paying my debt, I am faine to rubbe and mollifie his stony fingers with divers sorts of oyles, and to wrap them in playsters and salves, so that I soyle my white and dainty hands with the corruption of filthy clouts, not using my selfe like a wife, but more like a servant. And you my sister seem likewise to be in bondage and servitude, wherefore I cannot abide to see our younger sister in such great felicity: saw you not I pray you how proudly and arrogantly shee handled us even now? And how in vaunting her selfe shee uttered her presumptuous minde, how she cast a little gold into our laps, and being weary of our company, commanded that we should be borne and blown away?

Verily I live not, nor am a woman, but I will deprive her of all her blisse. And if you my sister bee so far bent as I, let us consult together, and not to utter our minde to any person, no not to our parents, nor tell that ever we saw her. For it sufficeth that we have seene her, whom it repenteth to have seene. Neither let us declare her good fortune to our father, nor to any other, since as they seeme not happy whose riches are unknowne: so shall she know that shee hath sisters no Abjects, but worthier than she.

But now let us goe home to our husbands and poore houses, and when wee are better instructed, let us returne to suppresse her pride. So this evill counsell pleased these two evill women, and they hid the treasure which Psyches gave them, and tare their haire, renewing their false and forged teares. When their father and mother beheld them weep and lament still, they doubled their sorrowes and griefes, but full of yre and forced with Envy, they tooke their voyage homeward, devising the slaughter and destruction of their sister.

In the meane season the husband of Psyches did warne

CHAPTER XXII

The most pleasant and delectable tale of the marriage of Cupid and Psyches

THE MARRIAGE OF

CHAPTER XXII

The most pleasant and delectable tale of the marriage of Cupid and Psyches

her againe in the night with these words: Seest thou not (quoth he) what perill and danger evill fortune doth threaten unto thee, whereof if thou take not good heed it will shortly come upon thee. For the unfaithfull harlots doe greatly endeavor to set their snares to catch thee, and their purpose is to make and perswade thee to behold my face, which if thou once fortune to see, as I have often told, thou shalt see no more. Wherfore if these naughty hagges, armed with wicked minds, doe chance to come againe (as I thinke no otherwise but that they will) take heed that thou talke not with them, but simply suffer them to speake what they will, howbeit if thou canst not refraine thy selfe, beware that thou have no communication of thy husband, nor answer a word if they fortune to question of me, so will we encrease our stocke, and this young and tender childe, couched in this young and tender belly of thine, if thou conceale my secrets, shall be made an immortall god, otherwise a mortal creature. Then Psyches was very glad that she should bring forth a divine babe, and very joyfull in that she should be honored as a mother. She reckened and numbered carefully the days and months that passed, and beeing never with child before, did marvel greatly that in so short a time her belly should swel so big. But those pestilent and wicked furies breathing out their Serpentine poyson, took shipping to bring their enterprise to passe. Then Psyches was warned again by her husband in this sort: Behold the last day, the extream case, and the enemies of thy blood, hath armed themselves against us, pitched their campe, set their host in array, and are marching towards us, for now thy two sisters have drawn their swords, and are ready to slay thee. O with what force are we assailed this day! O sweet Psyches I pray thee to take pitty on thy selfe, of me, and deliver thy husband and this infant within thy belly from so great danger, and see not neither heare these cursed women, which are not worthy to be called thy sisters, for their great hatred and breach of sisterly amity, for they wil come like Syrens to the mountains, and yeeld out their pittious and lamentable cries. When Psyches had heard these words shee sighed sorrowfully and said, O deare

CUPID AND PSYCHES

husband, this long time have you had experience and triall of my faith, and doubt you not but that I will persever in the same, wherefore command your winde Zephyrus, that hee may doe as hee hath done before, to the intent that where you have charged me not to behold your venerable face, yet that I may comfort my selfe with the sight of my sisters. I pray you by these beautifull haires, by these round cheeks delicate and tender, by your pleasant hot breast, whose shape and face I shall learne at length by the childe in my belly, grant the fruit of my desire, refresh your deare Spowse Psyches with joy, who is bound and linked unto you for ever. I little esteeme to see your visage and figure, little doe I regard the night and darkenesse thereof, for you are my only light.

CHAPTER XXII The most pleasant and delectable tale of the marriage of Cupid and Psyches

Her husband being as it were inchanted with these words and compelled by violence of her often embracing, wiping away her teares with his haire, did yeeld unto his wife. And when morning came, departed as hee was accustomed to doe.

Now her sisters arrived on land, and never rested til they came to the rock, without visiting their parents, and leapt down rashly from the hill themselves. Then Zephyrus according to the divine commandment brought them down, though it were against his wil, and laid them in the vally without any harm: by and by they went into the palace to their sister without leave, and when they had eftscone embraced their prey, and thanked her with flattering words for the treasure which she gave them, they said, O deare sister Psyches, know you that you are now no more a childe, but a mother: O what great joy beare you unto us in your belly? What a comfort will it be unto all the house? How happy shall we be, that shall see this Infant nourished amongst so great plenty of Treasure? That if he be like his parents, as it is necessary he should, there is no doubt but a new Cupid shall be borne. By this kinde of meanes they went about to winne Psyches by little and little, but because they were wearie with travell, they sate them downe in chaires, and after that they had washed their bodies in baines they went into a Parlour, where all kinde of meats

THE MARRIAGE OF

CHAPTER XXII

The most pleasant and delectable tale of the marriage of Cupid and Psyches

were ready prepared. Psyches commanded one to play with his harpe, it was done. Then immediately others sung, others tuned their instruments, but no person was seene, by whose sweet harmony and modulation the sisters of Psyches were greatly delighted.

Howbeit the wickednesse of these cursed women was nothing suppressed by the sweet noyse of these instruments, but they setled themselves to worke their treasons against Psyches, demanding who was her husband, and of what Parentage. Then shee having forgotten by too much simplicity, what she had spoken before of her husband, invented a new answer, and said that her husband was of a great province, a merchant, and a man of a middle age, having his beard interspersed with gray haires. Which when shee had spoken (because she would have no further talke) she filled their laps full of Gold and Silver, and bid Zephyrus to bear them away.

In their returne homeward they murmured within themselves, saying, How say you sister to so apparant a lye of Psyches? First she sayd that her husband was a young man of flourishing yeares, and had a flaxen beard, and now she sayth that he is halfe gray with age. What is he that in so short a space can become so old? You shall finde it no otherwise my sister, but that either this cursed queane hath invented a great lie, or else that she never saw the shape of her husband. And if it be so that she never saw him, then verily she is married to some god, and hath a yong god in her belly. But if it be a divine babe, and fortune to come to the eares of my mother (as God forbid it should) then may I go and hang my selfe: wherfore let us go to our parents, and with forged lies let us colour the matter.

After they were thus inflamed, and had visited their Parents, they returned againe to the mountaine, and by the ayd of the winde Zephyrus were carried downe into the valley, and after they had streined their eye lids, to enforce themselves to weepe, they called unto Psyches in this sort, Thou (ignorant of so great evill) thinkest thy selfe sure and happy, and sittest at home nothing regarding thy peril, whereas wee goe about thy affaires, and are carefull lest any harme should

CUPID AND PSYCHES

CHAPTER XXII

The most pleasant and delectable tale of the marriage of Cupid and Psyches

happen unto you: for we are credibly informed, neither can we but utter it unto you, that there is a great serpent full of deadly poyson, with a ravenous and gaping throat, that lieth with thee every night. Remember the Oracle of Apollo, who pronounced that thou shouldest be married to a dire and fierce Serpent, and many of the Inhabitants hereby, and such as hunt about in the countrey, affirme that they saw him yesternight returning from pasture and swimming over the River, whereby they doe undoubtedly say, that hee will not pamper thee long with delicate meats, but when the time of delivery shall approach he will devoure both thee and thy child: wherefore advise thy selfe whether thou wilt agree unto us that are carefull of thy safety, and so avoid the perill of death, and bee contented to live with thy sisters, or whether thou wilt remaine with the Serpent, and in the end be swallowed into the gulfe of his body. And if it be so that thy solitary life, thy conversation with voices, this servile and dangerous pleasure, and the love of the Serpent doe more delight thee, say not but that we have played the parts of naturall sisters in warning thee.

Then the poore and simple miser Psyches was mooved with the feare of so dreadfull words, and being amazed in her mind, did cleane forget the admonitions of her husband, and her owne promises made unto him, and throwing her selfe headlong into extreame misery, with a wanne and sallow countenance, scantly uttering a third word, at length gan say in this sort: O my most deare sisters, I heartily thanke you for your great kindenesse toward me, and I am now verily perswaded that they which have informed you hereof hath informed you of nothing but truth, for I never saw the shape of my husband, neither know I from whence he came, only I heare his voice in the night, insomuch that I have an uncertaine husband, and one that loveth not the light of the day: which causeth me to suspect that he is a beast, as you affirme. Moreover, I doe greatly feare to see him, for he doth menace and threaten great evill unto mee, if I should goe about to spy and behold his shape, wherefore my loving sisters if you have any wholsome remedy for your sister in danger, give it now presently. Then they opened the gates

THE MARRIAGE OF

CHAPTER XXII

The most pleasant and delectable tale of the marriage of Cupid and Psyches

of their subtill mindes, and did put away all privy guile, and egged her forward in her fearefull thoughts, perswading her to doe as they would have her: whereupon one of them began and sayd, Because that wee little esteeme any perill or danger, to save your life, we intend to shew you the best way and meane as we may possibly do. Take a sharpe razor and put it under the pillow of your bed; and see that you have ready a privy burning lampe with oyle, hid under some part of the hanging of the chamber, and finely dissembling the matter, when according to his custome hee commeth to bed and sleepeth soundly, arise you secretly, and with your bare feet goe and take the lampe, with the Razor in your right hand, and with valiant force cut off the head of the poysonous serpent, wherein we will aid and assist you: and when by the death of him you shall be made safe, we wil marry you to some comely man.

After they had thus inflamed the heart of their sister, fearing lest some danger might happen unto them by reason of their evill counsell, they were carried by the wind Zephyrus to the top of the mountaine, and so they ran away and tooke shipping.

When Psyches was left alone (saving that she seemed not to be alone, being stirred by so many furies) she was in a tossing minde like the waves of the sea, and although her wil was obstinate, and resisted to put in execution the counsell of her Sisters, yet she was in doubtfull and divers opinions touching her calamity. Sometime she would, sometime she would not, sometime she is bold, sometime she feareth, somtime shee mistrusteth, somtime she is mooved, somtime she hateth the beast, somtime she loveth her husband: but at length night came, when as she prepared for her wicked intent.

Soon after her husband came, and when he had kissed and embraced her he fel asleep. Then Psyches (somwhat feeble in body and mind, yet mooved by cruelty of fate) received boldnes and brought forth the lampe, and tooke the razor, so by her audacity she changed her mind: but when she took the lamp and came to the bed side, she saw the most meeke and sweetest beast of all beasts, even faire Cupid couched

CUPID AND PSYCHES

fairly, at whose sight the very lampe encreased his light for joy, and the razor turned his edge.

But when Psyches saw so glorious a body shee greatly feared, and amazed in mind, with a pale countenance all trembling fel on her knees and thought to hide the razor, yea verily in her owne heart, which doubtlesse she had done, had it not through feare of so great an enterprise fallen out of her hand. And when she saw and beheld the beauty of the divine visage shee was well recreated in her mind, she saw his haires of gold, that yeelded out a sweet savor, his neck more white than milk, his purple cheeks, his haire hanging comely behinde and before, the brightnesse whereof did darken the light of the lamp, his tender plume feathers, dispersed upon his sholders like shining flours, and trembling hither and thither, and his other parts of his body so smooth and so soft, that it did not repent Venus to beare such a childe. At the beds feet lay his bow, quiver, and arrowes, that be the weapons of so great a god: which when Psyches did curiously behold, she marvelling at her husbands weapons, took one of the arrows out of the quiver, and pricked her selfe withall, wherwith she was so grievously wounded that the blood followed, and thereby of her owne accord shee added love upon love; then more broyling in the love of Cupid shee embraced him and kissed him and kissed him a thousand times, fearing the measure of his sleepe. But alas while shee was in this great joy, whether it were for envy, for desire to touch this amiable body likewise, there fell out a droppe of burning oyle from the lampe upon the right shoulder of the god. O rash and bold lampe, the vile ministery of love, how darest thou bee so bold as to burne the god of all fire? When as he invented thee, to the intent that all lovers might with more joy passe the nights in pleasure.

The god beeing burned in this sort, and perceiving that promise and faith was broken, hee fled away without utterance of any word, from the eyes and hands of his most unhappy wife. But Psyches fortuned to catch him as hee was rising, by the right thigh, and held him fast as hee flew above in the aire, untill such time as constrained by wearinesse shee let goe and fell downe upon the ground. But Cupid followed

CHAPTER XXII

The most pleasant and delectable tale of the marriage of Cupid and Psyches

THE MARRIAGE OF

CHAPTER XXII

The most pleasant and delectable tale of the marriage of Cupid and Psyches

her downe, and lighted upon the top of a Cypresse tree, and angerly spake unto her in this manner: O simple Psyches, consider with thy selfe how I, little regarding the commandement of my mother (who willed mee that thou shouldst bee married to a man of base and miserable condition) did come my selfe from heaven to love thee, and wounded myne owne body with my proper weapons, to have thee to my Spowse: And did I seeme a beast unto thee, that thou shouldst go about to cut off my head with a razor, who loved thee so well? Did not I alwayes give thee a charge? Did not I gently will thee to beware? But those cursed aiders and Counsellors of thine shall be worthily rewarded for their paines. As for thee thou shalt be sufficiently punished by my absence. When hee had spoken these words he tooke his flight into the aire. Then Psyches fell flat on the ground, and as long as she could see her husband she cast her eyes after him into the aire, weeping and lamenting pitteously: but when hee was gone out of her sight shee threw her selfe into the next running river, for the great anguish and dolour that shee was in for the lack of her husband; howbeit the water would not suffer her to be drowned, but tooke pitty upon her, in the honour of Cupid which accustomed to broyle and burne the river, and threw her upon the bank amongst the herbs.

Then Pan the rusticall god sitting on the river side, embracing and [teaching] the goddesse Canna to tune her songs and pipes, by whom were feeding the young and tender Goats, after that he perceived Psyches in sorrowfull case, not ignorant (I know not by what meanes) of her miserable estate, endeavored to pacifie her in this sort: O faire maid, I am a rusticke and rude heardsman, howbeit by reason of my old age expert in many things, for as farre as I can learne by conjecture (which according as wise men doe terme is called divination) I perceive by your uncertaine gate, your pale hew, your sobbing sighes, and your watery eyes, that you are greatly in love. Wherefore hearken to me, and goe not about to slay your selfe, nor weepe not at all, but rather adore and worship the great god Cupid, and winne him unto you by your gentle promise of service.

CUPID AND PSYCHES

When the god of Shepheards had spoken these words, she gave no answer, but made reverence to him as to a god, and so departed.

CHAPTER XXII

The most pleasant and delectable tale of the marriage of Cupid and Psyches

After that Psyches had gone a little way, she fortuned unawares to come to a city where the husband of one of her Sisters did dwell. Which when Psyches did understand, shee caused that her sister had knowledge of her comming, and so they met together, and after great embracing and salutation, the sister of Psyches demaunded the cause of her travell thither. Marry (quoth she) doe you not remember the counsell you gave me, whereby you would that I should kill the beast which under colour of my husband did lie with mee every night? You shall understand, that as soone as I brought forth the lampe to see and behold his shape, I perceived that he was the sonne of Venus, even Cupid himselfe that lay with mee. Then I being stricken with great pleasure, and desirous to embrace him, could not throughly asswage my delight, but alas by evill chance the boyling oyle of the lampe fortuned to fall on his shoulder, which caused him to awake, and seeing me armed with fire and weapons, gan say, How darest thou be so bold to doe so great a mischiefe? depart from me and take such things as thou didst bring: for I will have thy sister (and named you) to my wife, and she shall be placed in thy felicity, and by and by hee commaunded Zephyrus to carry me away from the bounds of his house.

Psyches had scantly finished her tale, but her sister pierced with the pricke of carnall desire and wicked envy, ran home, and feigning to her husband that shee had heard word of the death of her parents, tooke shipping and came to the mountaine. And although there blew a contrary winde, yet being brought in a vaine hope, she cried, O Cupid take me a more worthy wife, and thou Zephyrus beare downe thy mistresse, and so she cast her selfe headlong from the mountaine: but shee fell not into the valley neither alive nor dead, for all the members and parts of her body were torne amongst the rockes, wherby she was made a prey unto the birds and wild beasts, as she worthily deserved.

Neither was the vengeance of the other delayed, for Psyches travelling in that country, fortuned to come to

THE MARRIAGE OF

CHAPTER XXII

The most pleasant and delectable tale of the marriage of Cupid and Psyches

another city where her other sister did dwel; to whom when shee had declared all such things as she told to her other sister, shee ran likewise unto the rock and was slaine in like sort. Then Psyches travelled about in the countrey to seeke her husband Cupid, but he was gotten into his mothers chamber, and there bewailed the sorrowfull wound which he caught by the oyle of a burning lamp.

Then the white bird the Gull, which swims on the waves of the water, flew toward the Ocean sea, where he found Venus washing and bathing her selfe: to whom she declared that her son was burned and in danger of death, and moreover that it was a common brute in the mouth of every person (who spake evill of all the family of Venus) that her son doth nothing but haunt harlots in the mountain, and she her self lasciviously use to ryot in the sea: wherby they say that they are now become no more gratious, pleasant, nor gentle, but incivile, monstrous and horrible. Moreover, that marriages are not for any amity, or for love of procreation, but full of envy, discord, and debate. This the curious Gul did clatter in the ears of Venus, reprehending her son. But Venus began to cry and sayd, What hath my sonne gotten any Love? I pray thee gentle bird that doest serve me so faithfully, tell me what she is, and what is her name that hath troubled my son in such sort? whether shee be any of the Nymphs, of the number of the goddesses, of the company of the Muses, or of the mistery of the Graces? To whom the bird answered, Madam I know not what shee is, but this I know that she is called Psyches. Then Venus with indignation cried out, What is it she? the usurper of my beauty, the Vicar of my name? What did he think that I was a bawd, by whose shew he fell acquainted with the maid? And immediately she departed and went to her chamber, where she found her son wounded as it was told unto her, whom when she beheld she cries out in this sort,

Is this an honest thing, is this honourable to thy parents? is this reason, that thou hast violated and broken the commandement of thy mother and soveraign mistresse: and whereas thou shouldst have vexed my enemy with loathsom love, thou hast done otherwise?

CUPID AND PSYCHES

For beeing of tender and unripe yeares, thou hast with too licentious appetite embraced my most mortall Foe, to whome I shall bee made a mother, and shee a Daughter. Thou presumest and thinkest, thou trifling boy, thou Varlet, and without all reverence, that thou art most worthy and excellent, and that I am not able by reason of myne age to have another son, which if I should have, thou shouldst well understand that I would beare a more worthier than thou. But to worke thee a greater despight, I do determine to adopt one of my servants, and to give him these wings, this fire, this bow, and these Arrowes, and all other furniture which I gave to thee, not to this purpose, neither is any thing given thee of thy father for this intent: but first thou hast beene evill brought up, and instructed in thy youth thou hast thy hands ready and sharpe. Thou hast often offended thy antients, and especially me that am thy mother, thou hast pierced mee with thy darts, thou contemnest me as a widow, neither dost thou regard thy valiant and invincible father, and to anger me more, thou art amorous of harlots and wenches: but I will cause that thou shalt shortly repent thee, and that this marriage shalbe dearely bought. To what a point am [I] now driven? What shall I do? Whether shall I goe? How shall I represse this beast? Shall I aske ayd of myne enemy Sobriety, whom I have often offended to engender thee? Or shall I seeke for counsel of every poore rusticall woman? No, no, yet had I rather dye, howbeit I will not cease my vengeance, to her must I have recourse for helpe, and to none other (I meane to Sobriety), who may correct thee sharpely, take away thy quiver, deprive thee of thy arrowes, unbend thy bow, quench thy fire, and which is more, subdue thy body with punishment: and when that I have rased and cut off this thy haire, which I have dressed with myne owne hands, and made to glitter like gold, and when I have clipped thy wings, which I my selfe have caused to burgen, then shall I thinke to have revenged my selfe sufficiently upon thee for the injury which thou hast done. When shee had spoken these words shee departed in a great rage out of her chamber.

Immediatelie as she was going away came Juno and Ceres,

CHAPTER XXII
The most pleasant and delectable tale of the marriage of Cupid and Psyches

THE MARRIAGE OF

CHAPTER XXII
The most pleasant and delectable tale of the marriage of Cupid and Psyches

demaunding the cause of her anger. Then Venus answered, Verily you are come to comfort my sorrow, but I pray you with all diligence to seeke out one whose name is Psyches, who is a vagabond, and runneth about the Countries, and (as I thinke) you are not ignorant of the brute of my son Cupid, and of his demeanour, which I am ashamed to declare. Then they understanding the whole matter, endeavoured to mitigate the ire of Venus in this sort: What is the cause Madam, or how hath your son so offended, that you shold so greatly accuse his love, and blame him by reason that he is amorous? and why should you seeke the death of her, whom he doth fancie? We most humbly intreat you to pardon his fault, if hee have accorded to the mind of any maiden: what do you not know that he is a young man? Or have you forgotten of what yeeres he is? Doth he seeme alwayes unto you to be a childe? You are his mother, and a kind woman, will you continually search out his dalliance? Will you blame his luxury? Will you bridle his love? and will you reprehend your owne art and delights in him? What God or man is hee, that can endure that you should sowe or disperse your seed of love in every place, and to make restraint thereof within your owne doores? certes you will be the cause of the suppression of the publike paces of young Dames. In this sort this goddesse endeavoured to pacifie her mind, and to excuse Cupid with al their power (although he were absent) for feare of his darts and shafts of love. But Venus would in no wise asswage her heat, but (thinking that they did rather trifle and taunt at her injuries) she departed from them, and tooke her voiage towards the sea in all haste. In the meane season Psyches hurled her selfe hither and thither, to seeke her husband, the rather because she thought that if he would not be appeased with the sweet flattery of his wife, yet he would take mercy on her at her servile and continuall prayers. And (espying a Church on the top of a high hill) she said, What can I tell whether my husband and master be there or no? wherefore she went thitherward, and with great paine and travell, moved by hope, after that she climbed to the top of the mountaine, she came to the temple, and went in,

CUPID AND PSYCHES

CHAPTER XXII
The most pleasant and delectable tale of the marriage of Cupid and Psyches

wheras behold she espied sheffes of corn lying on a heap, blades withered with garlands, and reeds of barly, moreover she saw hooks, sithes, sickles, and other instruments, to reape, but every thing lay out of order, and as it were cast in by the hands of laborers, which when Psyches saw she gathered up and put every thing in order, thinking that she would not despise or contemne the temples of any of the Gods, but rather get the favour and benevolence of them all: by and by Ceres came in, and beholding her busie and curious in her chapell, cried out a far off, and said, O Psyches needfull of mercy, Venus searcheth for thee in every place to revenge her selfe and to punish thee grievously, but thou hast more mind to be heere, and carest for nothing lesse, then for thy safety. Then Psyches fell on her knees before her, watring her feet with her teares, wiping the ground with her haire, and with great weeping and lamentation desired pardon, saying, O great and holy Goddesse, I pray thee by thy plenteous and liberall right hand, by the joyfull ceremonies of thy harvest, by the secrets of thy Sacrifice, by the flying chariots of thy dragons, by the tillage of the ground of Sicilie, which thou hast invented, by the marriage of Proserpin, by the diligent inquisition of thy daughter, and by the other secrets which are within the temple of Eleusis in the land of Athens, take pitty on me thy servant Psyches, and let me hide my selfe a few dayes amongst these sheffes of corne, untill the ire of so great a Goddesse be past, or untill that I be refreshed of my great labour and travell. Then answered Ceres, Verely Psyches, I am greatly moved by thy prayers and teares, and desire with all my heart to aide thee, but if I should suffer thee to be hidden here, I should increase the displeasure of my Cosin, with whom I have made a treatie of peace, and an ancient promise of amity: wherefore I advise thee to depart hence and take it not in evil part in that I will not suffer thee to abide and remaine here within my temple. Then Psyches driven away contrary to her hope, was double afflicted with sorrow, and so she returned back againe. And behold she perceived a far off in a vally a Temple standing within a Forest, faire and curiously wrought, and minding to over-passe no place

THE MARRIAGE OF

CHAPTER XXII

The most pleasant and delectable tale of the marriage of Cupid and Psyches

whither better hope did direct her, and to the intent she would desire pardon of every God, she approached nigh unto the sacred doore, whereas she saw pretious riches and vestiments ingraven with letters of gold, hanging upon branches of trees, and the posts of the temple testifying the name of the goddesse Juno, to whom they were dedicate, then she kneeled downe upon her knees, and imbraced the Alter with her hands, and wiping her teares, gan pray in this sort: O deere spouse and sister of the great God Jupiter which art adored and worshipped amongst the great temples of Samos, called upon by women with child, worshipped at high Carthage, because thou wast brought from heaven by the lyon, the rivers of the floud Inachus do celebrate thee: and know that thou art the wife of the great god, and the goddesse of goddesses; all the east part of the world have thee in veneration, all the world calleth thee Lucina: I pray thee to be my advocate in my tribulations, deliver me from the great danger which pursueth me, and save me that am weary with so long labours and sorrow, for I know that it is thou that succorest and helpest such women as are with child and in danger. Then Juno hearing the prayers of Psyches, appeared unto her in all her royalty, saying, Certes Psyches I would gladly help thee, but I am ashamed to do any thing contrary to the will of my daughter in law Venus, whom alwaies I have loved as mine owne child, moreover I shall incurre the danger of the law, intituled, *De servo corrupto*, whereby I am forbidden to retaine any servant fugitive, against the will of his Master. Then Psyches cast off likewise by Juno, as without all hope of the recovery of her husband, reasoned with her selfe in this sort: Now what comfort or remedy is left to my afflictions, when as my prayers will nothing availe with the goddesses? what shall I do? whither shall I go? In what cave or darknesse shall I hide my selfe, to avoid the furor of Venus? Why do I not take a good heart, and offer my selfe with humilitie unto her, whose anger I have wrought? What do I know whether he (whom I seeke for) be in his mothers house or no? Thus being in doubt, poore Psyches prepared her selfe to her owne danger, and devised how she might make her

CUPID AND PSYCHES

orison and prayer unto Venus. After that Venus was weary with searching by Sea and Land for Psyches, shee returned toward heaven, and commanded that one should prepare her Chariot, which her husband Vulcanus gave unto her by reason of marriage, so finely wrought that neither gold nor silver could be compared to the brightnesse therof. Four white pigeons guided the chariot with great diligence, and when Venus was entred in, a number of sparrowes flew chirping about, making signe of joy, and all other kind of birds sang sweetly, foreshewing the comming of the great goddesse: the clouds gave place, the heavens opened, and received her joyfully, the birds that followed nothing feared the Eagle, Hawkes, or other ravenous foules of the aire. Incontinently she went unto the royall Pallace of God Jupiter, and with a proud and bold petition demanded the service of Mercury, in certaine of her affaires, whereunto Jupiter consented: then with much joy shee descended from Heaven with Mercury, and gave him an earnest charge to put in execution her words, saying: O my Brother, borne in Arcadia, thou knowest well, that I (who am thy sister) did never enterprise to doe any thing without thy presence, thou knowest also how long I have sought for a girle and cannot finde her, wherefore there resteth nothing else save that thou with thy trumpet doe pronounce the reward to such as take her: see thou put in execution my commandement, and declare that whatsoever he be that retaineth her wittingly, against my will shall not defend himselfe by any meane or excusation: which when she had spoken, she delivered unto him a libell, wherein was contained the name of Psyches, and the residue of his publication, which done, she departed away to her lodging. By and by, Mercurius (not delaying the matter) proclaimed throughout all the world, that whatsoever hee were that could tell any tydings of a Kings fugitive Daughter, the servant of Venus, named Psyches, should bring word to Mercury, and for reward of his paines, he should receive seaven sweet kisses of Venus. After that Mercury had pronounced these things, every man was enflamed with desire to search out Psyches.

This proclamation was the cause that put all doubt from

CHAPTER XXII

The most pleasant and delectable tale of the marriage of Cupid and Psyches

THE MARRIAGE OF

CHAPTER XXII
The most pleasant and delectable tale of the marriage of Cupid and Psyches

Psyches, who was scantly come in the sight of the house of Venus, but one of her servants called Custome came out, who espying Psyches, cried with a loud voyce, saying : O wicked harlot as thou art, now at length thou shalt know that thou hast a mistresse above thee. What, dost thou make thy selfe ignorant, as though thou didst not understand what travell wee have taken in searching for thee? I am glad that thou art come into my hands, thou art now in the gulfe of hell, and shalt abide the paine and punishment of thy great contumacy, and therewithall she tooke her by the haire, and brought her in, before the presence of the goddesse Venus. When Venus spied her, shee began to laugh, and as angry persons accustome to doe, she shaked her head, and scratched her right eare saying, O goddesse, goddesse, you are now come at length to visit your husband that is in danger of death, by your meanes : bee you assured, I will handle you like a daughter : where be my maidens, Sorrow and Sadnesse? To whom (when they came) she delivered Psyches to be cruelly tormented; then they fulfilled the commandement of their Mistresse, and after they had piteously scourged her with rods and whips, they presented her againe before Venus; then she began to laugh againe, saying : Behold she thinketh (that by reason of her great belly, which she hath gotten by playing the whore) to move me to pitty, and to make me a grandmother to her childe. Am not I happy, that in the flourishing time of al mine age, shall be called a grandmother, and the sonne of a vile harlot shall bee accounted the nephew of Venus : Howbeit I am a foole to tearm him by the name of my son, since as the marriage was made betweene unequall persons, in the field without witnesses, and not by the consent of parents, wherefore the marriage is illegitimate, and the childe (that shall be borne) a bastard ; if we fortune to suffer thee to live so long till thou be delivered. When Venus had spoken these words she leaped upon the face of poore Psyches, and (tearing her apparell) tooke her by the haire, and dashed her head upon the ground. Then she tooke a great quantity of wheat, of barly, poppy seede, peason, lintles, and beanes, and mingled them altogether on a heape saying:

CUPID AND PSYCHES

Thou evill favoured girle, thou seemest unable to get the grace of thy lover, by no other meanes, but only by diligent and painefull service, wherefore I will prove what thou canst doe: see that thou separate all these graines one from another, disposing them orderly in their quantity, and let it be done before night. When she had appointed this taske unto Psyches, she departed to a great banket that was prepared that day. But Psyches went not about to dissever the graine, (as being a thing impossible to be brought to passe by reason it lay so confusedly scattered) but being astonyed at the cruell commandement of Venus, sate still and said nothing. Then the little pismire the emote, taking pitty of her great difficulty and labour, cursing the cruellnesse of the daughter of Jupiter, and of so evill a mother, ran about, hither and thither, and called to all her friends, Yee quick sons of the ground, the mother of all things, take mercy on this poore maid, espouse to Cupid, who is in great danger of her person, I pray you helpe her with all diligence. Incontinently one came after another, dissevering and dividing the graine, and after that they had put each kinde of corne in order, they ranne away againe in all haste. When night came, Venus returned home from the banket wel tippled with wine, smelling of balme, and crowned with garlands of roses, who when shee had espied what Psyches had done, gan say, This is not the labour of thy hands, but rather of his that is amorous of thee: then she gave her a morsel of brown bread, and went to sleep. In the mean season, Cupid was closed fast in the surest chamber of the house, partly because he should not hurt himself with wanton dalliance, and partly because he should not speake with his love: so these two lovers were divided one from another. When night was passed Venus called Psyches, and said, Seest thou yonder Forest that extendeth out in length with the river? there be great sheepe shining like gold, and kept by no manner of person. I command thee that thou go thither and bring me home some of the wooll of their fleeces. Psyches arose willingly not to do her commandement, but to throw her selfe headlong into the water to end her sorrows. Then a green reed inspired by divine inspiration, with a gratious tune and

CHAPTER XXII
The most pleasant and delectable tale of the marriage of Cupid and Psyches

THE MARRIAGE OF

CHAPTER XXII
The most pleasant and delectable tale of the marriage of Cupid and Psyches

melody gan say, O Psyches I pray thee not to trouble or pollute my water by the death of thee, and yet beware that thou goe not towards the terrible sheepe of this coast, untill such time as the heat of the sunne be past, for when the sunne is in his force, then seeme they most dreadfull and furious, with their sharpe hornes, their stony foreheads and their gaping throats, wherewith they arme themselves to the destruction of mankinde. But untill they have refreshed themselves in the river, thou maist hide thy selfe here by me, under this great plaine tree, and as soone as their great fury is past, thou maist goe among the thickets and bushes under the wood side and gather the lockes of their golden Fleeces, which thou shalt finde hanging upon the briers. Then spake the gentle and benigne reed, shewing a mean to Psyches to save her life, which she bore well in memory, and with all diligence went and gathered up such lockes as shee found, and put them in her apron, and carried them home to Venus. Howbeit the danger of this second labour did not please her, nor give her sufficient witnesse of the good service of Psyches, but with a sower resemblance of laughter, did say: Of a certaine I know that this is not thy fact, but I will prove if that thou bee of so stout, so good a courage, and singular prudency as thou seemest to bee. Then Venus spake unto Psyches againe saying: Seest thou the toppe of yonder great Hill, from whence there runneth downe waters of blacke and deadly colour, which nourisheth the floods of Stix, Cocytus? I charge thee to goe thither, and bring me a vessell of that water: wherewithall she gave her a bottle of Christall, menacing and threatning her rigorously. Then poor Psyches went in all haste to the top of the mountaine, rather to end her life, then to fetch any water, and when she was come up to the ridge of the hill, she perceived that it was impossible to bring it to passe: for she saw a great rocke gushing out most horrible fountaines of waters, which ran downe and fell by many stops and passages into the valley beneath: on each side shee did see great Dragons, which were stretching out their long and bloody Neckes, that did never sleepe, but appointed to keepe the river there: the waters seemed to themselves likewise saying, Away, away, what wilt thou doe?

CUPID AND PSYCHES

flie, flie, or else thou wilt be slaine. Then Psyches (seeing the impossibility of this affaire) stood still as though she were transformed into a stone, and although she was present in body, yet was she absent in spirit and sense, by reason of the great perill which she saw, insomuch that she could not comfort her self with weeping, such was the present danger that she was in. But the royall bird of great Jupiter, the Eagle remembring his old service which he had done, when as by the pricke of Cupid he brought up the boy Ganimedes, to the heavens, to be made butler of Jupiter, and minding to shew the like service in the person of the wife of Cupid, came from the high-house of the Skies, and said unto Psyches, O simple woman without all experience, doest thou thinke to get or dip up any drop of this dreadfull water? No, no, assure thy selfe thou art never able to come nigh it, for the Gods themselves do greatly feare at the sight thereof. What, have you not heard, that it is a custome among men to sweare by the puissance of the Gods, and the Gods do sweare by the majesty of the river Stix? But give me thy bottle, and sodainly he tooke it, and filled it with the water of the river, and taking his flight through those cruell and horrible dragons, brought it unto Psyches: who being very joyfull thereof, presented it to Venus, who would not yet be appeased, but menacing more and more said, What, thou seemest unto me a very witch and enchauntresse, that bringest these things to passe, howbeit thou shalt do nothing more. Take this box and to Hell to Proserpina, and desire her to send me a little of her beauty, as much as will serve me the space of one day, and say that such as I had is consumed away since my sonne fell sicke, but returne againe quickly, for I must dresse my selfe therewithall, and goe to the Theatre of the Gods: then poore Psyches perceived the end of all fortune, thinking verely that she should never returne, and not without cause, when as she was compelled to go to the gulfe and furies of hell. Wherefore without any further delay, she went up to an high tower to throw her selfe downe headlong (thinking that it was the next and readiest way to hell) but the tower (as inspired) spake unto her saying, O poore miser, why goest thou about to slay thy

CHAPTER XXII

The most pleasant and delectable tale of the marriage of Cupid and Psyches

THE MARRIAGE OF

CHAPTER XXII
The most pleasant and delectable tale of the marriage of Cupid and Psyches

selfe? Why dost thou rashly yeeld unto thy last perill and danger? know thou that if thy spirit be once separated from thy body, thou shalt surely go to hell, but never to returne againe, wherefore harken to me; Lacedemon a Citie in Greece is not farre hence: go thou thither and enquire for the hill Tenarus, whereas thou shalt find a hold leading to hell, even to the Pallace of Pluto, but take heede thou go not with emptie hands to that place of darknesse: but carrie two sops sodden in the flour of barley and Honney in thy hands, and two halfepence in thy mouth. And when thou hast passed a good part of that way, thou shalt see a lame Asse carrying of wood, and a lame fellow driving him, who will desire thee to give him up the sticks that fall downe, but passe thou on and do nothing; by and by thou shalt come unto a river of hell, whereas Charon is ferriman, who will first have his fare paied him, before he will carry the soules over the river in his boat, whereby you may see that avarice raigneth amongst the dead, neither Charon nor Pluto will do any thing for nought: for if it be a poore man that would passe over and lacketh money, he shal be compelled to die in his journey before they will shew him any reliefe, wherefore deliver to carraine Charon one of the halfepence (which thou bearest for thy passage) and let him receive it out of thy mouth. And it shall come to passe as thou sittest in the boat thou shalt see an old man swimming on the top of the river, holding up his deadly hands, and desiring thee to receive him into the barke, but have no regard to his piteous cry: when thou art passed over the floud, thou shalt espie old women spinning, who will desire thee to helpe them, but beware thou do not consent unto them in any case, for these and like baits and traps will Venus set to make thee let fall one of thy sops, and thinke not that the keeping of thy sops is a light matter, for if thou leese one of them thou shalt be assured never to returne againe to this world. Then shalt thou see a great and marvailous dogge, with three heads, barking continually at the soules of such as enter in, but he can do them no other harme, he lieth day and night before the gate of Proserpina, and keepeth the house of Pluto with great diligence, to whom if thou cast one of thy sops, thou

CUPID AND PSYCHES

CHAPTER XXII
The most pleasant and delectable tale of the marriage of Cupid and Psyches

maist have accesse to Proserpina without all danger: shee will make thee good cheere, and entertaine thee with delicate meate and drinke, but sit thou upon the ground, and desire browne bread, and then declare thy message unto her, and when thou hast received such beauty as she giveth, in thy returne appease the rage of the dogge with thy other sop, and give thy other halfe penny to covetous Charon, and come the same way againe into the world as thou wentest: but above all things have a regard that thou looke not in the boxe, neither be not too curious about the treasure of the divine beauty. In this manner the tower spake unto Psyches, and advertised her what she should do: and immediatly she tooke two halfe pence, two sops, and all things necessary, and went to the mountaine Tenarus to go towards hell. After that Psyches had passed by the lame Asse, paid her halfe pennie for passage, neglected the old man in the river, denyed to helpe the women spinning, and filled the ravenous mouth of the dogge with a sop, shee came to the chamber of Proserpina. There Psyches would not sit in any royall seate, nor eate any delicate meates, but kneeled at the feete of Proserpina, onely contented with course bread, declared her message, and after she had received a mysticall secret in a boxe, she departed, and stopped the mouth of the dogge with the other sop, and paied the boat-man the other halfe penny. When Psyches was returned from hell, to the light of the world, shee was ravished with great desire, saying, Am not I a foole, that knowing that I carrie heere the divine beauty, will not take a little thereof to garnish my face, to please my love withall? And by and by shee opened the boxe where she could perceive no beauty nor any thing else, save onely an infernall and deadly sleepe, which immediatly invaded all her members as soone as the boxe was uncovered, in such sort that shee fell downe upon the ground, and lay there as a sleeping corps.

But Cupid being now healed of his wound and Maladie, not able to endure the absence of Psyches, got him secretly out at a window of the chamber where hee was enclosed, and (receiving his wings,) tooke his flight towards his loving wife, whom when he had found, hee wiped away the sleepe from

THE MARRIAGE OF

CHAPTER XXII
The most pleasant and delectable tale of the marriage of Cupid and Psyches

her face, and put it againe into the boxe, and awaked her with the tip of one of his arrows, saying: O wretched Caitife, behold thou wert well-nigh perished againe, with the overmuch curiositie: well, goe thou, and do thy message to my Mother, and in the meane season, I will provide for all things accordingly: wherewithall he tooke his flight into the aire, and Psyches brought her present to Venus.

Cupid being more and more in love with Psyches, and fearing the displeasure of his Mother, did pearce into the heavens, and arrived before Jupiter to declare his cause: then Jupiter after that hee had eftsoone embraced him, gan say in this manner: O my well beloved sonne, although thou haste not given due reverence and honour unto me as thou oughtest to doe, but haste rather spoiled and wounded this my brest (whereby the laws and order of the Elements and Planets be disposed) with continuall assaults, of Terren luxury and against all laws, and the discipline Julia, and the utility of the publike weale, in transforming my divine beauty into serpents, fire, savage beasts, birds, and into Bulles: Howbeit remembring my modesty, and that I have nourished thee with mine owne proper hands, I will doe and accomplish all thy desire, so that thou canst beware of spitefull and envious persons. And if there be any excellent Maiden of comely beauty in the world, remember yet the benefit which I shall shew unto thee by recompence of her love towards me againe. When he had spoken these words he commanded Mercury to call all the gods to counsell, and if any of the celestiall powers did faile of appearance he would be condemned in ten thousand pounds: which sentence was such a terrour to all the goddesses, that the high Theatre was replenished, and Jupiter began to speake in this sort: O yee gods, registred in the bookes of the Muses, you all know this young man Cupid whom I have nourished with mine owne hands, whose raging flames of his first youth, I thought best to bridle and restraine. It sufficeth that hee is defamed in every place for his adulterous living, wherefore all occasion ought to bee taken away by meane of marriage: he hath chosen a Maiden that fancieth him well, and hath bereaved her of her virginity, let him have her still, and possesse her according to his owne

CUPID AND PSYCHES

pleasure: then he returned to Venus, and said, And you my daughter, take you no care, neither feare the dishonour of your progeny and estate, neither have regard in that it is a mortall marriage, for it seemeth unto me just, lawfull, and legitimate by the law civill. Incontinently after, Jupiter commanded Mercury to bring up Psyches, the spouse of Cupid, into the Pallace of heaven. And then he tooke a pot of immortality, and said, Hold Psyches, and drinke, to the end thou maist be immortall, and that Cupid may be thine everlasting husband. By and by the great banket and marriage feast was sumptuously prepared, Cupid sate downe with his deare spouse betweene his armes: Juno likewise with Jupiter, and all the other gods in order, Ganimedes filled the pot of Jupiter, and Bacchus served the rest. Their drinke was Nectar, the wine of the gods, Vulcanus prepared supper, the howers decked up the house with roses and other sweet smells, the graces threw about balme, the Muses sang with sweet harmony, Apollo tuned pleasantly to the Harpe, Venus danced finely: Satirus and Paniscus plaid on their pipes; and thus Psyches was married to Cupid, and after she was delivered of a child whom we call Pleasure.

CHAPTER XXII

The most pleasant and delectable tale of the marriage of Cupid and Psyches

This the trifling old woman declared unto the captive maiden: but I poore Asse, not standing farre of, was not a little sorry in that I lacked pen and inke to write so worthy a tale.

THE SIXTH BOOKE

THE TWENTY-THIRD CHAPTER

How Apuleius carried away the Gentlewoman, and how they were taken againe by the theeves, and what a kind of death was invented for them.

BY and by the theeves came home laden with treasure, and many of them which were of strongest courage (leaving behind such as were lame and wounded, to heale and aire themselves) said they would returne backe againe to fetch the rest of their pillage, which they had hidden in a certaine cave, and so they snatched up their dinner greedily, and brought us forth into the way and beate us before them with staves. About night (after that we had passed over many hilles and dales) we came to a great cave, where they laded us with mighty burthens, and would not suffer us to refresh our selves any season but brought us againe in our way, and hied so fast homeward, that what with their haste and their cruell stripes, I fell downe upon a stone by the way side, then they beate me pittifully in lifting me up, and hurt my right thigh and my left hoofe, and one of them said, What shall we do with this lame Ill favoured Asse, that is not worth the meate he eats? And other said, Since the time that we had him first he never did any good, and I thinke he came unto our house with evill lucke, for we have had great wounds since, and losse of our valiant captaines, and other said, As soone as he hath brought home his burthen, I will surely throw him out upon the mountaine to be a pray for wild beasts: While these gentlemen reasoned together of my death, we fortuned to come home, for the feare that I was in, caused my feet to turne into wings: after that we were discharged of our burthens, they went to their fellowes that were wounded, and told them of our great tardity

OF LUCIUS APULEIUS

and slownesse by the way, neither was I brought into small anguish, when I perceived my death prepared before my face: Why standest thou still Lucius? Why dost thou not looke for thy death? Knowst thou not that the theeves have ordained to slay thee? seest thou not these sharpe and pointed flints which shall bruise and teare thee in peeces, if by adventure thou happen upon them? Thy gentle Magitian hath not onely given thee the shape and travell of an Asse, but also a skinne so soft and tender as it were a swallow: why dost thou not take courage and runne away to save thy selfe? Art thou afraid of the old woman more then halfe dead, whom with a stripe of thy heele thou maist easily dispatch? But whither shall I fly? What lodging shall I seek? See my Assy cogitation. Who is he that passeth by the way and will not take me up? While I devised these things, I brake the halter wherewith I was tyed and ran away with all my force, howbeit I could not escape the kitish eyes of the old woman, for shee ran after me, and with more audacity then becommeth her kind age, caught me by the halter and thought to pull me home: but I not forgetting the cruell purpose of the theeves, was mooved with small pity, for I kicked her with my hinder heeles to the ground and had welnigh slaine her, who (although shee was throwne and hurled downe) yet shee held still the halter, and would not let me goe; then shee cryed with a loud voyce and called for succour, but she little prevayled, because there was no person that heard her, save onely the captive gentlewoman, who hearing the voice of the old woman, came out to see what the matter was, and perceiving her hanging at the halter, tooke a good courage and wrested it out of her hand, and (entreating me with gentle words) got upon my backe. Then I began to runne, and shee gently kicked mee forward, whereof I was nothing displeased, for I had as great a desire to escape as shee: insomuch that I seemed to scowre away like a horse. And when the Gentlewoman did speake, I would answere her with my neighing, and oftentimes (under colour to rub my backe) I would sweetly kisse her tender feet. Then shee fetching a sigh from the bottome of her heart, lifted up her eyes to the heavens, saying: O soveraigne Gods, deliver mee

CHAPTER XXIII

How Apuleius carried away the Gentlewoman, and how they were taken againe by the theeves, and what a kind of death was invented for them

THE SIXTH BOOKE

CHAPTER XXIII
How Apuleius carried away the Gentlewoman, and how they were taken againe by the theeves, and what a kind of death was invented for them

if it be your pleasure, from these present dangers: and thou cruell fortune cease thy wrath, let the sorrow suffice thee which I have already sustained. And thou little Asse, that art the occasion of my safety and liberty, if thou canst once render me safe and sound to my parents, and to him that so greatly desireth to have mee to his wife, thou shalt see what thankes I will give: with what honour I will reward thee, and how I will use thee. First, I will bravely dresse the haires of thy forehead, and then will I finely combe thy maine, I will tye up thy rugged tayle trimly, I will decke thee round about with golden trappes, in such sort that thou shalt glitter like the starres of the skie, I will bring thee daily in my apron the kirnels of nuts, and will pamper thee up with delicates; I will set store by thee, as by one that is the preserver of my life: Finally, thou shalt lack no manner of thing. Moreover amongst thy glorious fare, thy great ease, and the blisse of thy life, thou shalt not be destitute of dignity, for thou shalt be chronicled perpetually in memory of my present fortune, and the providence divine. All the whole history shall be painted upon the wall of our house, thou shalt be renowned throughout all the world. And it shall be registred in the bookes of Doctours, that an Asse saved the life of a young maiden that was captive amongst Theeves: Thou shalt be numbred amongst the ancient miracles: wee beleeve that by like example of truth Phryxus saved himselfe from drowning upon the Ram, Arion escaped upon a Dolphin, and that Europa was delivered by the Bull. If Jupiter transformed himselfe into a Bull, why may it not be that under the shape of this Asse, is hidden the figure of a man, or some power divine? While that the Virgin did thus sorrowfully unfold her desires, we fortuned to come to a place where three wayes did meet, and shee tooke me by the halter, and would have me to turne on the right hand to her fathers house: but I (knowing that the theeves were gone that way to fetch the residue of their pillage) resisted with my head as much as I might, saying within my selfe: What wilt thou doe unhappy maiden? Why wouldst thou goe so willingly to hell? Why wilt thou runne into destruction by meane of my feet? Why dost thou seek thine own

OF LUCIUS APULEIUS

harme, and mine likewise? And while we strived together whether way we might take, the theeves returned, laiden with their pray, and perceived us a farre off by the light of the Moon: and after they had known us, one of them gan say, Whither goe you so hastely? Be you not affraid of spirits? And you (you harlot) doe you not goe to see your parents? Come on, we will beare you company? And therewithall they tooke me by the halter, and drave me backe againe, beating me cruelly with a great staffe (that they had) full of knobs: then I returning againe to my ready destruction, and remembring the griefe of my hoofe, began to shake my head, and to waxe lame, but he that led me by the halter said, What, dost thou stumble? Canst thou not goe? These rotten feet of thine ran well enough, but they cannot walke: thou couldest mince it finely even now with the gentlewoman, that thou seemedst to passe the horse Pegasus in swiftnesse. In saying of these words they beat mee againe, that they broke a great staffe upon mee. And when we were come almost home, we saw the old woman hanging upon a bow of a Cipresse tree; then one of them cut downe the bowe whereon shee hanged, and cast her into the bottome of a great ditch: after this they bound the maiden and fell greedily to their victuals, which the miserable old woman had prepared for them. At which time they began to devise with themselves of our death, and how they might be revenged; divers was the opinions of this divers number: the first said, that hee thought best the Mayd should be burned alive: the second said she should be throwne out to wild beasts: the third said, she should be hanged upon a gibbet: the fourth said she should be flead alive: thus was the death of the poore Maiden scanned betweene them foure. But one of the theeves after every man had declared his judgement, did speake in this manner: It is not convenient unto the oath of our company, to suffer you to waxe more cruell then the quality of the offence doth merit, for I would that shee should not be hanged nor burned, nor throwne to beasts, nor dye any sodaine death, but by my counsell I would have her punished according to her desert. You know well what you have determined already of this dull

CHAPTER XXIII
How Apuleius carried away the Gentlewoman, and how they were taken againe by the theeves, and what a kind of death was invented for them

THE SIXTH BOOKE

CHAPTER XXIII
How Apuleius carried away the Gentlewoman, and how they were taken againe by the theeves, and what a kind of death was invented for them

Asse, that eateth more then he is worth, that faineth lamenesse, and that was the cause of the flying away of the Maid: my mind is that he shall be slaine to morrow, and when all the guts and entrailes of his body is taken out, let the Maide be sowne into his belly, then let us lay them upon a great stone against the broiling heate of the Sunne, so they shall both sustaine all the punishments which you have ordained: for first the Asse shall be slaine as you have determined, and she shall have her members torne and gnawne with wild beasts, when as she is bitten and rent with wormes, shee shall endure the paine of the fire, when as the broyling heat of the Sunne shall scorch and parch the belly of the Asse, shee shall abide the gallows when the Dogs and Vultures shall have the guts of her body hanging in their ravenous mouthes. I pray you number all the torments which she shall suffer: First shee shall dwell within the paunch of an Asse: secondly her nosethrilles shall receive a carraine stinke of the beast: thirdly shee shall dye for hunger: last of all, shee shall finde no meane to ridde her selfe from her paines, for her hands shall be sowen up within the skinne of the Asse: This being said, all the Theeves consented, and when I (poore Asse) heard and understood all their device, I did nothing else but lament and bewayle my dead carkasse, which should be handled in such sort on the next morrow.

THE
SEVENTH BOOKE
of LUCIUS APULEIUS of
THE GOLDEN ASSE

THE SEVENTH BOOKE

THE TWENTY-FOURTH CHAPTER

How hee that was left behinde at Hippata did bring newes concerning the robbery of Miloes house, came home and declared to his Company, that all the fault was laid to one Apuleius his charge.

AS soone as night was past, and the cleare Chariot of the Sunne had spred his bright beames on every coast, came one of the company of the theeves, (for so his and their greeting together did declare) who at the first entry into the Cave (after hee had breathed himselfe, and was able to speake) told these tydings unto his companions in this sort. Sirs, as touching the house of Milo of Hippata, which we forcibly entred and ransackt the last day, we may put away all feare, and doubt nothing at all. For after that ye by force of armes, had spoyled and taken away all things in the house, and returned hither into our Cave, I (thrusting my selfe amongst the presse of the people, and shewing my selfe as though I were sad and sorrowfull for the mischance) consulted with them for the boulting out of the matter, and devising what meanes might be wrought for the apprehension of the theeves, to the intent I might learne and see all that was done to make relation thereof unto you as you willed me, insomuch that the whole fact at length by mani-

THE SEVENTH BOOKE

CHAPTER XXIV
How hee that was left behinde at Hippata did bring newes concerning the robbery of Miloes house, etc.

fest and evident proofes as also by the common opinion and judgement of the people, was laid to one Lucius Apuleius charge as manifest author of this common robbery, who a few dayes before by false and forged letters and colored honesty, fell so farre in favour with this Milo, that he entertained him into his house, and received him as a chiefe of his familiar friends, which Lucius after that he had sojourned there a good space, and won the heart of Miloes Maid, by fained love, did throughly learne the waies and doores of all the house, and curiously viewed the cofers and chests, wherein was laid the whole substance of Milo: neither was there small cause given to judge him culpable, since as the very same night that this robbery was done he fled away, and could not be found in no place: and to the intent hee might cleane escape, and better prevent such as made hew and crie after him, he tooke his white horse and gallopped away, and after this, his servant was found in the house, who (accused as accessary to the fellony and escape of his Master) was committed to the common gaole, and the next day following was cruelly scourged and tormented till hee was welnigh dead, to the intent hee should confesse the matter, but when they could wreast or learne no such thing of him, yet sent they many persons after, towardes Lucius Countrey to enquire him out, and so to take him prisoner. As he declared these things, I did greatly lament with my selfe, to thinke of mine old and pristine estate, and what felicity I was sometimes in, in comparison to the misery that I presently susteined, being changed into a miserable Asse, then had I no small occasion to remember, how the old and ancient Writers did affirme, that fortune was starke blind and without eies, because she alwaies bestoweth her riches upon evill persons, and fooles, and chooseth or favoureth no mortall person by judgement, but is alwaies conversant, especially with such as if she could see, she should most shunne, and forsake, yea and that which is more worse, she soweth such evill or contrary opinions in men, that the wicked doe glory with the name of good, and contrary the good and innocent be detracted and slandred as evill. Furthermore I, who by her great cruelty, was turned into a foure footed Asse, in most vile and abject

OF LUCIUS APULEIUS

manner: yea, and whose estate seemed worthily to be lamented and pittied of the most hard and stonie hearts, was accused of theft and robbing of my deare host Milo, which villany might rather be called parricide then theft, yet might not I defend mine owne cause or denie the fact any way, by reason I could not speake; howbeit least my conscience should seeme to accuse me by reason of silence, and againe being enforced by impatience I endevored to speake, and faine would have said, Never did I that fact, and verely the first word, never, I cried out once or twise, somewhat handsome, but the residue I could in no wise pronounce, but still remaining in one voice, cried, Never, never, never. Howbeit I settled my hanging lips as round as I could to speake the residue: but why should I further complaine of the crueltie of my fortune, since as I was not much ashamed, by reason that my servant and my horse, was likewise accused with me of the robbery.

CHAPTER XXIV

How hee that was left behinde at Hippata did bring newes concerning the robbery of Miloes house, etc.

While I pondered with my selfe all these things, a great care [came] to my remembrance, touching the death, which the theeves provised for me and the maiden, and still as I looked downe to my belly, I thought of my poore gentlewoman that should be closed within me. And the theefe which a little before had brought the false newes against me, drew out of the skirt of his coate, a thousand crowns, which he had rifled from such as hee met, and brought it into the common treasury. Then hee carefully enquired how the residue of his companions did. To whom it was declared that the most valiant was murdred and slaine in divers manners, whereupon he perswaded them to remit all their affaires a certaine season, and to seeke for other fellowes to be in their places, that by the exercise of new lads, the terror of their martiall band might be reduced to the old number, assuring them that such as were unwilling, might be compelled by menaces and threatnings, and such as were willing might be incouraged forward with reward. Further he said, that there were some, which (seeing the profite which they had) would forsake their base and servile estate, and rather bee contented to live like tyrants amongst them. Moreover he declared, that for his part he had spoken with

THE SEVENTH BOOKE

CHAPTER XXIV
How hee that was left behinde at Hippata did bring newes concerning the robbery of Miloes house, etc.

a certaine tall man, a valiant companion, but of young age, stout in body, and couragious in fight, whom he had fully perswaded to exercise his idle hands, dull with slothfullnesse, to his greater profit, and (while he might) to receive the blisse of better Fortune, and not to hold out his sturdy arme to begge for a penny, but rather to take as much gold and silver as hee would. Then every one consented, that hee that seemed so worthy to be their companion, should be one of their company, and that they would search for others to make up the residue of the number, whereupon he went out, and by and by (returning againe) brought in a tall young man (as he promised) to whom none of the residue might bee compared, for hee was higher then they by the head, and of more bignesse in body, his beard began to burgen, but hee was poorely apparelled, insomuch that you might see all his belly naked. As soone as he was entred in he said, God speed yee souldiers of Mars and my faithfull companions, I pray you make me one of your band, and I will ensure you, that you shall have a man of singular courage and lively audacity: for I had rather receive stripes upon my backe, then money or gold in my hands. And as for death (which every man doth feare) I passe nothing at all, yet thinke you not that I am an abject or a begger, neither judge you my vertue and prowesse by ragged clothes, for I have beene a Captaine of a great company, and subdued all the countrey of Macedonia. I am the renowned theefe Hemes the Thracian, whose name all countreyes and nations do so greatly feare: I am the sonne of Theron the noble theefe, nourished with humane bloud, entertained amongst the stoutest; finally I am inheritour and follower of all my fathers vertues, yet I lost in a short time all my company and all my riches, by one assault, which I made upon a Factor of the Prince, which sometime had beene Captaine of two hundred men, for fortune was cleane against me: harken and I will tell you the whole matter.

There was a certaine man in the court of the Emperour, which had many offices, and in great favour, who at last by the envy of divers persons, was banished away and compelled

OF LUCIUS APULEIUS

CHAPTER XXIV

How hee that was left behinde at Hippata did bring newes concerning the robbery of Miloes house, etc.

to forsake the court: his wife Platina, a woman of rare faith and singular shamefastnes having borne ten children to her husband, despised all worldly Pompe and delicacy, and determined to follow her husband, and to be partaker of his perils and danger, wherefore shee cut off her haire, disguised her selfe like a man, and tooke with her all her treasure, passing through the hands of the souldiers, and the naked swords without any feare, whereby she endured many miseries, and was partaker of much affliction, to save the life of her husband, such was her love which she bare unto him. And when they had escaped many perillous dangers, as well by land as by sea, they went together towards Zacynthe, to continue there according as fortune had appointed. But when they were arived on the sea coast of Actium (where we in our returne from Macedony were roving about) when night came, they returned into a house not far distant from their ship, where they lay all night. Then we entred in and tooke away all their substance, but verely we were in great danger: for the good matron perceiving us incontinently by the noise of the gate, went into the chamber, and called up every man by his name, and likewise the neighbors that dwelled round about, insomuch that by reason of the feare that every one was in, we hardly escaped away, but this most holy woman, faithfull and true to her husband (as the truth must be declared) returned to Cæsar, desiring his aid and puissance, and demanding vengeance of the injury done to her husband, who granted all her desire: then went my company to wracke, insomuch that every man was slaine, so great was the authority and word of the Prince. Howbeit, when all my band was lost, and taken by search of the Emperours army, I onely stole away and delivered my selfe from the violence of the souldiers, for I clothed my selfe in a womans attire, and mounted upon an Asse, that carryed barly sheafes, and (passing through the middle of them all) I escaped away, because every one deemed that I was a woman by reason I lacked a beard. Howbeit I left not off for all this, nor did degenerate from the glory of my father, or mine own vertue, but freshly comming from the bloody skirmish, and disguised like a woman, I invaded townes and castles

141

THE SEVENTH BOOKE

CHAPTER XXIV
How hee that was left behinde at Hippata did bring newes concerning the robbery of Miloes house, etc.

alone to get some pray. And therewithall he pulled out two thousand crownes, which he had under his coate, saying: Hold here the dowry which I present unto you, hold eke my person, which you shall alwayes find trusty and faithfull, if you willingly receive me: and I will ensure you that in so doing, within short space I will make and turne this stony house of yours into gold. Then by and by every one consented to make him their Captaine, and so they gave him better garments, and threw away his old. When they had changed his attire, hee imbraced them one after another, then placed they him in the highest roome of the table, and drunke unto him in token of good lucke.

THE TWENTY-FIFTH CHAPTER
How the death of the Asse, and the Gentlewoman was stayed.

AFTER supper they began to talke, and declare unto him the going away of the Gentlewoman, and how I bare her upon my backe, and what death was ordained for us two. Then he desired to see her, whereupon the Gentlewoman was brought forth fast bound, whom as soone as he beheld, he turned himselfe wringing his nose, and blamed them saying: I am not so much a beast, or so rash a fellow to drive you quite from your purpose, but my conscience will not suffer me to conceale any thing that toucheth your profit, since I am as carefull for you, howbeit if my counsell doe displease you, you may at your liberty proceed in your enterprise. I doubt not but all theeves, and such as have a good judgement, will preferre their owne lucre and gain above all things in the world, and above their vengeance, which purchaseth damage to divers persons. Therefore if you put this virgin in the Asses belly, you shall but execute your indignation against her, without all

OF LUCIUS APULEIUS

manner of profit: But I would advise you to carry the virgin to some towne and to sell her: and such a brave girle as she is, may be sold for a great quantity of money. And I my selfe know certaine bawdy Marchants, amongst whom peradventure one will give us summes of gold for her. This is my opinion touching this affaire: but advise you what you intend to do, for you may rule me in this case. In this manner the good theefe pleaded and defended our cause, being a good Patron to the silly virgin, and to me poore Asse. But they staied hereupon a good space, with long deliberation, which made my heart (God wot) and spirit greatly to quaile. Howbeit in the end they consented to his opinion, and by and by the Maiden was unloosed of her bonds, who seeing the young man, and hearing the name of brothels and bawdy Merchants, began to wax joyfull, and smiled with her selfe. Then began I to deeme evill of the generation of women, when as I saw the Maiden (who was appointed to be married to a young Gentleman, and who so greatly desired the same) was now delighted with the talke of a wicked brothel house, and other things dishonest. In this sort the consent and manners of women depended in the judgement of an Asse.

CHAPTER XXV
How the death of the Asse, and the Gentlewoman was stayed

THE TWENTY-SIXTH CHAPTER

How all the Theeves were brought asleepe by their new companion.

THEN the young man spake againe, saying, Masters, why goe wee not about to make our prayers unto Mars, touching this selling of the Maiden, and to seeke for other companions. But as farre as I see, here is no other manner of beast to make sacrifice withall, nor wine sufficient for us to drinke. Let me have (quoth hee) tenne more with me, and wee will goe to the next Castle, to provide for meat

143

THE SEVENTH BOOKE

CHAPTER XXVI
How all the Theeves were brought asleepe by their new companion

and other things necessary. So he and tenne more with him, went their way: In the meane season, the residue made a great fire and an Alter with greene turffes in the honour of Mars. By and by after they came againe, bringing with them bottles of wine, and a great number of beasts, amongst which there was a big Ram Goat, fat, old, and hairy, which they killed and offered unto Mars. Then supper was prepared sumptuously, and the new companion said unto the other, You ought to accompt me not onely your Captaine in robbery and fight, but also in pleasures and jolity, whereupon by and by with pleasant cheere he prepared meat, and trimming up the house he set all things in order, and brought the pottage and dainty dishes to the Table: but above all he plyed them wel with great pots and jugs of wine. Sometimes (seeming to fetch somewhat) hee would goe to the Maiden and give her pieces of meate, which he privily tooke away, and would drinke unto her, which she willingly tooke in good part. Moreover, hee kissed her twice or thrice, whereof she was well pleased, but I (not well contented thereat) thought in my selfe: O wretched Maid, thou hast forgotten thy marriage, and doest esteeme this stranger and bloudy theefe above thy husband which thy Parents ordained for thee, now perceive I well thou hast no remorse of conscience, but more delight to tarry and play the harlot heere amongst so many swords. What? knowest thou not how the other theeves if they knew thy demeanour, would put thee to death as they had once appointed, and so worke my destruction likewise? Well now I perceive thou hast a pleasure in the dammage and hurt of other. While I did angerly devise with my selfe all these things, I perceived by certaine signes and tokens (not ignorant to so wise an Asse) that he was not the notable theefe Hemus, but rather Lepolemus her husband, for after much communication he beganne to speake more franckly, not fearing at all my presence, and said, Be of good cheere my sweete friend Charites, for thou shalt have by and by all these thy enemies captive unto thee. Then hee filled wine to the theeves more and more, and never ceased, till as they were all overcome with abundance of meat and drinke, when as hee himselfe ab-

OF LUCIUS APULEIUS

stained and bridled his owne appetite. And truely I did greatly suspect, least hee had mingled in their cups some deadly poyson, for incontinently they all fell downe asleepe on the ground one after an other, and lay as though they had beene dead.

CHAPTER XXVI
How all the Theeves were brought asleepe by their new companion

THE TWENTY-SEVENTH CHAPTER

How the Gentlewoman was carried home by her husband while the theeves were asleepe, and how much Apuleius was made of.

HEN the theeves were all asleepe by their great and immoderate drinking, the young man Lepolemus took the Maiden and set her upon my backe, and went homeward. When we were come home, all the people of the Citie, especially her Parents, friends, and family, came running forth joyfully, and all the children and Maidens of the towne gathered together to see this virgin in great triumph sitting upon an Asse. Then I (willing to shew as much joy as I might, as present occasion served) I set and pricked up my long eares, I ratled my nosethrils, and cryed stoutly, nay rather I made the towne to ring againe with my shrilling sound: when wee were come to her fathers house, shee was received into a chamber honourably: as for me, Lepolemus (accompanied with a great number of Citizens) did presently after drive me backe againe with other horses to the cave of the theeves, where wee found them all asleepe lying on the ground as wee left them; then they first brought out all the gold, and silver, and other treasure of the house, and laded us withall, which when they had done, they threw many of the theeves downe into the bottome of deepe ditches, and the residue they slew with their swords: after this wee returned home glad and merry of so great vengeance upon them, and the riches which wee carried was commited to the publike treasurie. This done, the Maid was married to

T

THE SEVENTH BOOKE

CHAPTER XXVII

How the Gentlewoman was carried home by her husband while the theeves were asleepe, and how much Apuleius was made of

Lepolemus, according to the law, whom by so much travell he had valiantly recovered: then my good Mistresse looked about for me, and asking for me commanded the very same day of her marriage, that my manger should be filled with barly, and that I should have hay and oats aboundantly, and she would call me her little Camell. But how greatly did I curse Fotis, in that shee transformed me into an Asse, and not into a dogge, because I saw the dogges had filled their paunches with the reliks and bones of so worthy a supper. The next day this new wedded woman (my Mistresse) did greatly commend me before her Parents and husband, for the kindnesse which I had shewed unto her, and never leaved off, untill such time as they promised to reward me with great honours. Then they called together all their friends, and thus it was concluded: one said, that I should be closed in a stable and never worke, but continually to be fedde and fatted with fine and chosen barly and beanes, and good littour, howbeit another prevailed, who wishing my liberty, perswaded them that it was better for me to runne in the fields amongst the lascivious horses and mares, whereby I might engender some mules for my Mistresse: then he that had in charge to keepe the horse, was called for, and I was delivered unto him with great care, insomuch that I was right pleasant and joyous, because I hoped that I should carry no more fardels nor burthens, moreover I thought that when I should thus be at liberty, in the spring time of the yeere when the meddows and fields were greene, I should find some roses in some place, whereby I was fully perswaded that if my Master and Mistresse did render to me so many thanks and honours being an Asse, they would much more reward me being turned into a man: but when hee (to whom the charge of me was so straightly committed) had brought me a good way distant from the City, I perceived no delicate meates nor no liberty which I should have, but by and by his covetous wife and most cursed queane made me a mill Asse, and (beating me with a cudgill full of knots) would wring bread for her selfe and her husband out of my skinne. Yet was she not contented to weary me and make me a drudge with carriage and grinding of her owne corne, but I

OF LUCIUS APULEIUS

CHAPTER XXVII

How the Gentlewoman was carried home by her husband while the theeves were asleepe, and how much Apuleius was made of

was hired of her neighbours to beare their sackes likewise, howbeit shee would not give me such meate as I should have, nor sufficient to sustaine my life withall, for the barly which I ground for mine owne dinner she would sell to the Inhabitants by. And after that I had laboured all day, she would set before me at night a little filthy branne, nothing cleane but full of stones. Being in this calamity, yet fortune worked me other torments, for on a day I was let loose into the fields to pasture, by the commandement of my master. O how I leaped for joy, how I neighed to see my selfe in such liberty, but especially since I beheld so many Mares, which I thought should be my wives and concubines; and I espied out and chose the fairest before I came nigh them; but this my joyfull hope turned into utter destruction, for incontinently all the stone Horses which were well fedde and made strong by ease of pasture, and thereby much more puissant then a poore Asse, were jealous over me, and (having no regard to the law and order of God Jupiter) ranne fiercely and terribly against me; one lifted up his forefeete and kicked me spitefully, another turned himselfe, and with his hinder heeles spurned me cruelly, the third threatning with a malicious neighing dressed his eares and shewing his sharpe and white teeth bit me on every side. In like sort have I read in Histories how the King of Thrace would throw his miserable ghests to be torne in peeces and devoured of his wild Horses, so niggish was that Tyrant of his provender, that he nourished them with the bodies of men.

THE SEVENTH BOOKE

THE TWENTY-EIGHTH CHAPTER
How Apuleius was made a common Asse to fetch home wood, and how he was handled by a boy.

AFTER that I was thus handled by horses, I was brought home againe to the Mill, but behold fortune (insatiable of my torments) had devised a new paine for me. I was appointed to bring home wood every day from a high hill, and who should drive me thither and home againe, but a boy that was the veriest hangman in all the world, who was not contented with the great travell that I tooke in climbing up the hill, neither pleased when he saw my hoofe torne and worne away by sharpe flintes, but he beat me cruelly with a great staffe, insomuch that the marrow of my bones did ake for woe, for he would strike me continually on the right hip, and still in one place, whereby he tore my skinne and made of my wide sore a great hole or trench, or rather a window to looke out at, and although it runne downe of blood, yet would he not cease beating me in that place: moreover he laded me with such great burthens of wood that you would thinke they had beene rather prepared for Elephants then for me, and when he perceived that my wood hanged more on one side then another, (when he should rather take away the heavy sides, and so ease me, or else lift them up to make them equall with the other) he laid great stones upon the weaker side to remedy the matter, yet could he not be contented with this my great misery and immoderate burthens of wood, but when hee came to any river (as there were many by the way) he to save his feete from water, would leape upon my loynes likewise, which was no small loade upon loade. And if by adversity I had fell downe in any dirty or myrie place, when he should have pulled me out either with ropes, or lifted me up by the taile, he would never helpe me, but lay me on from top to toe

OF LUCIUS APULEIUS

CHAPTER XXVIII

How Apuleius was made a common Asse to fetch home wood, and how he was handled by a boy

with a mighty staffe, till he had left no haire on all my body, no not so much as on mine eares, whereby I was compelled by force of blowes to stand up. The same hangman boy did invent another torment for me: he gathered a great many sharp thornes as sharp as needles and bound them together like a fagot, and tyed them at my tayle to pricke me, then was I afflicted on every side, for if I had indeavoured to runne away, the thorns would have pricked me, if I had stood still, the boy would have beaten mee, and yet the boy beate mee to make me runne, whereby I perceived that the hangman did devise nothing else save onely to kill me by some manner of meanes, and he would sweare and threaten to do me worse harme, and because hee might have some occasion to execute his malicious minde, upon a day (after that I had endeavoured too much by my patience) I lifted up my heeles and spurned him welfavouredly. Then he invented this vengeance against me, after that he had well laded me with shrubs and rubble, and trussed it round upon my backe, hee brought me out into the way: then hee stole a burning coale out of a mans house of the next village, and put it into the middle of the rubbell; the rubbell and shrubs being very dry, did fall on a light fire and burned me on every side. I could see no remedy how I might save my selfe, and in such a case it was not best for me to stand still: but fortune was favourable towards me, perhaps to reserve me for more dangers, for I espyed a great hole full of raine water that fell the day before, thither I ranne hastily and plunged my selfe therein, in such sort that I quenched the fire, and was delivered from that present perill, but the vile boy to excuse himselfe declared to all the neighbours and shepheards about, that I willingly tumbled in the fire as I passed through the village. Then he laughed upon me saying: How long shall we nourish and keepe this fiery Asse in vaine?

THE SEVENTH BOOKE

THE TWENTY-NINTH CHAPTER
How Apuleius was accused of Lechery by the boy.

A FEW dayes after, the boy invented another mischiefe : For when he had sold all the wood which I bare, to certaine men dwelling in a village by, he lead me homeward unladen : And then he cryed that he was not able to rule me, and that hee would not drive mee any longer to the hill for wood, saying : Doe you not see this slow and dull Asse, who besides all the mischiefes that he hath wrought already, inventeth daily more and more. For he espyeth any woman passing by the way, whether she be old or marryed, or if it be a young child, hee will throw his burthen from his backe, and runneth fiercely upon them. And after that he hath thrown them downe, he will stride over them to commit his buggery and beastly pleasure, moreover hee will faine as though hee would kisse them, but he will bite their faces cruelly, which thing may worke us great displeasure, or rather to be imputed unto us as a crime : and even now when he espyed an honest maiden passing by the high way, he by and by threw downe his wood and runne after her : And when he had throwne her down upon the ground, he would have ravished her before the face of all the world, had it not beene that by reason of her crying out, she was succored and pulled from his heeles, and so delivered. And if it had so come to passe that this fearefull maid had beene slaine by him, what danger had we beene in ? By these and like lies, he provoked the shepheards earnestly against me, which grieved mee (God wot) full sore that said nothing. Then one of the shepheards said : Why doe we not make sacrifice of this common adulterous Asse ? My sonne (quoth he) let us kill him and throw his guts to the dogges, and reserve his flesh for the labourers supper. Then let us cast dust upon his skinne, and carry it home to

OF LUCIUS APULEIUS

our master, and say that the Woolves have devoured him. The boy that was my evill accuser made no delay, but prepared himselfe to execute the sentence of the shepheard, rejoycing at my present danger, but O how greatly did I then repent that the stripe which I gave him with my heele had not killed him. Then he drew out his sword and made it sharp upon the whetstone to slay me, but another of the shepheards gan say, Verely it is a great offence to kill so faire an Asse, and so (by accusation of luxurie and lascivious wantonnesse) to lack so necessarie his labour and service, where otherwise if ye would cut off his stones, he might not onely be deprived of his courage but also become gentle, that we should be delivered from all feare and danger. Moreover he would be thereby more fat and better in flesh. For I know my selfe as well many Asses, as also most fierce horses, that by reason of their wantonnesse have beene most mad and terrible, but (when they were gelded and cut) they have become gentle and tame, and tractable to all use. Wherefore I would counsell you to geld him. And if you consent thereto, I will by and by, when I go to the next market fetch mine irons and tooles for the purpose: And I ensure you after that I have gelded and cut off his stones, I will deliver him unto you as tame as a lambe. When I did perceive that I was delivered from death, and reserved to be gelded, I was greatly sorrie, insomuch that I thought all the hinder part of my body and my stones did ake for woe, but I sought about to kill my selfe by some manner of meanes, to the end if I should die, I would die with unperished members.

CHAPTER XXIX

How Apuleius was accused of Lechery by the boy

THE SEVENTH BOOKE

THE THIRTIETH CHAPTER
How the boy that lead Apuleius to the field, was slaine in the wood.

HILE I devised with my selfe in what manner I might end my life, the roperipe boy on the next morrow lead me to the same hill againe, and tied me to a bow of a great Oke, and in the meane season he tooke his hatchet and cut wood to load me withall, but behold there crept out of a cave by, a marvailous great Beare, holding out his mighty head, whom when I saw, I was sodainly stroken in feare, and (throwing all the strength of my body into my hinder heeles) lifted up my strained head and brake the halter, wherewith I was tied. Then there was no need to bid me runne away, for I scoured not onely on foot, but tumbled over the stones and rocks with my body till I came into the open fields, to the intent I would escape from the terrible Beare, but especially from the boy that was worse then the Beare. Then a certaine stranger that passed by the way (espying me alone as a stray Asse) tooke me up and roade upon my backe, beating me with a staffe (which he bare in his hand) through a wide and unknowne lane, whereat I was nothing displeased, but willingly went forward to avoid the cruell paine of gelding, which the shepherds had ordained for me, but as for the stripes I was nothing moved, since I was accustomed to be beaten so every day. But evill fortune would not suffer me to continue in so good estate long: For the shepheards looking about for a Cow that they had lost (after they had sought in divers places) fortuned to come upon us unwares, who when they espied and knew me, they would have taken me by the halter, but he that rode upon my backe resisted them saying, O Lord masters, what intend you to do? Will you rob me? Then said the shepheards, What? thinkest thou we handle thee

OF LUCIUS APULEIUS

otherwise then thou deservest, which hast stollen away our Asse? Why dost thou not rather tell us where thou hast hidden the boy whom thou hast slaine? And therewithall they pulled him downe to the ground, beating him with their fists, and spurning him with their feete. Then he answered unto them saying, that he saw no manner of boy, but onely found the Asse loose and straying abroad, which he tooke up to the intent to have some reward for the finding of him and to restore him againe to his Master. And I would to God (quoth he) that this Asse (which verely was never seene) could speake as a man to give witnesse of mine innocency: Then would you be ashamed of the injury which you have done to me. Thus (reasoning for himselfe) he nothing prevailed, for they tied the halter about my necke, and (maugre his face) pulled me quite away, and lead me backe againe through the woods of the hill to the place where the boy accustomed to resort. And after they could find him in no place, at length they found his body rent and torne in peeces, and his members dispersed in sundry places, which I well knew was done by the cruell Beare: and verely I would have told it if I might have spoken, but (which I could onely do) I greatly rejoyced at his death, although it came too late. Then they gathered together the peeces of his body and buried them. By and by they laid the fault to my new Master, that tooke me up by the way, and (bringing him home fast bound to their houses) purposed on the next morrow to accuse him of murther, and to lead him before the Justices to have judgement of death.

CHAPTER XXX

How the boy that lead Apuleius to the field, was slaine in the wood

THE SEVENTH BOOKE

THE THIRTY-FIRST CHAPTER
How Apuleius was cruelly beaten by the Mother of the boy that was slaine.

IN the meane season, while the Parents of the boy did lament and weepe for the death of their sonne, the shepheard (according to his promise) came with his instruments and tooles to geld me. Then one of them said, Tush we little esteeme the mischiefe he did yesterday, but now we are contented that to morrow his stones shall not onely be cut off, but also his head. So was it brought to passe, that my death was delayed till the next morrow, but what thanks did I give to that good boy, who (being so slaine) was the cause of my pardon for one short day. Howbeit I had no time then to rest my selfe, for the Mother of the boy, weeping and lamenting for his death, attired in mourning vesture, tare her haire and beat her breast, and came presently into the stable, saying, Is it reason that this carelesse beast should do nothing all day but hold his head in the manger, filling and belling his guts with meat without compassion of my great miserie, or remembrance of the pittifull death of his slaine Master: and contemning my age and infirmity, thinketh that I am unable to revenge his mischiefs, moreover he would perswade me, that he were not culpable. Indeed, it is a convenient thing to looke and plead for safety, when as the conscience doeth confesse the offence, as theeves and malefactors accustome to do. But O good Lord, thou cursed beast, if thou couldest utter the contents of thine owne mind, whom (though it were the veriest foole in all the world) mightest thou perswade that this murther was voide or without thy fault, when as it lay in thy power, either to keepe off the theeves with thy heeles, or else to bite and teare them with thy teeth? Couldest not thou (that so often in his life time diddest spurne

OF LUCIUS APULEIUS

and kicke him) defend him now at the point of death by the like meane? Yet at least, thou shouldest have taken him upon thy backe, and so brought him from the cruell hands of the theeves: where contrary thou runnest away alone, forsaking thy good Master, thy pastor and conductor. Knowest thou not, that such as denie their wholsome help and aid to them which lie in danger of death, ought to be punished, because they have offended against good manners, and the law naturall? but I promise thee, thou shalt not long rejoyce at my harmes, thou shalt feele the smart of thy homicide and offence, I will see what I can doe. And therewithall she unclosed her apron, and bound all my feete together, to the end I might not help my selfe, then she tooke a great barre, which accustomed to bar the stable doore, and never ceased beating me till she was so weary that the bar fell out of her hands, whereupon she (complaining of the soone faintnesse of her armes) ran to her fire and brought a firebrand and thrust it under my taile, burning me continually, till such time as (having but one remedy) I all arayed her face and eies with my durty dunge, whereby (what with the stinke thereof, and what with the filthinesse that fell in her eies) she was welnigh blinded: so I enforced the queane to leave off, otherwise I had died as Meleager did by the sticke, which his mad mother Althea cast into the fire.

CHAPTER XXXI

How Apuleius was cruelly beaten by the Mother of the boy that was slaine

THE
EIGHTH BOOKE
of LUCIUS APULEIUS of
THE GOLDEN ASSE

THE EIGHTH BOOKE

THE THIRTY-SECOND CHAPTER
How a young man came and declared the miserable death of Lepolemus and his wife Charites.

ABOUT midnight came a young man, which seemed to be one of the family of the good woman Charites, who sometimes endured so much misery and calamity with mee amongst the theeves, who after that hee had taken a stoole, and sate downe before the fire-side, in the company of the servants, began to declare many terrible things that had happened unto the house of Charites, saying : O yee house-keepers, shepheards and cow-heards, you shall understand that wee have lost our good mistris Charites miserably and by evill adventure : and to the end you may learne and know all the whole matter, I purpose to tell you the circumstance of every point, whereby such as are more learned then I (to whom fortune hath ministred more copious stile) may painte it out in paper in forme of an History. There was a young Gentleman dwelling in the next City, borne of good parentage, valiant in prowesse, and riche in substance, but very much given and adicted to whorehunting, and continuall revelling. Whereby he fell in company with Theeves, and had his hand ready to the effusion of humane blood; his name was Thrasillus. The matter was this according to the report of every man. Hee demanded Charites in marriage, who although he were

THE EIGHTH BOOKE

CHAPTER XXXII

How a young man came and declared the miserable death of Lepolemus and his wife Charites

a man more comely then the residue that wooed her, and also had riches abundantly, yet because he was of evill fame, and a man of wicked manners and conversation, he had the repulse and was put off by Charites, and so she married with Lepolemus. Howbeit this young man secretly loved her, yet moved somewhat at her refusall, hee busily searched some meanes to worke his damnable intent. And (having found occasion and opportunity to accomplish his purpose, which he had long time concealed) brought to passe, that the same day that Charites was delivered by the subtill meane and valiant audacity of her husband, from the puissance of the Theeves, he mingled himselfe among the assembly, faining that he was glad of the new marriage, and comming home againe of the maiden, whereby (by reason that he came of so noble parents) he was received and entertained into the house as one of their chiefe and principall friends: Howbeit under cloake of a faithfull welwiller, hee dissimuled his mischievous mind and intent: in continuance of time by much familiarity and often conversation and banketting together, he fell more and more in favour, like as we see it fortuneth to Lovers, who first doe little delight themselves in love: till as by continuall acquaintance they kisse and imbrace each other. Thrasillus perceiving that it was a hard matter to breake his minde secretly to Charites, whereby he was wholly barred from the accomplishment of his luxurious appetite, and on the other side perceiving that the love of her and her husband was so strongly lincked together, that the bond betweene them might in no wise be dissevered, moreover, it was a thing impossible to ravish her, although he had consented thereto, yet was hee still provoked forward by vehement lust, when as hee saw himselfe unable to bring his purpose to passe. Howbeit at length the thing which seemed so hard and difficill, thorough hope of his fortified love, did now appeare easie and facill: but marke I pray you diligently to what end the furious force of his inordinate desire came. On a day Lepolemus went to the chase with Thrasillus, to hunt for Goates, for his wife Charites desired him earnestly to meddle with no other beasts, which were of more fierce and wilde nature. When they were come within the chase

OF LUCIUS APULEIUS

to a great thicket fortressed about with bryers and thornes, they compassed round with their Dogs, and beset every place with nets: by and by warning was given to let loose. The Dogs rushed in with such a cry, that all the Forrest rang againe with the noyse, but behold there leaped out no Goat, nor Deere, nor gentle Hinde, but an horrible and dangerous wild Boare, hard and thicke skinned, bristeled terribly with thornes, foming at the mouth, grinding his teeth, and looking direfully with fiery eyes. The Dogs that first set upon him, he tare and rent with his tuskes, and then he ranne quite through the nets, and escaped away. When wee saw the fury of this beast, wee were greatly striken with feare, and because wee never accustomed to chase such dreadfull Boares, and further because we were unarmed and without weapons, we got and hid our selves under bushes and trees. Then Thrasillus having found opportunity to worke his treason, said to Lepolemus: What stand we here amazed? Why show we our selves like dastards? Why leese we so worthy a prey with our feminine hearts? Let us mount upon our Horses, and pursue him incontinently: take you a hunting staffe, and I will take a chasing speare. By and by they leaped upon their Horses, and followed the beast. But hee returning against them with furious force, pryed with his eyes, on whom hee might first assayle with his tuskes: Lepolemus strooke the beast first on the backe with his hunting staffe. Thrasillus faining to ayde and assist him, came behind, and cut off the hinder legges of Lepolemus Horse, in such sort that hee fell downe to the ground with his master: and sodainely the Boare came upon Lepolemus, and furiously tare and rent him with his teeth. Howbeit, Thrasillus was not sufficed to see him thus wounded, but when he desired his friendly help, he thrust Lepolemus through the right thigh with his speare, the more because he thought the wound of the speare would be taken for a wound of the Boars teeth, then he killed the beast likewise. And when he was thus miserably slaine, every one of us came out of our holes, and went towards our slaine master. But although that Thrasillus was joyfull of the death of Lepolemus, whom he did greatly hate, yet he

CHAPTER XXXII

How a young man came and declared the miserable death of Lepolemus and his wife Charites

THE EIGHTH BOOKE

CHAPTER XXXII
How a young man came and declared the miserable death of Lepolemus and his wife Charites

cloked the matter with a sorrowfull countenance, he fained a dolorous face, he often imbraced the body which himselfe slew, he played all the parts of a mourning person, saving there fell no teares from his eyes. Thus hee resembled us in each point, who verily and not without occasion had cause to lament for our master, laying all the blame of this homicide unto the Boare. Incontinently after the sorrowfull newes of the death of Lepolemus, came to the eares of all the family, but especially to Charites, who after she had heard such pitifull tydings, as a mad and raging woman, ran up and down the streets, crying and howling lamentably. All the Citizens gathered together, and such as they met bare them company running towards the chasse. When they came to the slaine body of Lepolemus, Charites threw her selfe upon him weeping and lamenting grievously for his death, in such sort, that she would have presently ended her life, upon the corps of her slaine husband, whom shee so entirely loved, had it not beene that her parents and friends did comfort her, and pulled her away. The body was taken up, and in funerall pompe brought to the City and buried. In the meane season, Thrasillus fained much sorrow for the death of Lepolemus, but in his heart he was well pleased and joyfull. And to counterfeit the matter, he would come to Charites and say: O what a losse have I had of my friend, my fellow, my companion Lepolemus? O Charites comfort your selfe, pacifie your dolour, refraine your weeping, beat not your breasts: and with such other and like words and divers examples he endeavoured to suppresse her great sorrow, but he spake not this for any other intent but to win the heart of the woman, and to nourish his odious love with filthy delight. Howbeit, Charites after the buriall of her husband sought the meanes to follow him, and (not sustaining the sorrows wherein she was wrapped) got her secretly into a chamber and purposed to finish her life there with dolour and tribulation. But Thrasillus was very importunate, and at length brought to passe, that at the intercession of the Parents and friends of Charites, she somewhat refreshed her fallen members with refection of meate and baine. Howbeit, she did it more at the commandement of her Parents, then for any thing else: for

OF LUCIUS APULEIUS

she could in no wise be merry, nor receive any comfort, but
tormented her selfe day and night before the Image of her
husband which she made like unto Bacchus, and rendred
unto him divine honours and services. In the meane season
Thrasillus not able to refraine any longer, before Charites
had asswaged her dolor, before her troubled mind had
pacified her fury, even in the middle of all her griefes, while
she tare her haire and rent her garments, demanded her in
marriage, and so without shame, he detected the secrets and
unspeakeable deceipts of his heart. But Charites detested
and abhorred his demand, and as she had beene stroken
with some clap of thunder, with some storme, or with the
lightning of Jupiter, she presently fell downe to the ground
all amazed. Howbeit when her spirits were revived and that
she returned to her selfe, perceiving that Thrasillus was so
importunate, she demanded respite to deliberate and to take
advise on the matter. In the meane season, the shape of
Lepolemus that was slaine so miserably, appeared to Charites
saying, O my sweet wife (which no other person can say but
I) I pray thee for the love which is betweene us two, if
there be any memorie of me in thy heart, or remembrance
of my pittifull death, marry with any other person, so
that thou marry not with the traitour Thrasillus, have no
conference with him, eate not with him, lie not with
him, avoid the bloudie hand of mine enemie, couple not
thy selfe with a paricide, for those wounds (the bloud
whereof thy teares did wash away) were not the wounds of
the teeth of the Boare, but the speare of Thrasillus, that
deprived me from thee. Thus spake Lepolemus, unto his
loving wife, and declared the residue of the damnable fact.
Then Charites, awaking from sleepe, began to renew her
dolour, to teare her garments, and to beate her armes with
her comely hands, howbeit she revealed the vision which she
saw to no manner of person, but dissimuling that she knew
no part of the mischiefe, devised with her selfe how she
might be revenged on the traitor, and finish her owne life to
end and knit up all sorrow. Incontinently came Thrasillus,
the detestable demander of sodaine pleasure, and wearied
the closed eares of Charites with talke of marriage, but she

CHAPTER
XXXII

How a young
man came and
declared the
miserable
death of Lepo-
lemus and his
wife Charites

THE EIGHTH BOOKE

CHAPTER XXXII

How a young man came and declared the miserable death of Lepolemus and his wife Charites

gently refused his communication, and coloring the matter, with passing craft in the middest of his earnest desires gan say, Thrasillus you shall understand that yet the face of your brother and my husband, is alwayes before mine eies, I smell yet the Cinamon sent of his pretious body, I yet feele Lepolemus alive in my heart: wherefore you shall do well if you grant to me miserable woman, necessarie time to bewaile his death, that after the residue of a few monethes, the whole yeare may be expired, which thing toucheth as well my shame as your wholsome profit, lest peradventure by your speed and quicke marriage we should justly raise and provoke the spirit of my husband to worke our destruction. Howbeit, Thrasillus was not contented with this promise, but more and more came upon her: Insomuch, that she was enforced to speake to him in this manner: My friend Thrasillus, if thou be so contented untill the whole yeare be compleate and finished, behold here is my bodie, take thy pleasure, but in such sort and so secret that no servant of the house may perceive it. Then Thrasillus trusting to the false promises of the woman, and preferring his inordinate pleasure above all things in the world, was joyfull in his heart and looked for night, when as he might have his purpose. But come thou about midnight (quoth Charites) disguised without companie, and doe but hisse at my chamber doore, and my nourse shall attend and let thee in. This counsell pleased Thrasillus marveilously, who (suspecting no harme) did alwaies looke for night, and the houre assigned by Charites. The time was scarce come, when as (according to her commandement) he disguised himselfe, and went straight to the chamber, where he found the nourse attending for him, who (by the appointment of her Mistresse) fed him with flattering talke, and gave him mingled and doled drinke in a cup, excusing the absence of her Mistresse Charites, by reason that she attended on her Father being sick, untill such time, that with sweet talke and operation of the wine, he fell in a sound sleepe: Now when he lay prostrate on the ground readie to all adventure, Charites (being called for) came in, and with manly courage and bold force stood over the sleeping murderer, saying: Behold the faithfull companion of my

OF LUCIUS APULEIUS

husband, behold this valiant hunter; behold me deere spouse, this is the hand which shed my bloud, this is the heart which hath devised so many subtill meanes to worke my destruction, these be the eies whom I have ill pleased, behold now they foreshew their owne destinie: sleepe carelesse, dreame that thou art in the hands of the mercifull, for I will not hurt thee with thy sword or any other weapon: God forbid that I should slay thee as thou slewest my husband, but thy eies shall faile thee, and thou shalt see no more, then that whereof thou dreamest: Thou shalt thinke the death of thine enemie more sweet then thy life; Thou shalt see no light, thou shalt lacke the aide of a leader, thou shalt not have me as thou hopest, thou shalt have no delight of my marriage, thou shalt not die, and yet living thou shalt have no joy, but wander betweene light and darknesse as an unsure Image: thou shalt seeke for the hand that pricked out thine eies, yet shalt thou not know of whom thou shouldest complaine: I will make sacrifice with the bloud of thine eies upon the grave of my husband. But what gainest thou through my delay? Perhaps thou dreamest that thou embracest me in thy armes: leave off the darknesse of sleepe and awake thou to receive a penall deprivation of thy sight, lift up thy face, regard thy vengeance and evill fortune, reckon thy miserie; so pleaseth thine eies to a chast woman, that thou shalt have blindnesse to thy companion, and an everlasting remorse of thy miserable conscience. When she had spoken these words, she tooke a great needle from her head and pricked out both his eies: which done, she by and by caught the naked sword which her husband Lepolemus accustomed to weare, and ranne throughout all the Citie like a mad woman towards the Sepulchre of her husband. Then all we of the house, with all the Citizens, ranne incontinently after her to take the sword out of her hand, but she clasping about the tombe of Lepolemus, kept us off with her naked weapon, and when she perceived that every one of us wept and lamented, she spake in this sort: I pray you my friends weepe not, nor lament for me, for I have revenged the death of my husband, I have punished deservedly the wicked breaker of our marriage; now is it time

CHAPTER XXXII

How a young man came and declared the miserable death of Lepolemus and his wife Charites

THE EIGHTH BOOKE

CHAPTER XXXII

How a young man came and declared the miserable death of Lepolemus and his wife Charites

to seeke out my sweet Lepolemus, and presently with this sword to finish my life. And therewithall after she had made relation of the whole matter, declared the vision which she saw and told by what meane she deceived Thrasillus, thrusting her sword under her right brest, and wallowing in her owne bloud, at length with manly courage yeelded up the Ghost. Then immediately the friends of miserable Charites did bury her body within the same Sepulchre. Thrasillus hearing all the matter, and knowing not by what meanes he might end his life, for he thought his sword was not sufficient to revenge so great a crime, at length went to the same Sepulchre, and cryed with a lowd voice, saying: O yee dead spirites whom I have so highly and greatly offended, vouchsafe to receive me, behold I make Sacrifice unto you with my whole body: which said, hee closed the Sepulchre, purposing to famish himselfe, and to finish his life there in sorrow. These things the young man with pitifull sighes and teares, declared unto the Cowheards and Shepheards, which caused them all to weepe: but they fearing to become subject unto new masters, prepared themselves to depart away.

THE THIRTY-THIRD CHAPTER

How Apuleius was lead away by the Horsekeeper: and what danger he was in.

BY and by the Horsekeeper, to whom the charge of me was committed, brought forth all his substance, and laded me and other Horses withall, and so departed thence: we bare women, children, pullets, sparrowes, kiddes, whelpes, and other things which were not able to keepe pace with us, and that which I bare upon my backe, although it was a mighty burthen, yet seemed it very light, because I was driven away from him that most terribly had appointed to kill me. When we had passed over

OF LUCIUS APULEIUS

a great mountaine full of trees, and were come againe into the open fields, behold we approached nigh to a faire and rich Castell, where it was told unto us that we were not able to passe in our journey that night, by reason of the great number of terrible Wolves which were in the Country about, so fierce and cruell that they put every man in feare, in such sort that they would invade and set upon such which passed by like theeves, and devoure both them and their beasts. Moreover, we were advertised that there lay in the way where we should passe, many dead bodies eaten and torne with wolves. Wherefore we were willed to stay there all night, and on the next morning, to goe close and round together, whereby we might passe and escape all dangers. But (notwithstanding this good counsell) our caitife drivers were so covetous to goe forward, and so fearefull of pursuite, that they never stayed till the morning: But being welnigh midnight, they made us trudge in our way apace. Then I fearing the great danger which might happen, ran amongst the middle of the other Horses, to the end I might defend and save my poore buttockes from the Wolves, whereat every man much marvelled to see, that I scowred away swifter then the other Horses. But such was my agility, not to get me any prayse, but rather for feare: at that time I remembred with my selfe, that the valiant Horse Pegasus did fly in the ayre more to avoyd the danger of dreadfull Chimera, then for any thing else. The shepheards which drave us before them were well armed like warriours: one had a speare, another had a sheepehooke, some had darts, some clubbes, some gathered up great stones, some held up their sharp Javelings, and some feared away the Woolves with light firebrands. Finally wee lacked nothing to make up an Army, but onely Drummes and Trumpets. But when we had passed these dangers, not without small feare, wee fortuned to fall into worse, for the Woolves came not upon us, either because of the great multitude of our company, or else because [of] our firebrands, or peradventure they were gone to some other place, for wee could see none, but the Inhabitants of the next villages (supposing that wee were Theeves by reason of the great multitude) for the defence of their owne substance,

CHAPTER XXXIII
How Apuleius was lead away by the Horse-keeper: and what danger he was in

THE EIGHTH BOOKE

CHAPTER XXXIII

How Apuleius was lead away by the Horsekeeper: and what danger he was in

and for the feare that they were in, set great and mighty masties upon us, which they had kept and nourished for the safety of their houses, who compassing us round about leaped on every side, tearing us with their teeth, in such sort that they pulled many of us to the ground: verily it was a pittifull sight to see so many Dogs, some following such as flyed, some invading such as stood still, some tearing those which lay prostrate, but generally there were none which escaped cleare: Behold upon this another danger ensued, the Inhabitants of the Towne stood in their garrets and windowes, throwing great stones upon our heads, that wee could not tell whether it were best for us to avoyd the gaping mouthes of the Dogges at hand or the perill of the stones afarre, amongst whome there was one that hurled a great flint upon a woman, which sate upon my backe, who cryed out pitiously, desiring her husband to helpe her. Then he (comming to succour and ayd his wife) beganne to speake in this sort: Alas masters, what mean you to trouble us poore labouring men so cruelly? What meane you to revenge your selves upon us, that doe you no harme? What thinke you to gaine by us? You dwell not in Caves or Dennes: you are no people barbarous, that you should delight in effusion of humane blood. At these words the tempest of stones did cease, and the storme of the Dogges vanished away. Then one (standing on the toppe of a great Cypresse tree) spake unto us saying: Thinke you not masters that we doe this to the intent to rifle or take away any of your goods, but for the safeguard of our selves and family: now a Gods name you may depart away. So we went forward, some wounded with stones, some bitten with Dogs, but generally there was none which escaped free.

OF LUCIUS APULEIUS

THE THIRTY-FOURTH CHAPTER
How the shepheards determined to abide in a certaine wood to cure their wounds.

HEN we had gone a good part of our way, we came to a certaine wood invironed with great trees and compassed about with pleasant meddowes, whereas the Shepheards appointed to continue a certaine space to cure their wounds and sores; then they sate downe on the ground to refresh their wearie minds, and afterwards they sought for medicines, to heale their bodies: some washed away their blood with the water of the running River: some stopped their wounds with Spunges and cloutes, in this manner every one provided for his owne safety. In the meane season wee perceived an old man, who seemed to be a Shepheard, by reason of the Goates and Sheep that fed round about him. Then one of our company demanded whether he had any milke, butter, or cheese to sell. To whom he made answere saying: Doe you looke for any meate or drinke, or any other refection here? Know you not in what place you be?

And therewithall he tooke his sheepe and drave them away as fast as he might possible. This answere made our shepheards greatly to feare, that they thought of nothing else, but to enquire what Country they were in: Howbeit they saw no manner of person of whom they might demand. At length as they were thus in doubt, they perceived another old man with a staffe in his hand very weary with travell, who approching nigh to our company, began to weepe and complaine saying: Alas masters I pray you succour me miserable caitife, and restore my nephew to me againe, that by following a sparrow that flew before him, is fallen into a ditch hereby, and verily I thinke he is in danger of death. As for me, I am not able to helpe him out by reason of mine

THE EIGHTH BOOKE

CHAPTER XXXIV
How the shepheards determined to abide in a certaine wood to cure their wounds

old age, but you that are so valiant and lusty may easily helpe me herein, and deliver me my boy, my heire and guide of my life. These words made us all to pity him: And then the youngest and stoutest of our company, who alone escaped best the late skirmish of Dogges and stones, rose up and demanded in what ditch the boy was fallen: Mary (quod he) yonder, and pointed with his finger, and brought him to a great thicket of bushes and thornes where they both entred in. In the meane season, after we cured our wounds, we tooke up our packs, purposing to depart away. And because we would not goe away without the young man our fellow: The shepheards whistled and called for him, but when he gave no answer, they sent one out of their company to seeke him out, who after a while returned againe with a pale face and sorrowfull newes, saying that he saw a terrible Dragon eating and devouring their companion: and as for the old man, hee could see him in no place. When they heard this, (remembring likewise the words of the first old man that shaked his head, and drave away his sheep) they ran away beating us before them, to fly from this desart and pestilent Country.

THE THIRTY-FIFTH CHAPTER

How a woman killed her selfe and her child, because her husband haunted harlots.

AFTER that we had passed a great part of our journey, we came to a village where we lay all night, but harken, and I will tell you what mischiefe happened there: you shall understand there was a servant to whom his Master had committed the whole government of his house, and was Master of the lodging where we lay: this servant had married a Maiden of the same house, howbeit he was greatly in love with a harlot of the towne, and accustomed to resort unto her, wherewith his wife

OF LUCIUS APULEIUS

was so highly displeased and became so jealous, that she gathered together all her husbands substance, with his tales and books of account, and threw them into a light fire: she was not contented with this, but she tooke a cord and bound her child which she had by her husband, about her middle and cast her selfe headlong into a deepe pit. The Master taking in evill part the death of these twaine, tooke his servant which was the cause of this murther by his luxurie, and first after that he had put off all his apparell, he annointed his body with honey, and then bound him sure to a fig-tree, where in a rotten stocke a great number of Pismares had builded their neasts, the Pismares after they had felt the sweetnesse of the honey came upon his body, and by little and little (in continuance of time) devoured all his flesh, in such sort, that there remained on the tree but his bare bones: this was declared unto us by the inhabitants of the village there, who greatly sorrowed for the death of this servant: then we avoiding likewise from this dreadfull lodging, incontinently departed away.

CHAPTER XXXV
How a woman killed her selfe and her child, because her husband haunted harlots

THE THIRTY-SIXTH CHAPTER
How Apuleius was cheapned by divers persons, and how they looked in his mouth to know his age.

AFTER this we came to a faire Citie very populous, where our shepheards determined to continue, by reason that it seemed a place where they might live unknowne, far from such as should pursue them, and because it was a countrey very plentifull of corne and other victuals, where when we had remained the space of three dayes, and that I poore Asse and the other horses were fed and kept in the stable to the intent we might seeme more saleable, we were brought out at length to the market, and by and by a crier sounded with his horne

171

THE EIGHTH BOOKE

CHAPTER XXXVI

How Apuleius was cheapned by divers persons, and how they looked in his mouth to know his age

to notifie that we were to be sold: all my companion horses were bought up by Gentlemen, but as for me I stood still forsaken of all men. And when many buiers came by and looked in my mouth to know mine age, I was so weary with opening my jawes that at length (unable to endure any longer) when one came with a stinking paire of hands, and grated my gummes with his filthy fingers, I bit them cleane off, which thing caused the standers by to forsake me as being a fierce and cruell beast: the crier when he had gotten a hoarse voice with crying, and saw that no man would buy me, began to mocke me saying, To what end stand we here with this wilde Asse, this feeble beast, this slow jade with worne hooves, good for nothing but to make sives of his skin? Why do we not give him to some body, for he earneth not his hay? In this manner he made all the standers by to laugh exceedingly, but my evill fortune which was ever so cruell against me, whom I by travell of so many countreys could in no wise escape, did more and more envie me, with invention of new meanes to afflict my poore body in giving me a new Master as spitefull as the rest. There was an old man somewhat bald, with long and gray haire, one of the number of those that go from door to door, throughout all the villages, bearing the Image of the goddesse Syria, and playing with Cimbals to get the almes of good and charitable folks, this old man came hastely towards the cryer, and demanded where I was bred: Marry (quoth he) in Cappadocia: Then he enquired what age I was of, the cryer answered as a Mathematician, which disposed to me my Planets, that I was five yeares old, and willed the old man to looke in my mouth: For I would not willingly (quoth he) incur the penalty of the law Cornelia, in selling a free Citizen for a servile slave, buy a Gods name this faire beast to ride home on, and about in the countrey: But this curious buier did never stint to question of my qualities, and at length he demanded whether I were gentle or no: Gentle (quoth the crier) as gentle as a Lambe, tractable to all use, he will never bite, he will never kicke, but you would rather thinke that under the shape of an Asse there were some well advised man, which verely you may easily conject, for if you would thrust your nose in his taile you shall perceive how

OF LUCIUS APULEIUS

patient he is: Thus the cryer mocked the old man, but he perceiving his taunts and jests, waxed very angry saying, Away doting cryer, I pray the omnipotent and omniparent goddesse Syria, Saint Sabod, Bellona, with her mother Idea, and Venus, with Adonis, to strike out both thine eies, that with taunting mocks hast scoffed me in this sort: Dost thou thinke that I will put a goddesse upon the backe of any fierce beast, whereby her divine Image should be throwne downe on the ground, and so I poore miser should be compelled (tearing my haire) to looke for some Physition to helpe her? When I heard him speake thus, I thought with my selfe sodainly to leap upon him like a mad Asse, to the intent he should not buy me, but incontinently there came another Marchant that prevented my thought, and offered 17 Pence for me, then my Master was glad and received the mony, and delivered me to my new Master who was called Phelibus, and he caried his new servant home, and before he came to his house, he called out his daughters saying, Behold my daughters, what a gentle servant I have bought for you: then they were marvailous glad, and comming out pratling and shouting for joy, thought verely that he had brought home a fit and conveniable servant for their purpose, but when they perceived that it was an Asse, they began to provoke him, saying, that he had not bought a servant for his Maidens, but rather an Asse for himselfe. Howbeit (quoth they) keepe him not wholly for your owne riding, but let us likewise have him at commandement. Therewithall they led me into the stable, and tied me to the manger: there was a certaine yong man with a mighty body, wel skilled in playing on instruments before the gods to get money, who (as soone as he had espied me) entertained me verie well, for he filled my racke and maunger full of meat, and spake merrily saying, O master Asse, you are very welcome, now you shall take my office in hand, you are come to supply my roome, and to ease me of my miserable labour: but I pray God thou maist long live and please my Master well, to the end thou maist continually deliver me from so great paine. When I heard these words I did prognosticate my miserie to come.

CHAPTER XXXVI
How Apuleius was cheapned by divers persons, and how they looked in his mouth to know his age

The day following I saw there a great number of persons

THE EIGHTH BOOKE

CHAPTER XXXVI

How Apuleius was cheapned by divers persons, and how they looked in his mouth to know his age

apparelled in divers colours, having painted faces, miters on their heads, vestiments coloured like saffron, Surplesses of silke, and on their feet yellow shooes, who attired the goddesse in a robe of Purple, and put her upon my backe. Then they went forth with their armes naked to their shoulders, bearing with them great swords and mightie axes, and dancing like mad persons. After that we had passed many small villages, we fortuned to come to one Britunis house, where at our first entrie they began to hurle themselves hither and thither, as though they were mad. They made a thousand gestures with their feete and their hands, they would bite themselves, finally, every one tooke his weapon and wounded his armes in divers places.

Amongst whom there was one more mad then the rest, that fet many deepe sighes from the bottome of his heart, as though he had beene ravished in spirite, or replenished with divine power. And after that, he somewhat returning to himselfe, invented and forged a great lye, saying, that he had displeased the divine majesty of the goddesse, by doing of some thing which was not convenable to the order of their holy religion, wherefore he would doe vengeance of himselfe: and therewithall he tooke a whip, and scourged his owne body, that the bloud issued out aboundantly, which thing caused me greatly to feare, to see such wounds and effusion of bloud, least the same goddesse desiring so much the bloud of men, should likewise desire the bloud of an Asse. After they were wearie with hurling and beating themselves, they sate downe, and behold, the inhabitants came in, and offered gold, silver, vessels of wine, milke, cheese, flower, wheate and other things: amongst whom there was one, that brought barly to the Asse that carried the goddesse, but the greedie whoresons thrust all into their sacke, which they brought for the purpose and put it upon my backe, to the end I might serve for two purposes, that is to say, for the barne by reason of my corne, and for the Temple by reason of the goddesse. In this sort, they went from place to place, robbing all the Countrey over. At length they came to a certaine Castle where under colour of divination, they brought to passe that they obtained a fat sheepe of a poore husbandman for the

OF LUCIUS APULEIUS

goddesse supper and to make sacrifice withall. After that the banket was prepared, they washed their bodies, and brought in a tall young man of the village, to sup with them, who had scarce tasted a few pottage, when hee began to discover their beastly customes and inordinate desire of luxury. For they compassed him round about, sitting at the table, and abused the young man, contrary to all nature and reason. When I beheld this horrible fact, I could not but attempt to utter my mind and say, O masters, but I could pronounce no more but the first letter O, which I roared out so valiantly, that the young men of the towne seeking for a straie Asse, that they had lost the same night, and hearing my voice, whereby they judged that I had beene theirs, entred into the house unwares, and found these persons committing their vilde abhomination, which when they saw, they declared to all the inhabitants by, their unnaturall villany, mocking and laughing at this the pure and cleane chastity of their religion. In the meane season, Phelibus and his company, (by reason of the bruit which was dispersed throughout all the region there of their beastly wickednesse) put all their trumpery upon my backe, and departed away about midnight. When we had passed a great part of our journey, before the rising of the Sun, we came into a wild desart, where they conspired together to slay me. For after they had taken the goddesse from my backe and set her gingerly upon the ground, they likewise tooke off my harnesse, and bound me surely to an Oake, beating me with their whip, in such sort that all my body was mortified. Amongst whom there was one that threatned to cut off my legs with his hatchet, because by my noyse I diffamed his chastity, but the other regarding more their owne profit then my utility, thought best to spare my life, because I might carry home the goddesse. So they laded me againe, driving me before them with their naked swords, till they came to a noble City : where the principall Patrone bearing high reverence unto the goddesse, came in great devotion before us with Tympany, Cymbals, and other instruments, and received her, and all our company with much sacrifice and veneration. But there I remember, I thought my selfe in most danger, for there was one that brought to

CHAPTER XXXVI

How Apuleius was cheapned by divers persons, and how they looked in his mouth to know his age

THE EIGHTH BOOKE

CHAPTER XXXVI
How Apuleius was cheapned by divers persons, and how they looked in his mouth to know his age

the Master of the house, a side of a fat Bucke for a present, which being hanged behind the kitchin doore, not far from the ground, was cleane eaten up by a gray hound, that came in. The Cooke when he saw the Venison devoured, lamented and wept pitifully. And because supper time approached nigh, when as he should be reproved of too much negligence, he tooke a halter to hang himselfe: but his wife perceiving whereabout he went, ran incontinently to him, and taking the halter in both her hands, stopped him of his purpose, saying, O husband, are you out of your wits? pray husband follow my counsel, cary this strange Asse out into some secret place and kill him, which done, cut off one of his sides, and sawce it well like the side of the Bucke, and set it before your Master. Then the Cooke hearing the counsell of his wife, was well pleased to slay me to save himselfe: and so he went to the whetstone, to sharpe his tooles accordingly.

THE
NINTH BOOKE
of LUCIUS APULEIUS of
THE GOLDEN ASSE

THE NINTH BOOKE

THE THIRTY-SEVENTH CHAPTER
How Apuleius saved himselfe from the Cooke, breaking his halter, and of other things that happened.

IN this manner the traiterous Cooke prepared himselfe to slay me: and when he was ready with his knives to doe his feat, I devised with my selfe how I might escape the present perill, and I did not long delay: for incontinently I brake the halter wherewith I was tied, and flinging my heeles hither and thither to save my selfe, at length I ran hastily into a Parlour, where the Master of the house was feasting with the Priests of the goddesse Syria, and disquieted all the company, throwing downe their meats and drinks from the table. The Master of the house dismayed at my great disorder, commanded one of his servants to take me up, and locke me in some strong place, to the end I might disturb them no more. But I little regarded my imprisonment, considering that I was happily delivered from the hands of the traiterous Cooke. Howbeit fortune, or the fatall disposition of the divine providence, which neither can be avoided by wise counsell, neither yet by any wholesome remedie, invented a new torment, for by and by a young ladde came running into the Parlour all trembling, and declared to the Master of the house, that there was a madde Dog running about in the streetes, which had

THE NINTH BOOKE

CHAPTER XXXVII

How Apuleius saved himselfe from the Cooke, breaking his halter, and of other things that happened

done much harme, for he had bitten many grey hounds and Horses in the Inne by: And he spared neither man nor beast. For there was one Mitilius a Mulettour, Epheseus, a Cooke, Hyppanius a chamberlaine, and Appolonius a Physition, who (thinking to chase away the madde Dogge) were cruelly wounded by him, insomuch that many Horses and other beasts infected with the venyme of his poysonous teeth became madde likewise. Which thing caused them all at the table greatly to feare, and thinking that I had beene bitten in like sort, came out with speares, Clubs, and Pitchforks purposing to slay me, and I had undoubtedly beene slaine, had I not by and by crept into the Chamber, where my Master intended to lodge all night. Then they closed and locked fast the doores about me, and kept the chamber round, till such time as they thought that the pestilent rage of madnesse had killed me. When I was thus shutte in the chamber alone, I laid me downe upon the bed to sleepe, considering it was long time past, since I lay and tooke my rest as a man doth. When morning was come, and that I was well reposed, I rose up lustily. In the meane season, they which were appointed to watch about the chamber all night, reasoned with themselves in this sort, Verely (quoth one) I think that this rude Asse be dead. So think I (quoth another) for the outragious poyson of madnes hath killed him, but being thus in divers opinions of a poore Asse, they looked through a crevis, and espied me standing still, sober and quiet in the middle of the chamber; then they opened the doores, and came towards me, to prove whether I were gentle or no. Amongst whom there was one, which in my opinion, was sent from Heaven to save my life, that willed the other to set a bason of faire water before me, and thereby they would know whether I were mad or no, for if I did drinke without feare as I accustomed to do, it was a signe that I was whole, and in mine Assie wits, where contrary if I did flie and abhorre the tast of the water, it was an evident proofe of my madnes, which thing he said that he had read in ancient and credible books, whereupon they tooke a bason of cleere water, and presented it before me: but I as soone as I perceived the wholsome water of my life, ran incontinently, thrusting my

OF LUCIUS APULEIUS

head into the bason, drank as though I had beene greatly athirst; then they stroked me with their hands, and bowed mine eares, and tooke me by the halter, to prove my patience, but I taking each thing in good part, disproved their mad presumption, by my meeke and gentle behaviour: when I was thus delivered from this double danger, the next day I was laded againe with the goddesse Siria, and other trumpery, and was brought into the way with Trumpets and Cymbals to beg in the villages which we passed by according to our custome. And after that we had gone through a few towns and Castles, we fortuned to come to a certaine village, which was builded (as the inhabitants there affirme) upon the foundation of a famous ancient Citie. And after that we had turned into the next Inne, we heard of a prettie jest committed in the towne there, which I would that you should know likewise.

CHAPTER XXXVII
How Apuleius saved himselfe from the Cooke, breaking his halter, and of other things that happened

THE THIRTY-EIGHTH CHAPTER

Of the deceipt of a Woman which made her husband Cuckold.

HERE was a man dwelling in the towne very poore, that had nothing but that which he got by the labour and travell of his hands: his wife was a faire young woman, but very lascivious, and given to the appetite and desire of the flesh. It fortuned on a day, that while this poore man was gone betimes in the morning to the field about his businesse, according as he accustomed to doe, his wives lover secretly came into his house to have his pleasure with her. And so it chanced that during the time that shee and he were basking together, her husband suspecting no such matter, returned home praising the chast continency of his wife, in that hee found his doores fast closed, wherefore as his custome was, he whistled to declare his comming. Then his crafty wife ready with shifts, caught

THE NINTH BOOKE

CHAPTER XXXVIII
Of the deceipt of a Woman which made her husband Cuckold

her lover and covered him under a great tub standing in a corner, and therewithall she opened the doore, blaming her husband in this sort: Commest thou home every day with empty hands, and bringest nothing to maintaine our house? thou hast no regard for our profit, neither providest for any meate or drinke, whereas I poore wretch doe nothing day and night but occupie my selfe with spinning, and yet my travell will scarce find the Candels which we spend. O how much more happy is my neighbour Daphne, that eateth and drinketh at her pleasure, and passeth the time with her amorous lovers according to her desire. What is the matter (quoth her husband) though our Master hath made holiday at the fields, yet thinke not but I have made provision for our supper; doest thou not see this tub that keepeth a place here in our house in vaine, and doth us no service? Behold I have sold it to a good fellow (that is here present) for five pence, wherefore I pray thee lend me thy hand, that I may deliver him the tub. His wife (having invented a present shift) laughed on her husband, saying: What marchant I pray you have you brought home hither, to fetch away my tub for five pence, for which I poore woman that sit all day alone in my house have beene proferred so often seaven: her husband being well apayed of her words demanded what he was that had bought the tub: Looke (quoth she) he is gone under, to see where it be sound or no: then her lover which was under the tub, began to stirre and rustle himselfe, and because his words might agree to the words of the woman, he sayd: Dame will you have me tell the truth, this tub is rotten and crackt as me seemeth on every side. And then turning to her husband sayd: I pray you honest man light a Candle, that I may make cleane the tub within, to see if it be for my purpose or no, for I doe not mind to cast away my money wilfully: he by and by (being made a very Oxe) lighted a candle, saying, I pray you good brother put not your selfe to so much paine, let me make the tub cleane and ready for you. Whereupon he put off his coate, and crept under the tub to rub away the filth from the sides. In the meane season this minion lover cast his wife on the bottome of the tub, and had his pleasure with her over his

OF LUCIUS APULEIUS

head, and as he was in the middest of his pastime, hee turned his head on this side and that side, finding fault with this and with that, till as they had both ended their businesse, when as he delivered seaven pence for the tub, and caused the good man himselfe to carry it on his backe againe to his Inne.

CHAPTER XXXVIII
Of the deceipt of a Woman which made her husband Cuckold

THE THIRTY-NINTH CHAPTER

How the Priests of the goddesse Siria were taken and put in prison, and how Apuleius was sold to a Baker.

AFTER that we had tarried there a few dayes at the cost and charges of the whole Village, and had gotten much mony by our divination and prognostication of things to come: The priests of the goddesse Siria invented a new meanes to picke mens purses, for they had certaine lofts, whereon were written: *Coniuncti terram proscindunt boves ut in futurum læta germinent sata:* that is to say: The Oxen tied and yoked together, doe till the ground to the intent it may bring forth his increase: and by these kind of lottes they deceive many of the simple sort, for if one had demanded whether he should have a good wife or no, they would say that his lot did testifie the same, that he should be tyed and yoked to a good woman and have increase of children. If one demanded whether he should buy lands and possession, they said that he should have much ground that should yeeld his increase. If one demanded whether he should have a good and prosperous voyage, they said he should have good successe, and it should be for the increase of his profit. If one demanded whether hee should vanquish his enemies, and prevaile in pursuite of theeves, they said that this enemy should be tyed and yoked to him: and his pursuite after theeves should be prosperous. Thus by the telling of fortunes, they gathered

THE NINTH BOOKE

CHAPTER XXXIX

How the Priests of the goddesse Siria were taken and put in prison, and how Apuleius was sold to a Baker

a great quantity of money, but when they were weary with giving of answers, they drave me away before them next night, through a lane which was more dangerous and stony then the way which we went the night before, for on the one side were quagmires and foggy marshes, on the other side were falling trenches and ditches, whereby my legges failed me, in such sort that I could scarce come to the plaine field pathes. And behold by and by a great company of inhabitants of the towne armed with weapons and on horsebacke overtooke us, and incontinently arresting Philebus and his Priests, tied them by the necks and beate them cruelly, calling them theeves and robbers, and after they had manacled their hands: Shew us (quoth they) the cup of gold, which (under the colour of your solemne religion) ye have taken away, and now ye thinke to escape in the night without punishment for your fact. By and by one came towards me, and thrusting his hand into the bosome of the goddesse Siria, brought out the cup which they had stole. Howbeit for all they appeared evident and plaine they would not be confounded nor abashed, but jesting and laughing out the matter, gan say: Is it reason masters that you should thus rigorously intreat us, and threaten for a small trifling cup, which the mother of the goddesse determined to give to her sister for a present? Howbeit for all their lyes and cavellations, they were carryed backe unto the towne, and put in prison by the Inhabitants, who taking the cup of gold, and the goddesse which I bare, did put and consecrate them amongst the treasure of the temple. The next day I was carryed to the market to be sold, and my price was set at seaven pence more then Philebus gave for me. There fortuned to passe by a Baker of the next village, who after that he had bought a great deale of corne, bought me likewise to carry it home, and when he had well laded me therewith, he drave me through a thorny and dangerous way to his bakehouse; there I saw a great company of horses that went in the mill day and night grinding of corne, but lest I should be discouraged at the first, my master entertained me well, for the first day I did nothing but fare daintily, howbeit such mine ease and felicity did not long endure, for

# OF LUCIUS APULEIUS

CHAPTER XXXIX

How the Priests of the goddesse Siria were taken and put in prison, and how Apuleius was sold to a Baker

the next day following I was tyed to the mill betimes in the morning with my face covered, to the end in turning and winding so often one way, I should not become giddy, but keepe a certaine course, but although when I was a man I had seen many such horsemills and knew well enough how they should be turned, yet feining my selfe ignorant of such kind of toile, I stood still and would not goe, whereby I thought I should be taken from the mill as an Asse unapt, and put to some other light thing, or else to be driven into the fields to pasture, but my subtilty did me small good, for by and by when the mill stood still, the servants came about me, crying and beating me forward, in such sort that I could not stay to advise my selfe, whereby all the company laughed to see so suddaine a change. When a good part of the day was past, that I was not able to endure any longer, they tooke off my harnesse, and tied me to the manger, but although my bones were weary, and that I needed to refresh my selfe with rest and provender, yet I was so curious that I did greatly delight to behold the bakers art, insomuch that I could not eate nor drinke while I looked on.

O good Lord what a sort of poore slaves were there; some had their skinne blacke and blew, some had their backes striped with lashes, some were covered with rugged sackes, some had their members onely hidden: some wore such ragged clouts, that you might perceive all their naked bodies, some were marked and burned in the heads with hot yrons, some had their haire halfe clipped, some had lockes on their legges, some very ugly and evill favoured, that they could scarce see, their eyes and face were so blacke and dimme with smoake, like those that fight in the sands, and know not where they strike by reason of dust: And some had their faces all mealy. But how should I speake of the horses my companions, how they being old and weake, thrust their heads into the manger: they had their neckes all wounded and worne away: they rated their nosethrilles with a continuall cough, their sides were bare with their harnesse and great travell, their ribs were broken with beating, their hooves were battered broad with incessant labour, and their

THE NINTH BOOKE

CHAPTER XXXIX
How the Priests of the goddesse Siria were taken and put in prison, and how Apuleius was sold to a Baker

skinne rugged by reason of their lancknesse. When I saw this dreadfull sight, I began to feare, least I should come to the like state: and considering with my selfe the good fortune which I was sometime in when I was a man, I greatly lamented, holding downe my head, and would eate no meate, but I saw no comfort or consolation of my evill fortune, saving that my mind was somewhat recreated to heare and understand what every man said, for they neither feared nor doubted my presence. At that time I remembred how Homer the divine authour of ancient Poetry, described him to be a wise man, which had travelled divers countries and nations, wherefore I gave great thanks to my Asse for me, in that by this meanes I had seene the experience of many things, and was become more wise (notwithstanding the great misery and labour which I daily sustained): but I will tell you a pretty jest, which commeth now to my remembrance, to the intent your eares may be delighted in hearing the same.

THE FORTIETH CHAPTER

How Apuleius was handled by the Bakers wife, which was a harlot.

THE Baker which bought me was an honest and sober man; but his wife was the most pestilent woman in all the world, insomuch that he endured many miseries and afflictions with her, so that I my selfe did secretly pitty his estate, and bewaile his evill fortune: for she had not one fault alone, but all the mischiefes that could be devised: shee was crabbed, cruell, lascivious, drunken, obstinate, niggish, covetous, riotous in filthy expenses, and an enemy to faith and chastity, a despiser of all the Gods, whom other did honour, one that affirmed that she had a God by her selfe, wherby she deceived all men, but especially her poore husband, one that abandoned her body with continual

OF LUCIUS APULEIUS

whoredome. This mischievous queane hated me in such sort, that shee commanded every day before she was up, that I should be put into the mill to grind : and the first thing which she would doe in the morning, was to see me cruelly beaten, and that I should grind when the other beasts did feed and take rest. When I saw that I was so cruelly handled, she gave me occasion to learne her conversation and life, for I saw oftentimes a yong man which would privily goe into her chamber, whose face I did greatly desire to see, but I could not by reason mine eyes were covered every day. And verily if I had beene free and at liberty, I would have discovered all her abhomination. She had an old woman, a bawd, a messenger of mischiefe that daily haunted to her house, and made good cheere with her to the utter undoing and impoverishment of her husband, but I that was greatly offended with the negligence of Fotis, who made me an Asse, in stead of a Bird, did yet comfort my selfe by this onely meane, in that to the miserable deformity of my shape, I had long eares, whereby I might heare all things that was done: On a day I heard the old bawd say to the Bakers wife:

CHAPTER XL

How Apuleius was handled by the Bakers wife, which was a harlot

Dame you have chosen (without my counsell) a young man to your lover, who as me seemeth, is dull, fearefull, without any grace, and dastardlike coucheth at the frowning looke of your odious husband, whereby you have no delight nor pleasure with him : how farre better is the young man Philesiterus who is comely, beautifull, in the flower of his youth, liberall, courteous, valiant and stout against the diligent pries and watches of your husband, whereby to embrace the worthiest dames of this country, and worthy to weare a crowne of gold, for one part that he played to one that was jealous over his wife. Hearken how it was and then judge the diversity of these two Lovers: Know you not one Barbarus a Senator of our towne, whom the vulgar people call likewise Scorpion for his severity of manners? This Barbarus had a gentlewoman to his wife, whom he caused daily to be enclosed within his house, with diligent custody. Then the Bakers wife said, I know her very well, for we two dwelleth together in one house: Then you know (quoth

THE NINTH BOOKE

CHAPTER XL
How Apuleius was handled by the Bakers wife, which was a harlot

the old woman) the whole tale of Philesiterus? No verily (said she) but I greatly desire to know it: therefore I pray you mother tell me the whole story. By and by the old woman which knew well to babble, began to tell as followeth.

THE FORTY-FIRST CHAPTER

How Barbarus being jealous over his wife, commanded that shee should be kept close in his house, and what happened.

YOU shall understand that on a day this Barbarus preparing himselfe to ride abroad, and willing to keepe the chastity of his wife (whom he so well loved) alone to himselfe, called his man Myrmex (whose faith he had tryed and proved in many things) and secretly committed to him the custody of his wife, willing him that he should threaten, that if any man did but touch her with his finger as he passed by, he would not onely put him in prison, and bind him hand and foote, but also cause him to be put to death, or else to be famished for lacke of sustenance, which words he confirmed by an oath of all the Gods in heaven, and so departed away: When Barbarus was gone, Myrmex being greatly astonied of his masters threatnings, would not suffer his mistresse to goe abroad, but as she sate all day a Spinning, he was so carefull that he sate by her; when night came he went with her to the baines, holding her by the garment, so faithfull he was to fulfill the commandement of his master: Howbeit the beauty of this matron could not be hidden from the burning eyes of Philesiterus, who considering her great chastity, and how she was diligently kept by Myrmex, thought it impossible to have his purpose, yet (indevouring by all kind of meanes to enterprise the matter, and remembring the fragility of man, that might be intised and currupted with money, since

OF LUCIUS APULEIUS

as by gold the Adamant gates may be opened) on a day, when he found Myrmex alone, he discovered his love, desiring him to shew his favour, (otherwise he should certainly dye) with assurance that he need not to feare when as he might privily be let in and out in the night, without knowledge of any person. When he thought, with these and other gentle words to allure and prick forward the obstinate mind of Myrmex he shewed him glittering gold in his hand, saying that he would give his mistresse twenty crownes and him ten, but Myrmex hearing these words, was greatly troubled, abhorring in his mind to commit such a mischiefe: wherfore he stopped his eares, and turning his head departed away: howbeit the glittering view of these crownes could never out of his mind, but being at home he seemed to see the money before his eyes, which was so worthy a prey, wherefore poore Myrmex being in divers opinions could not tell what to doe, for on the one side he considered the promise which he made to his master, and the punishment that should ensue if he did contrary. On the other side he thought of the gaine, and the passing pleasure of the crownes of gold; in the end the desire of the money did more prevaile then the feare of death, for the beauty of the flowrishing crownes did so sticke in his mind, that where the menaces of his master compelled him to tarry at home, the pestilent avarice of gold egged him out a doores, wherefore putting all shame aside, without further delay, he declared all the whole matter to his Mistresse, who according to the nature of a woman, when she heard him speake of so great a summe, she bound chastity in a string, and gave authority to Myrmex to rule her in that case. Myrmex seeing the intent of his Mistresse, was very glad, and for great desire of the gold, he ran hastily to Philesiterus, declaring that his Mistresse was consented to his mind, wherefore he demanded the gold which he promised. Then incontinently Philesiterus delivered him tenne Crownes, and when night came, Myrmex brought him disguised into his mistresses Chamber. About Midnight when he and she were naked together, making sacrifice unto the Goddesse Venus, behold her husband (contrary to their expectation) came and knocked at the doore, calling with a loud voice to his Servant

CHAPTER XLI

How Barbarus being jealous over his wife, commanded that shee should be kept close in his house, and what happened

THE NINTH BOOKE

CHAPTER XLI

How Barbarus being jealous over his wife, commanded that she should be kept close in his house, and what happened

Myrmex : whose long tarrying increased the suspition of his Master, in such sort that he threatned to beat Myrmex cruelly : but he being troubled with feare, and driven to his latter shifts, excused the matter saying : that he could not find the key : by reason it was so darke. In the meane season Philesiterus hearing the noise at the doore, slipt on his coat and privily ran out of the Chamber. When Myrmex had opened the doore to his Master that threatned terribly, and had let him in, he went into the Chamber to his wife : In the meane while Myrmex let out Philesiterus, and barred the doores fast, and went againe to bed. The next morning when Barbarus awaked, he perceived two unknown slippers lying under his bed, which Philesiterus had forgotten when he went away. Then he conceived a great suspition and jealousie in mind, howbeit he would not discover it to his wife, neither to any other person, but putting secretly the slippers into his bosome, commanded his other Servants to bind Myrmex incontinently, and to bring him bound to the Justice after him, thinking verily that by the meane of the slippers he might boult out the matter. It fortuned that while Barbarus went towards the Justice in a fury and rage, and Myrmex fast bound, followed him weeping, not because he was accused before his master, but by reason he knew his owne conscience guilty : behold by adventure Philesiterus (going about earnest businesse) fortuned to meete with them by the way, who fearing the matter which he committed the night before, and doubting lest it should be knowne, did suddainly invent a meane to excuse Myrmex, for he ran upon him and beate him about the head with his fists, saying : Ah mischievous varlet that thou art, and perjured knave. It were a good deed if the Goddesse and thy master here, would put thee to death, for thou art worthy to be imprisoned and to weare out these yrons, that stalest my slippers away when thou werest at my baines yester night. Barbarus hearing this returned incontinently home, and called his servant Myrmex, commanding him to deliver the slippers againe to the right owner. The old woman had scant finished her tale when the Bakers wife gan say : Verily she is blessed and most blessed, that hath the fruition of so worthy a lover, but as for me

OF LUCIUS APULEIUS

poore miser, I am fallen into the hands of a coward, who is not onely afraid of my husband but also of every clap of the mill, and dares not doe nothing, before the blind face of yonder scabbed Asse. Then the old woman answered, I promise you certainly if you will, you shall have this young man at your pleasure, and therewithall when night came, she departed out of her chamber. In the meane season, the Bakers wife made ready a supper with abundance of wine and exquisite fare: so that there lacked nothing, but the comming of the young man, for her husband supped at one of her neighbours houses. When time came that my harnesse should be taken off and that I should rest my selfe, I was not so joyfull of my liberty, as when the vaile was taken from mine eyes, I should see all the abhomination of this mischievous queane. When night was come and the Sunne gone downe, behold the old bawd and the young man, who seemed to me but a child, by reason he had no beard, came to the doore. Then the Bakers wife kissed him a thousand times and received him courteously, placed him downe at the table: but he had scarce eaten the first morsell, when the good man (contrary to his wives expectation) returned home, for she thought he would not have come so soone: but Lord how she cursed him, praying God that he might breake his necke at the first entry in. In the meane season, she caught her lover and thrust him into the bin where she bolted her flower, and dissembling the matter, finely came to her husband demanding why he came home so soone. I could not abide (quod he) to see so great a mischiefe and wicked fact, which my neighbours wife committed, but I must run away: O harlot as she is, how hath she dishonoured her husband, I sweare by the goddesse Ceres, that if I had [not] seene it with mine eyes, I would never have beleeved it. His wife desirous to know the matter, desired him to tell what she had done: then hee accorded to the request of his wife, and ignorant of the estate of his own house, declared the mischance of another. You shall understand (quoth he) that the wife of the Fuller my companion, who seemed to me a wise and chast woman, regarding her own honesty and profit of her house, was found this night with her knave. For while we

CHAPTER XLI
How Barbarus being jealous over his wife, commanded that shee should be kept close in his house, and what happened

THE NINTH BOOKE

CHAPTER XLI

How Barbarus being jealous over his wife, commanded that shee should be kept close in his house, and what happened

went to wash our hands, hee and she were together: who being troubled with our presence ran into a corner, and she thrust him into a mow made with twigs, appoynted to lay on clothes to make them white with the smoake of fume and brymstone. Then she sate downe with us at the table to colour the matter: in the meane season the young man covered in the mow, could not forbeare sneesing, by reason of the smoake of the brymstone. The good man thinking it had beene his wife that sneesed, cryed, Christ helpe. But when he sneesed more, he suspected the matter, and willing to know who it was, rose from the table, and went to the mow, where hee found a young man welnigh dead with smoke. When hee understood the whole matter, he was so inflamed with anger that he called for a sword to kill him, and undoubtedly he had killed him, had I not restrained his violent hands from his purpose, assuring him, that his enemy would dye with the force of his brimstone, without the harme which he should doe. Howbeit my words would not appease his fury, but as necessity required he tooke the young man well nigh choked, and carried him out at the doores. In the meane season, I counsailed his wife to absent her selfe at some of her Neighbours houses, till the choller of her Husband was pacified, lest he should be moved against her, as he was against the young-man. And so being weary of their Supper, I forthwith returned home. When the Baker had told his tale, his impudent wife began to curse and abhorre the wife of the Fuller, and generally all other wives, which abandon their bodies with any other then with their owne Husbands, breaking the faith and bond of marriage, whereby she said, they were worthy to be burned alive. But knowing her owne guilty conscience and proper whoredome, lest her lover should be hurt lying in the bin, she willed her husband to goe to bed, but he having eaten nothing, said that he would sup before he went to rest: whereby shee was compelled to maugre her eies, to set such things on the Table as she had prepared for her Lover.

But I, considering the great mischiefe of this wicked queane, devised with my selfe how I might reveale the matter to my Master, and by kicking away the cover of the

OF LUCIUS APULEIUS

binne (where like a Snaile the young-man was couched) to
make her whoredome apparant and knowne. At length I
was ayded by the providence of God, for there was an old
man to whom the custody of us was committed, that drave
me poore Asse, and the other Horses the same time to the
water to drinke; then had I good occasion ministred, to
revenge the injury of my master, for as I passed by, I perceived the fingers of the young-man upon the side of the
binne, and lifting up my heeles, I spurned off the flesh
with the force of my hoofes, whereby he was compelled
to cry out, and to throw downe the binne on the ground,
and so the whoredome of the Bakers wife was knowne and
revealed. The Baker seeing this was not a little moved at
the dishonesty of his wife, but hee tooke the young-man
trembling for feare by the hand, and with cold and courteous
words spake in this sort: Feare not my Sonne, nor thinke
that I am so barbarous or cruell a person, that I would
stiffle thee up with the smoke of Sulphur as our neighbour
accustometh, nor I will not punish thee according to the
rigour of the law of Julia, which commandeth the Adulterers should be put to death: No no, I will not execute my
cruelty against so faire and comely a young-man as you be,
but we will devide our pleasure betweene us, by lying all
three in one bed, to the end there may be no debate nor
dissention betweene us, but that either of us may be contented, for I have alwayes lived with my wife in such tranquility, that according to the saying of the wise-men, whatsoever I say, she holdeth for law, and indeed equity will not
suffer, but that the husband should beare more authority
then the wife: with these and like words he lead the young-
man to his Chamber, and closed his wife in another Chamber.
On the next morrow, he called two of the most sturdiest
Servants of his house, who held up the young-man, while
he scourged his buttockes welfavouredly with rods like a
child. When he had well beaten him, he said: Art not
thou ashamed, thou that art so tender and delicate a child,
to desire the violation of honest marriages, and to defame
thy selfe with wicked living, whereby thou hast gotten the
name of an Adulterer? After he had spoken these and like

CHAPTER
XLI
How Bar-
barus being
jealous over
his wife, com-
manded that
shee should be
kept close in
his house, and
what hap-
pened

THE NINTH BOOKE

CHAPTER XLI
How Barbarus being jealous over his wife, commanded that shee should be kept close in his house, and what happened

words, he whipped him againe, and chased him out of his house. The young-man who was the comeliest of all the adulterers, ran away, and did nothing else that night save onely bewaile his striped and painted buttockes. Soone after the Baker sent one to his wife, who divorced her away in his name, but she beside her owne naturall mischiefe, (offended at this great contumely, though she had worthily deserved the same) had recourse to wicked arts and trumpery, never ceasing untill she had found out an Enchantresse, who (as it was thought) could doe what she would with her Sorcery and conjuration. The Bakers wife began to intreate her, promising that she would largely recompence her, if shee could bring one of these things to passe, eyther to make that her husband may be reconciled to her againe, or else if hee would not agree thereto, to send an ill spirit into him, to dispossesse the spirit of her husband. Then the witch with her abhominable science, began to conjure and to make her Ceremonies, to turne the heart of the Baker to his wife, but all was in vaine, wherefore considering on the one side that she could not bring her purpose to passe, and on the other side the losse of her gaine, she ran hastily to the Baker, threatning to send an evill spirit to kill him, by meane of her conjurations. But peradventure some scrupulous reader may demand me a question, how I, being an Asse, and tyed alwayes in the mill house, could know the secrets of these women: Verily I answer, notwithstanding my shape of an Asse, I had the sence and knowledge of a man, and curiously endeavoured to know out such injuries as were done to my master. About noone there came a woman into the Milhouse, very sorrowfull, raggedly attired, with bare feete, meigre, ill-favoured, and her hayre scattering upon her face: This woman tooke the Baker by the hand, and faining that she had some secret matter to tell him, went into a chamber, where they remained a good space, till all the corne was ground, when as the servants were compelled to call their master to give them more corne, but when they had called very often, and no person gave answer, they began to mistrust, insomuch that they brake open the doore: when they were come in, they could not find the woman, but onely their

OF LUCIUS APULEIUS

master hanging dead upon a rafter of the chamber, whereupon they cryed and lamented greatly, and according to the custome, when they had washed themselves, they tooke the body and buried it. The next day morrow, the daughter of the Baker, which was married but a little before to one of the next Village, came crying and beating her breast, not because she heard of the death of her father by any man, but because his lamentable spirit, with a halter about his necke appeared to her in the night, declaring the whole circumstance of his death, and how by inchantment he was descended into hell, which caused her to thinke that her father was dead. After that she had lamented a good space, and was somewhat comforted by the servants of the house, and when nine dayes were expired, as inheretrix to her father, she sold away all the substance of the house, whereby the goods chanced into divers mens hands.

CHAPTER XLI
How Barbarus being jealous over his wife, commanded that shee should be kept close in his house, and what happened

THE FORTY-SECOND CHAPTER

How Apuleius after the Baker was hanged, was sold to a Gardener, and what dreadfull things happened.

THERE was a poore Gardener amongst the rest, which bought me for the summe of fifty pence, which seemed to him a great price, but he thought to gayne it againe by the continuall travell of my body. The matter requireth to tell likewise, how I was handled in his service. This Gardener accustomed to drive me, every morning laded with hearbes to the next Village, and when he had sold his hearbes, hee would mount upon my backe and returne to the Garden, and while he digged the ground and watered the hearbes, and went about other businesse, I did nothing but repose my selfe with great ease, but when Winter approached with sharpe haile, raine and frosts, and I

195

THE NINTH BOOKE

CHAPTER XLII

How Apuleius after the Baker was hanged, was sold to a Gardener, and what dreadfull things happened

standing under a hedge side, was welnigh killed up with cold, and my master was so poore that he had no lodging for himselfe, much lesse had he any littor or place to cover me withall, for he himselfe alwayes lay under a little roofe shadowed with boughes. In the morning when I arose, I found my hoofes shriveled together with cold, and unable to passe upon the sharpe ice, and frosty mire, neither could I fill my belly with meate, as I accustomed to doe, for my master and I supped together, and had both one fare : howbeit it was very slender since as wee had nothing else saving old and unsavoury sallets which were suffered to grow for seed, like long broomes, and that had lost all their sweet sappe and juice.

It fortuned on a day that an honest man of the next village was benighted and constrained by reason of the rain to lodge (very lagged and weary) in our Garden, where although he was but meanely received, yet it served well enough considering time and necessity. This honest man to recompence our entertainment, promised to give my master some corne, oyle, and two bottels of wine : wherefore my master not delaying the matter, laded me with sackes and bottels, and rode to the Towne which was seaven miles off.

When we came to the honest mans house, he entertained and feasted my master exceedingly. And it fortuned while they eate and dranke together as signe of great amity there chanced a strange and dreadfull case : for there was a Hen which ran kackling about the yard, as though she would have layed an Egge. The good man of the house perceiving her, said : O good and profitable pullet that feedest us every day with thy fruit, thou seemest as though thou wouldest give us some pittance for our dinner : Ho boy put the Pannier in the corner that the Hen may lay. Then the boy did as his master commanded, but the Hen forsaking the Pannier, came toward her master and laid at his feet not an Egge, which every man knoweth, but a Chickin with feathers, clawes, and eyes, which incontinently ran peeping after his damme. By and by happened a more strange thing, which would cause any man to abhorre : under the Table where they sate, the ground opened, and there appeared a great well and fountain

OF LUCIUS APULEIUS

of bloud, insomuch that the drops thereof sparckled about the Table. At the same time while they wondred at this dreadfull sight one of the Servants came running out of the Seller, and told that all the wine was boyled out of the vessels, as though there had beene some great fire under. By and by a Weasel was seene that drew into the house a dead Serpent, and out of the mouth of a Shepheards dog leaped a live frog, and immediately after one brought word that a Ram had strangled the same dog at one bit. All these things that happened, astonied the good man of the house, and the residue that were present, insomuch that they could not tell what to doe, or with what sacrifice to appease the anger of the gods. While every man was thus stroken in feare, behold, one brought word to the good man of the house, that his three sonnes who had been brought up in good literature, and endued with good manners were dead, for they three had great acquaintance and ancient amity with a poore man which was their neighbour, and dwelled hard by them: and next unto him dwelled another young man very rich both in lands and goods, but bending from the race of his progenies dissentions, and ruling himselfe in the towne according to his owne will. This young royster did mortally hate this poore man, insomuch that he would kill his sheepe, steale his oxen, and spoyle his corne and other fruits before the time of ripenesse, yet was he not contented with this, but he would encroch upon the poore mans ground, and clayme all the heritage as his owne. The poore man which was very simple and fearefull, seeing all his goods taken away by the avarice of the rich man, called together and assembled many of his friends to shew them all his land, to the end he might have but so much ground of his fathers heritage, as might bury him. Amongst whom, he found these three brethren, as friends to helpe and ayd him in his adversity and tribulation.

Howbeit, the presence of these honest Citizens, could in no wise perswade him to leave his extort power, no nor yet to cause any temperance of his tongue, but the more they went about with gentle words to tell him his faults, the more would he fret and likewise fume, swearing all the oathes under

CHAPTER XLII

How Apuleius after the Baker was hanged, was sold to a Gardener, and what dreadfull things happened

THE NINTH BOOKE

CHAPTER XLII
How Apuleius after the Baker was hanged, was sold to a Gardener, and what dreadfull things happened

God, that he little regarded the presence of the whole City, whereupon incontinently he commanded his servants to take the poore man by the eares, and carry him out of his ground, which greatly offended all the standers by. Then one of the brethren spake unto him somewhat boldly, saying: It is but a folly to have such affiance in your riches, whereby you should use your tyranny against the poore, when as the law is common for all men, and a redresse may be had to suppresse your insolency. These words chafed him more then the burning oile, or flaming brimstone, or scourge of whipps, saying: that they should be hanged and their law too, before he would be subject unto any person: and therewithall he called out his bandogges and great masties, which accustomed to eate the carrion and carkases of dead beasts in the fields, and to set upon such as passe by the way; then he commanded they should be put upon all the assistance to teare them in peeces: who as soone as they heard the hisse of their master, ran fiercely upon them invading them on every side, insomuch that the more they flied to escape away, the more cruell and terrible were the dogges. It fortuned amongst all this fearefull company, that in running, the youngest of the three brethren stumbled at a stone, and fell down to the ground: Then the dogs came upon him and tare him in peeces with their teeth, whereby he was compelled to cry for succour: His other two brethren hearing his lamentable voice ran towards him to helpe him, casting their cloakes about their left armes, tooke up stones to chase away the dogs, but all was in vaine, for they might see their brother dismembred in every part of his body: Who lying at the very point of death, desired his brethren to revenge his death against that cruell tyrant: And therewithall he gave up the ghost. The other two brethren perceiving so great a murther, and neglecting their owne lives, like desperate persons dressed themselves against the tyrant, and threw a great number of stones at him, but the bloudy theefe exercised in such and like mischiefes, tooke a speare and thrust it cleane through the body: howbeit he fell not downe to the ground. For the speare that came out at his backe ran into the earth, and sustained him up. By and by

OF LUCIUS APULEIUS

CHAPTER XLII

How Apuleius after the Baker was hanged, was sold to a Gardener, and what dreadfull things happened

came one of these tyrants servants the most sturdiest of the rest to helpe his master, who at the first comming tooke up a stone and threw at the third brother, but by reason the stone ran along his arme it did not hurt him, which chanced otherwise then all mens expectation was: by and by the young man feigning that his arme was greatly wounded, spake these words unto the cruell bloud sucker: Now maist thou, thou wretch, triumph upon the destruction of all our family, now hast thou fed thy insatiable cruelty with the bloud of three brethren, now maist thou rejoyce at the fall of us Citizens, yet thinke not but that how farre thou dost remove and extend the bounds of thy land, thou shalt have some neighbor, but how greatly am I sorry in that I have lost mine arme wherewithall I minded to cut off thy head. When he had spoken these words, the furious theefe drew out his dagger, and running upon the young man thought verily to have slaine him, but it chanced otherwise: For the young man resisted him stoutly, and in buckling together by violence wrested the dagger out of his hand: which done, he killed the rich theefe with his owne weapon, and to the intent the young man would escape the hands of the servants which came running to assist their master, with the same dagger he cut his owne throat. These things were signified by the strange and dreadfull wonders which fortuned in the house of the good man, who after he had heard these sorrowfull tydings could in no wise weepe, so farre was he stroken with dolour, but presently taking his knife wherewith he cut his cheese and other meate before, he cut his owne throat likewise, in such sort that he fell upon the bord and imbraced the table with the streames of his bloud, in most miserable manner. Hereby was my master the Gardener deprived of his hope, and paying for his dinner the watry teares of his eyes, mounted upon my backe and so we went homeward the same way as wee came.

THE NINTH BOOKE

THE FORTY-THIRD CHAPTER
How Apuleius was found by his shadow.

AS wee passed by the way wee met with a tall souldier (for so his habite and countenance declared) who with proud and arrogant words spake to my master in this sort: *Quorsum vacuum ducis Asinum?* My master somewhat astonied at the strange sights which he saw before, and ignorant of the Latine tongue, roade on and spake never a word : The souldier unable to refraine his insolence, and offended at his silence, strake him on the shoulders as he sate on my backe ; then my master gently made answer that he understood not what he said, whereat the souldier angerly demanded againe, whether he roade with his Asse ? Marry (quoth he) to the next City : But I (quoth the souldier) have need of his helpe, to carry the trusses of our Captaine from yonder Castle, and therewithall he tooke me by the halter and would violently have taken me away : but my master wiping away the blood of the blow which he received of the souldier, desired him gently and civilly to take some pitty upon him, and to let him depart with his owne, swearing and affirming that his slow Asse, welnigh dead with sicknesse, could scarce carry a few handfuls of hearbs to the next towne, much lesse he was able to beare any greater trusses : but when he saw the souldier would in no wise be intreated, but ready with his staffe to cleave my masters head, my master fell downe at his feete, under colour to move him to some pitty, but when he saw his time, he tooke the souldier by the legs and cast him upon the ground: Then he buffetted him, thumped him, bit him, and tooke a stone and beat his face and his sides, that he could not turne and defend himselfe, but onely threaten that if ever he rose, he would choppe him in pieces. The Gardener when he heard him say so, drew out his javelin which hee had by his side, and when he had throwne it away, he knockt

OF LUCIUS APULEIUS

CHAPTER XLIII

How Apuleius was found by his shadow

and beate him more cruelly then he did before, insomuch that the souldier could not tell by what meanes to save himselfe, but by feining that he was dead. Then my master tooke the javelin and mounted upon my backe, riding in all hast to the next village, having no regard to goe to his Garden, and when he came thither, he turned into one of his friends house and declared all the whole matter, desiring him to save his life and to hide himselfe and his Asse in some secret place, untill such time as all danger were past. Then his friends not forgetting the ancient amity betweene them, entertained him willingly and drew me up a paire of staires into a chamber, my master crept into a chest, and lay there with the cover closed fast: The souldier (as I afterwards learned) rose up as one awaked from a drunken sleepe, but he could scarce goe by reason of his wounds: howbeit at length by little and little through ayd of his staffe he came to the towne, but hee would not declare the matter to any person nor complaine to any justice, lest he should be accused of cowardise or dastardnesse, yet in the end he told some of his companions of all the matter that happened: then they tooke him and caused him to be closed in some secret place, thinking that beside the injury which he had received, he should be accused of the breach of his faith, by reason of the losse of his speare, and when they had learned the signes of my master, they went to search him out: at last there was an unfaithfull neighbour that told them where he was, then incontinently the souldiers went to the Justice declaring that they had lost by the way a silver goblet of their Captaines, and that a Gardener had found it, who refusing to deliver the goblet, was hidden in one of his friends houses: by and by the Magistrates understanding the losse of the Captaine, came to the doores where we were, commanded our host to deliver my master upon paine of death: howbeit these threatnings could not enforce him to confesse that he was within his doores, but by reason of his faithfull promise and for the safeguard of his friend, he said, that hee saw not the Gardener a great while, neither knew where he was: the souldiers said contrary, whereby to know the verity of the matter, the Magistrates commanded their Seargants and

THE NINTH BOOKE

CHAPTER XLIII
How Apuleius was found by his shadow

ministers to search every corner of the house, but when they could find neither Gardener nor Asse, there was a great contention betweene the souldiers and our Host, for they sayd we were within the house : and he said no, but I that was very curious to know the matter, when I heard so great a noyse, put my head out of the window to learne what the stirre and tumult did signifie. It fortuned that one of the souldiers perceived my shadow, whereupon he began to cry, saying : that hee had certainly seene me ; then they were all glad and came up into the chamber, and pulled me downe like a prisoner. When they had found mee, they doubted nothing of the Gardener, but seeking about more narrowly, at length they found him couched in a chest. And so they brought out the poore gardener to the Justices, who was committed immediately to prison, but they could never forbeare laughing from the time they found me by my shadow, wherefore is risen a common Proverbe:
'The shadow of the Asse.'

THE
TENTH BOOKE
of LUCIUS APULEIUS of
THE GOLDEN ASSE

THE TENTH BOOKE

THE FORTY-FOURTH CHAPTER
How the souldier drave Apuleius away, and how he came to a Captaines house, and what happened there.

HE next day how my master the Gardener sped, I knew not, but the gentle souldier, who was well beaten for his cowardise, lead me to his lodging without the contradiction of any man: Where hee laded me well, and garnished my body (as seemed to me) like an Asse of armes. For on the one side I bare an helmet that shined exceedingly: On the other side a Target that glistered more a thousand folde. And on the top of my burthen he put a long speare, which things he placed thus gallantly, not because he was so expert in warre (for the Gardener proved the contrary) but to the end he might feare those which passed by, when they saw such a similitude of warre. When we had gone a good part of our journey, over the plaine and easie fields, we fortuned to come to a little towne, where we lodged at a certaine Captaines house. And there the souldier tooke me to one of the servants, while he himselfe went towards his captaine; who had the charge of a thousand men. And when we had remained there a few dayes, I understood of a wicked and mischievous fact committed there, which I have put in writing to the end you may know the same.

THE TENTH BOOKE

CHAPTER XLIV

How the souldier drave Apuleius away, and how he came to a Captaines house, and what happened there

The master of the house had a sonne instructed in good literature, and endued with vertuous manners, such a one as you would desire to have the like. Long time before his mother dyed, and when his father married a new wife, and had another child of the age of xii. yeares. The stepdame was more excellent in beauty then honesty: for she loved this young man her sonne in law, either because she was unchast by nature, or because she was enforced by fate of stepmother, to commit so great a mischiefe. Gentle reader, thou shalt not read of a fable, but rather a tragedy: This woman when her love began first to kindle in her heart, could easily resist her desire and inordinate appetite by reason of shame and feare, lest her intent should be knowne: But after it compassed and burned every part of her brest, she was compelled to yeeld unto the raging flame of Cupid, and under colour of the disease and infirmity of her body, to conceale the wound of her restlesse mind. Every man knoweth well the signes and tokens of love, and the malady convenient to the same: Her countenance was pale, her eyes sorrowfull, her knees weake, and there was no comfort in her, but continuall weeping and sobbing, insomuch that you would have thought that she had some spice of an ague, saving that she wept unmeasurably: the Phisitians knew not her disease, when they felt the beating of her veines, the intemperance of her heart, the sobbing sighes, and her often tossing of every side: No, no, the cunning Phisitian knew it not, but a scholler of Venus Court might easily conjecture the whole. After that she had beene long time tormented in her affliction, and was no more able to conceale her ardent desire, shee caused her sonne to be called for, (which word son she would faine put away if it were not for shame:) Then he nothing disobedient to the commandement of his mother, with a sad and modest countenance, came into the chamber of his stepdame, the mother of his brother, but she speaking never a word was in great doubt what she might doe, and could not tell what to say first, by reason of shame. The young man suspecting no ill, with humble courtesie demanded the cause of her present disease. Then she having found an occasion to utter her intent, with weeping eyes and covered face, began boldly to speake unto

OF LUCIUS APULEIUS

him in this manner: Thou, thou, art the originall cause of all my dolour: Thou art my comfort and onely health, for those thy comely eyes are so enfastned within my brest, that unlesse they succour me, I shall certainly die: Have pitty therefore upon me, be not the occasion of my destruction, neither let my conscience reclaime to offend thy father, when as thou shalt save the life of thy mother. Moreover since thou dost resemble thy fathers shape in every point, it giveth me cause the more to fancy thee: Now is ministred unto thee time and place: Now hast thou occasion to worke thy will, seeing that we are alone. And it is a common saying:

CHAPTER XLIV

How the souldier drave Apuleius away, and how he came to a Captaines house, and what happened there

Never knowne, never done.

This young man troubled in mind at so suddaine an ill, although hee abhorred to commit so beastly a crime, yet hee would not cast her off with a present deniall, but warily pacified her mind with delay of promise. Wherefore he promised to doe all according to her desire: And in the meane season, he willed his mother to be of good cheere, and comfort her selfe till as he might find some convenient time to come unto her, when his father was ridden forth: Wherewithall hee got him away from the pestilent sight of his stepdame. And knowing that this matter touching the ruine of all the whole house needed the counsell of wise and grave persons, he went incontinently to a sage old man and declared the whole circumstance of the matter. The old man after long deliberation, thought there was no better way to avoyd the storme of cruell fortune to come, then to run away. In the meane season this wicked woman impatient of her love, and the long delay of her sonne, egged her husband to ride abroad into farre countreyes. And then she asked the young-man the accomplishment of his promise, but he to rid himselfe entirely from her hands, would find alwayes excuses, till in the end she understood by the messengers that came in and out, that he nothing regarded her. Then she by how much she loved him before, by so much and more she hated him now. And by and by she called one of her servants, ready to all mischiefes: To whom she declared all her secrets. And there it was concluded

THE TENTH BOOKE

CHAPTER XLIV
How the souldier drave Apuleius away, and how he came to a Captaines house, and what happened there

betweene them two, that the surest way was to kill the young man: Whereupon this varlet went incontinently to buy poyson, which he mingled with wine, to the intent he would give it to the young man to drinke, and thereby presently to kill him. But while they were in deliberation how they might offer it unto him, behold here happened a strange adventure. For the young sonne of the woman that came from schoole at noone (being very thirsty) tooke the pot wherein the poyson was mingled, and ignorant of the venim, dranke a good draught thereof, which was prepared to kill his brother: whereby he presently fell downe to the ground dead. His schoole-master seeing his suddaine chance, called his mother, and all the servants of the house with a lowd voyce. Incontinently every man declared his opinion, touching the death of the child: but the cruell woman the onely example of stepmothers malice, was nothing moved by the bitter death of her sonne, or by her owne conscience of paracide, or by the misfortune of her house, or by the dolour of her husband, but rather devised the destruction of all her family. For by and by shee sent a messenger after her husband to tell him the great misfortune which happened after his departure. And when he came home, the wicked woman declared that his sonne had empoysoned his brother, because he would not consent to his will, and told him divers other leasings, adding in the end that hee threatned to kill her likewise, because she discovered the fact: Then the unhappy father was stroken with double dolour of the death of his two children, for on the one side he saw his younger sonne slaine before his eyes, on the other side, he seemed to see the elder condemned to dye for his offence: Againe, where he beheld his wife lament in such sort, it gave him further occasion to hate his sonne more deadly; but the funerals of his younger sonne were scarce finished, when the old man the father with weeping eyes even at the returne from the grave, went to the Justice and accused his sonne of the slaughter of his brother, and how he threatned to slay his wife, whereby the rather at his weeping and lamentation, he mooved all the Magistrates and people to pitty, insomuch that without any delay, or further inquisition they cryed all that hee should

OF LUCIUS APULEIUS

CHAPTER XLIV
How the souldier drave Apuleius away, and how he came to a Captaines house, and what happened there

be stoned to death, but the Justices fearing a farther inconvenience to arise by the particular vengeance, and to the end there might fortune no sedition amongst the people, prayed the decurions and other Officers of the City, that they might proceed by examination of witnesses, and with order of justice according to the ancient custome before the judging of any hasty sentence or judgement, without the hearing of the contrary part, like as the barbarous and cruell tyrants accustome to use: otherwise they should give an ill example to their successours. This opinion pleased every man, wherefore the Senatours and counsellers were called, who being placed in order according to their dignity, caused the accuser and defender to be brought forth, and by the example of the Athenian law, and judgement materiall, their Advocates were commanded to plead their causes briefly without preambles or motions of the people to pitty, which were too long a processe. And if you demand how I understood all this matter, you shall understand that I heard many declare the same, but to recite what words the accuser used in his invective, what answer the defender made, the orations and pleadings of each party, verily I am not able to doe: for I was fast bound at the manger. But as I learned and knew by others, I will God willing declare unto you. So it was ordered, that after the pleadings of both sides was ended, they thought best to try and boult out the verity by witnesses, all presumptions and likelihood set apart, and to call in the servant, who onely was reported to know all the matter: by and by the servant came in, who nothing abashed, at the feare of so great a judgement, or at the presence of the Judges, or at his owne guilty conscience, which hee so finely fained, but with a bold countenance presented himselfe before the Justices and confirmed the accusation against the young man, saying: O yee judges, on a day when this young man loathed and hated his stepmother, hee called mee, desiring mee to poyson his brother, whereby hee might revenge himselfe, and if I would doe it and keepe the matter secret, hee promised to give me a good reward for my paines: but when the young man perceived that I would not accord to his will, he threatned to slay mee, whereupon hee went himselfe and

THE TENTH BOOKE

CHAPTER XLIV

How the souldier drave Apuleius away, and how he came to a Captaines house, and what happened there

bought poyson, and after tempered it with wine, and then gave it me to give the child, which when I refused he offered it to his brother with his own hands. When the varlet with a trembling countenance had ended these words which seemed a likelihood of truth, the judgement was ended: neither was there found any judge or counseller, so mercifull to the young man accused, as would not judge him culpable, but that he should be put and sowne in a skin, with a dogge, a Cocke, a Snake, and an Ape, according to the law against parricides: wherefore they wanted nothing but (as the ancient custome was) to put white stones and black into a pot, and to take them out againe, to see whether the young-man accused should be acquitted by judgment or condemned, which was a thing irrevocable.

In the mean season he was delivered to the hands of the executioner. But there arose a sage and ancient Physitian, a man of a good conscience and credit throughout all the City, that stopped the mouth of the pot wherein the stones were cast, saying: I am right glad ye reverend Judges, that I am a man of name and estimation amongst you, whereby I am accompted such a one as will not suffer any person to be put to death by false and untrue accusations, considering there hath bin no homicide or murther committed by this yong man in this case, neither you (being sworn to judge uprightly) to be misinformed and abused by invented lyes and tales. For I cannot but declare and open my conscience, least I should be found to beare small honour and faith to the Gods, wherefore I pray you give eare, and I will shew you the whole truth of the matter. You shall understand that this servant which hath merited to be hanged, came one of these dayes to speake with me, promising to give me a hundred crownes, if I would give him present poyson, which would cause a man to dye suddenly, saying, that he would have it for one that was sicke of an incurable disease, to the end he might be delivered from all torment, but I smelling his crafty and subtill fetch, and fearing least he would worke some mischiefe withall, gave him a drinke: but to the intent I might cleare my selfe from all danger that might happen I would not presently take the money which he offered

OF LUCIUS APULEIUS

CHAPTER XLIV

How the souldier drave Apuleius away, and how he came to a Captaines house, and what happened there

But least any of the crownes should lacke weight or be found counterfeit, I willed him to seale the purse wherein they were put, with his manuell signe, whereby the next day we might goe together to the Goldsmith to try them, which he did; wherefore understanding that he was brought present before you this day, I hastily commanded one of my servants to fetch the purse which he had sealed, and here I bring it unto you to see whether he will deny his owne signe or no: and you may easily conject that his words are untrue, which he alleadged against the young man, touching the buying of the poyson, considering hee bought the poyson himselfe. When the Physitian had spoken these words you might perceive how the trayterous knave changed his colour, how hee sweat for feare, how he trembled in every part of his body: and how he set one leg upon another, scratching his head and grinding his teeth, whereby there was no person but would judge him culpable. In the end, when he was somewhat returned to his former subtilty, he began to deny all that was said, and stoutly affirmed, that the Physitian did lye. But the Physitian perceiving that he was rayled at and his words denyed, did never cease to confirme his sayings, and to disprove the varlet, till such time as the Officers by the commandement of the Judges, bound his hands and brought out the seale, wherewith he had sealed the purse, which augmented suspition which was conceived of him first. Howbeit, neither the feare of the wheele or any other torment according to the use of the Grecians, which were ready prepared, no, nor yet the fire could enforce him to confesse the matter, so obstinate and grounded was he in his mischievous mind. But the Physitian perceiving that the menaces of these torments did nothing prevaile, gan say: I cannot suffer or abide that this young man who is innocent, should against all law and conscience, be punished and condemned to die, and the other which is culpable, should escape so easily, and after mocke and flowte at your judgement: for I will give you an evident proofe and argument of this present crime. You shall understand, that when this caytiffe demanded of me a present and strong poyson, considering that it was not my part to give occasion of any others death, but rather to cure

THE TENTH BOOKE

CHAPTER XLIV

How the souldier drave Apuleius away, and how he came to a Captaines house, and what happened there

and save sicke persons by meane of medicines: and on the other side, fearing least if I should deny his request, I might minister a further cause of his mischiefe, either that he would buy poyson of some other, or else returne and worke his wicked intent, with a sword or some dangerous weapon, I gave him no poyson, but a doling drinke of Mandragora, which is of such force, that it will cause any man to sleepe as though he were dead. Neither is it any marvaile if this most desperate man, who is certainly assured to be put to death, ordained by an ancient custome, can suffer and abide these facill and easie torments, but if it be so that the child hath received the drinke as I tempered it with mine owne hands, he is yet alive and doth but sleepe, and after his sleepe he shall returne to life againe, but if he be dead indeed, then may you further enquire of the causes of his death. The opinion of this ancient Physitian was found good, and every man had a desire to goe to the Sepulchre where the child was layd; there was none of the Justices, none of any reputation of the towne, nor any of the common people, but went to see this strange sight. Amongst them all the father of the child remooved with his owne hands the stone of the Sepulchre, and found his Sonne rising up after his dead and soporiferous sleepe, whom when he beheld, he imbraced him in his armes, and presented him before the people, with great joy and consolation, and as he was wrapped and bound in his grave, so he brought him before the Judges, whereupon the wickednesse of the Servant, and the rest of the Servant, and the treason of the stepdame was plainely discovered, and the verity of the matter revealed, whereby the woman was perpetually exiled, the Servant hanged on a Gallowes, and the Physitian had the Crownes, which was prepared to buy the poyson. Behold how the fortune of the old man was changed, who thinking to be deprived of all his race and posterity, was in one moment made the Father of two Children.

But as for me, I was ruled and handled by fortune, according to her pleasure.

OF LUCIUS APULEIUS

THE FORTY-FIFTH CHAPTER
How Apuleius was sold to two brethren, whereof one was a Baker, and the other a Cooke, and how finely and daintily he fared.

HE Souldier that payed never a peny for me, by the commandement of his Captaine, was sent unto Rome, to cary Letters to the great Prince, and Generall of the Campe. Before he went, he sold me for eleven pence to two of his Companions, being Servants to a man of worship, whereof one was a Baker that baked sweet bread and delicates, the other a Cooke, which dressed fine and excellent meats for his Master. These two lived in common, and would drive me from place to place, to carry such things as was necessary, insomuch that I was received by these two, as a third Brother, and Companion, and I thought I was never better placed, then with them : for when night came that Supper was done, and their businesse ended, they would bring many good morsels into their Chamber for themselves. One would bring Pigs, Chickens, fish, and other good meates, the other fine bread, pasties, tarts, custards and other delicate Junkets dipped in hony. And when they had shut their chamber doore, and went to the bains : (O Lord) how I would fill my guts with these goodly dishes : neither was I so much a foole, or so very an Asse, to leave the dainty meats, and to grind my teeth upon hard hay. In this sort I continued a great space, for I played the honest Asse, taking but a little of one dish, and a little of another, wherby no man distrusted me. In the end, I was more hardier and began to devoure the whole messes of the sweet delicates, which caused the Baker and the Cooke to suspect, howbeit they nothing mistrusted me, but searched about to apprehend the theefe. At length they began to accuse one another of theft, and to set the dishes and morsels of meat in

THE TENTH BOOKE

CHAPTER XLV

How Apuleius was sold to two brethren, whereof one was a Baker, and the other a Cooke, and how finely and daintily he fared

order, one by another, because they would learne what was taken away, whereby one of them was compelled to say thus to his fellow: Is it reason to breake promise and faith in this sort, by stealing away the best meat, and to sell it to augment thy good, and yet neverthelesse to have thy part in the residue that is left: if our partnership doe mislike thee, we will be partners and brothers in other things, but in this we will breake off: for I perceive that the great losse which I sustain, will at length be a cause of great discord betweene us. Then answered the other, Verily I praise thy great constancy and subtilnesse, in that (when thou hast secretly taken away the meat) [thou] dost begin to complaine first, whereas I by long space of time have suffered thee, because I would not seeme to accuse my brother of theft, but I am right glad in that wee are fallen into communication of the matter, least by our silence, like contention might arise betweene us, as fortuned betweene Eteocles and his Brother. When they had reasoned together in this sort, they swore both earnestly, that neither of them stale or tooke away any jote of the meate, wherefore they concluded to search out the Theefe by all kind of meanes. For they could not imagin or thinke, the Asse who stood alone there, would eate any such meates, neither could they thinke that Mice or Flyes, were so ravenous, as to devouer whole dishes of meat, like the Birds Harpies which carried away the meates of Phineus the King of Archadia. In the meane season while I was fed with dainty morsels, I gathered together my flesh, my skin waxed soft, my haire began to shine, and was gallant on every part, but such faire and comely shape of my body, was cause of my dishonour, for the Baker and Cooke marvelled to see me so slick and fine, considering I did eate no hay at all. Wherefore on a time at their accustomed houre, they went to the baines, and locked their chamber doore. It fortuned that ere they departed away, they espyed me through a hole, how I fell roundly to my victuals: then they marvelled greatly, and little esteemed the losse of their meate, laughed exceedingly, calling the servants of the house, to shew them the greedy gorge and appetite of the Asse. Their laughing was so immoderate that the master of the house

OF LUCIUS APULEIUS

heard them, and demanded the cause of their laughter, and when hee understood all the matter, hee looked through the hole likewise, wherewith hee tooke such a delectation that hee commanded the doore to be opened, that hee might see mee at his pleasure. Then I perceiving every man laugh, was nothing abashed, but rather more bold, whereby I never rested eating, till such time as the master of the house commanded me to be brought into his parler as a novelty, and there caused all kinds of meates which were never touched to be set on the table, which (although I had eaten sufficiently before, yet to win the further favour of the master of the house) I did greedily devoure and made a cleane riddance of all the delicate meates. And to prove my nature wholly, they gave mee such meates as every Asse doth abhorre: for they put before mee beefe and vineger, birds and pepper, fish and verjuice: in the meane season they that beheld mee at the table did nothing but laugh. Then one of the servants of the house sayd to his master, I pray you sir give him some drinke to his supper: Marry (quoth hee) I thinke thou saist true, for it may be, that to his meate hee would drinke likewise a cup of wine. Hoe boy, wash yonder pot, and fill it with wine, which done, carry it to the Asse, and say that I have drunke to him. Then all the standers by looked on, to see what would come to passe: but I (as soone as I beheld the cup) staied not long, but gathering my lips together, supped up all the wine at one draught. The master being right joyfull hereat caused the Baker and Cooke which had bought me, to come before him, to whom he delivered foure times as much for me, as they paid, which done he commited me to one of his rich Libertines, and charged him to looke well to me, and that I should lacke nothing, who obeied his masters commandement in every point: and to the end he would creepe further into his favour, he taught me a thousand qualities. First he instructed me to sit at the table upon my taile, and how I should leape and dance, holding up my former feete: moreover hee taught me how I should answer when any body spake unto me, with nodding my head, which was a strange and marvailous thing, and if I did lacke

CHAPTER XLV

How Apuleius was sold to two brethren, whereof one was a Baker, and the other a Cooke, and how finely and daintily he fared

215

THE TENTH BOOKE

CHAPTER XLV

How Apuleius was sold to two brethren, whereof one was a Baker, and the other a Cooke, and how finely and daintily he fared

drinke, I should looke still upon the pot. All which things I did willingly bring to passe, and obeyed his doctrine: howbeit, I could have done all these things without his teaching, but I feared greatly lest in shewing my selfe cunning without a master, I should pretend some great and strange wonder, and thereby be throwne out to wild beasts. But my fame was spred about in every place, and the qualities which I could doe, insomuch that my master was renowned throughout all the Country by reason of mee. For every man would say: Behold the Gentleman that hath an Asse, that will eate and drinke with him, that will dance, and understand what is said to him, will shew his fantasie by signes. But first I will tell you (which I should have done before) who my master was, and of what country. His name was Thiasus, hee was borne at Corinth, which is a principall towne of Achaia, and he had passed many offices of honor, till hee had taken upon him the degree Quinquenuall, according as his birth and dignity required, who to shew his worthinesse, and to purchase the benevolence of every person, appointed publike joyes and triumphs, to endure the space of three dayes, and to bring his endeavour to passe, he came into Thessaly to buy excellent Beasts, and valiant fighters for the purpose.

OF LUCIUS APULEIUS

THE FORTY-SIXTH CHAPTER
How a certaine Matron fell in love with Apuleius, how hee had his pleasure with her, and what other things happened.

HEN he had bought such things as was necessary, he would not returne home into his Countrey in Chariots, or waggon, neither would he ride upon Thessalian Horses, or Jenets of France, or Spanish Mules, which be most excellent as can be found, but caused me to be garnished and trimmed with trappers and barbs of Gold, with brave harnesse, with purple coverings, with a bridle of silver, with pictured cloths, and with shrilling bells, and in this manner he rode upon me lovingly, speaking and intreating me with gentle words, but above all things he did greatly rejoyce in that I was his Servant to beare him upon my backe, and his Companion to feed with him at the Table: After long time when we had travelled as well by Sea as Land, and fortuned to arive at Corinth, the people of the Towne came about us on every side, not so much to doe honour to Thiasus, as to see me: For my fame was so greatly spread there, that I gained my master much money, and when the people was desirous to see me play prankes, they caused the Gates to be shut, and such as entered in should pay money, by meanes whereof I was a profitable companion to them every day: There fortuned to be amongst the Assembly a noble and rich Matron that conceived much delight to behold me, and could find no remedy to her passions and disordinate appetite, but continually desired to have her pleasure with me, as Pasiphae had with a Bull. In the end she promised a great reward to my keeper for the custody of me one night, who for gaine of a little money accorded to her desire, and when I had supped in a Parler with my Master, we departed away and went into our

THE TENTH BOOKE

CHAPTER XLVI

How a certaine Matron fell in love with Apuleius, etc.

Chamber, where we found the faire Matron, who had tarried a great space for our comming : I am not able to recite unto you how all things were prepared : there were foure Eunuches that lay on a bed of downe on the ground with Boulsters accordingly for us to lye on, the Coverlet was of cloth of Gold, and the pillowes soft and tender, whereon the delicate Matron had accustomed to lay her head. Then the Eunuches not minding to delay any longer the pleasure of their Mistresse, closed the doores of the Chamber and departed away : within the Chamber were Lamps that gave a cleare light all the place over : Then she put off all her Garments to her naked skinne, and taking the Lampe that stood next to her, began to annoint all her body with balme, and mine likewise, but especially my nose, which done, she kissed me, not as they accustome to doe at the stewes, or in brothell houses, or in the Curtiant Schooles for gaine of money, but purely, sincerely, and with great affection, casting out these and like loving words : Thou art he whom I love, thou art he whom I onely desire, without thee I cannot live, and other like preamble of talke as women can use well enough, when as they mind to shew or declare their burning passions and great affection of love : Then she tooke me by the halter and cast me downe upon the bed, which was nothing strange unto me, considering that she was so beautifull a Matron and I so wel boldened out with wine, and perfumed with balme, whereby I was readily prepared for the purpose : But nothing grieved me so much as to think, how I should with my huge and great legs imbrace so faire a Matron, or how I should touch her fine, dainty, and silken skinne, with my hard hoofes, or how it was possible to kisse her soft, pretty and ruddy lips, with my monstrous mouth and stony teeth, or how she, who was young and tender, could be able to receive me.

And I verily thought, if I should hurt the woman by any kind of meane, I should be throwne to the wild Beasts : But in the meane season she kissed me, and looked in my mouth with burning eyes, saying : I hold thee my cunny, I hold thee my nops, my sparrow, and therewithall she eftsoones imbraced my body round about, and had her pleasure with

OF LUCIUS APULEIUS

me, whereby I thought the mother of Minotarus did not causelesse quench her inordinate desire with a Bull. When night was passed, with much joy and small sleepe, the Matron went before day to my keeper, to bargaine with him another night, which he willingly granted, partly for gaine of money, and partly to finde new pastime for my master. Who after he was informed of all the history of my luxury, was right glad, and rewarded my keeper well for his paine, minding to shew before the face of all the people, what I could doe: but because they would not suffer the Matron to abide such shame, by reason of her dignity, and because they could finde no other that would endeavour so great a reproach, at length they obtained for money a poore woman, which was condemned to be eaten of wilde beasts, with whom I should openly have to doe: But first I will tell you what tale I heard concerning this woman. This woman had a husband, whose father minding to ride foorth, commanded his wife which he left at home great with child, that if she were delivered of a daughter, it should incontinently be killed. When the time of her delivery came, it fortuned that she had a daughter, whom she would not suffer to be slaine, by reason of the naturall affection which she bare unto her child, but secretly committed her to one of her neighbours to nurse. And when her husband returned home, shee declared unto him that shee was delivered of a daughter, whom (as hee commanded,) shee had caused to be put to death. But when this child came to age, and ready to be married, the mother knew not by what meanes shee should endow her daughter, but that her husband should understand and perceive it. Wherefore shee discovered the matter to her sonne, who was the husband of this woman, condemned to be eaten of wild beasts: For shee greatly feared least hee should unawares fancie or fall in love with his owne sister. The young man understanding the whole matter (to please and gratifie his mother) went immediately to the young mayden, keeping the matter secret in his heart, for feare of inconveniency, and (lamenting to see his sister forsaken both of mother and father) incontinently after endowed her with part of his owne goods, and would have married her

CHAPTER XLVI

How a certaine Matron fell in love with Apuleius, etc.

THE TENTH BOOKE

CHAPTER XLVI

How a certaine Matron fell in love with Apuleius, etc.

to one of his especiall and trusty friends : But although hee brought this to passe very secretly and sagely, yet in the end cruell fortune sowed great sedition in his house. For his wife who was now condemned to beasts, waxed jealous of her husband and began to suspect the young woman as a harlot and common queane, insomuch that shee invented all manner of meanes to dispatch her out of the way. And in the end shee invented this kind of mischiefe : She privily stale away her husbands ring, and went into the country, whereas she commanded one of her trusty servants to take the ring and carry it to the mayden. To whom he should declare that her brother did pray her to come into the country to him, and that she should come alone without any person. And to the end shee should not delay but come with all speed he should deliver her the ring, which should be a sufficient testimony of the message. This mayden as soone as she had received the ring of her brother, being very willing and desirous to obey his commandement : (For she knew no otherwise but that he had sent for her) went in all hast as the messenger willed her to doe. But when she was come to the snare and engine which was prepared for her, the mischievous woman, like one that were mad, and possessed with some ill spirit, when the poore maiden called for helpe with a loud voyce to her brother, the wicked harlot (weening that she had invented and feined the matter) tooke a burning firebrand and thrust it into her secret place, whereby she died miserably. The husband of this maiden but especially her brother, advertised of her death, came to the place where she was slain, and after great lamentation and weeping, they caused her to be buried honourably. This yong man her brother taking in ill part the miserable death of his sister, as it was convenient he should, conceived so great dolour within his mind and was strucken with so pestilent fury of bitter anguish, that he fell into the burning passions of a dangerous ague, whereby he seemed in such necessity, that he needed to have some speedy remedy to save his life. The woman that slew the Maiden having lost the name of wife together with her faith, went to a traiterous Physitian, who had killed a great many persons in his dayes and promised

OF LUCIUS APULEIUS

him fifty peeces of Gold, if he would give her a present poyson to kill her Husband out of hand, but in presence of her Husband, she feined that it was necessary for him to receive a certaine kind of drinke, which the Maisters and Doctours of Physicke doe call a sacred Potion, to the intent he might purge Choller, and scoure the interiour parts of his body. But the Physitian in stead of that drinke prepared a mortall and deadly poyson, and when he had tempered it accordingly, he tooke the pot in the presence of the family, and other neighbours and friends of the sick yong man, and offered it to his patient. But the bold and hardy woman, to the end she might accomplish her wicked intent, and also gaine the money which she had promised the Physitian, staid the pot with her hand, saying: I pray you master Physitian, minister not this drinke unto my deare Husband, untill such time as you have drunke some part thereof your selfe: For what know I, whether you have mingled any poyson in the drinke or no, wherein I would have you not to be offended: For I know that you are a man of wisedome and learning, but this I do to the intent the conscience and love that I beare to the health and safegard of my husband, may be apparant. The Physitian being greatly troubled at the wickednesse of this mischievous woman, as voyd of all counsell and leysure to consider of the matter, and least he might give any cause of suspition to the standers by, or shew any scruple of his guilty conscience, by reason of long delay, tooke the pot in his hand, and presently drunke a good draught thereof, which done, the young man having no mistrust, drunke up the residue. The Physitian would have gone immediatly home to receive a counterpoyson, to expell and drive out the first poyson: But the wicked woman persevering in her mischiefe, would not suffer him to depart a foot, untill such time as the poyson began to worke in him, and then by much prayer and intercession she licensed him to goe home: By the way the poyson invaded the intrailes and bowels of the whole body of the Physitian, in such sort that with great paine he came to his owne house, where he had scarce time to speake to his wife, and to will her to receive the promised salitary of the death of two persons,

CHAPTER XLVI

How a certaine Matron fell in love with Apuleius, etc.

THE TENTH BOOKE

CHAPTER XLVI

How a certaine Matron fell in love with Apuleius, etc.

but he yeelded up the ghost: And the other young man lived not long after, but likewise dyed, amongst the feined and deceitfull teares of his cursed wife. A few dayes after, when the young man was buried and the funerall ended, the Physitians wife demanded of her the fifty peeces of gold which she promised her husband for the drinke, whereat the ill disposed woman, with resemblance of honesty, answered her with gentle words, and promised to give her the fifty peeces of gold, if she would fetch her a little of that same drinke, to proceed and make an end of all her enterprise. The Physitians wife partly to winne the further favour of this rich woman, and partly to gaine the money, ranne incontinently home, and brought her a whole roote of poyson, which when she saw, having now occasion to execute her further malice, and to finish the damnable plot, began to stretch out her bloody hands to murther. She had a daughter by her husband (that was poysoned) who according to order of law, was appointed heire of all the lands and goods of her father: but this woman knowing that the mothers succoured their children, and received all their goods after their death, purposed to shew her selfe a like parent to her child, as she was a wife to her husband, whereupon she prepared a dinner with her owne hands, and empoysoned both the wife of the Physitian and her owne daughter: The child being young and tender dyed incontinently by force of the drinke, but the Physitians wife being stout and strong of complexion, feeling the poison to trill down into her body, doubted the matter, and thereupon knowing of certainty that she had received her bane, ran forthwith to the judges house, that what with her cryes, and exclamations, she raised up the people of the towne, and promising them to shew divers wicked and mischievous acts, caused that the doores and gates were opened. When she came in she declared from the beginning to the end the abhomination of this woman: but shee had scarce ended her tale, when opening her falling lips, and grinding her teeth together, she fell downe dead before the face of the Judge, who incontinently to try the truth of the matter, caused the cursed woman, and her servants to be pulled out of the house, and enforced by paine of torment to

OF LUCIUS APULEIUS

CHAPTER XLVI

How a certaine Matron fell in love with Apuleius, etc.

confesse the verity, which being knowne, this mischievous woman farre lesse then she deserved, but because there could be no more cruell a death invented for the quality of her offence, was condemned to be eaten with wild beasts. Behold with this woman was I appointed to have to doe before the face of the people, but I being wrapped in great anguish, and envying the day of the triumph, when we two should so abandon our selves together, devised rather to sley my selfe, then to pollute my body with this mischievous harlot, and so for ever to remaine defamed: but it was impossible for me so to doe, considering that I lacked hands, and was not able to hold a knife in my hoofes: howbeit standing in a pretty cabin, I rejoyced in my selfe to see that spring time was come, and that all things flourished, and that I was in good hope to find some Roses, to render me my humane shape. When the day of triumph came, I was led with great pompe and benevolence to the appointed place, where when I was brought, I first saw the preamble of that triumph, dedicated with dancers and merry taunting jests, and in the meane season was placed before the gate of the Theater, whereas on the one side I saw the greene and fresh grasse growing before the entry thereof, whereon I greatly desired to feed: on the other side I conceived a great delectation to see when the Theater gates were opened, how all things was finely prepared and set forth: For there I might see young children and maidens in the flowre of their youth of excellent beauty, and attired gorgiously, dancing and mooved in comely order, according to the order of Grecia, for sometime they would dance in length, sometime round together, sometime divide themselves into foure parts, and sometimes loose hands on every side: but when the trumpet gave warning that every man should retire to his place, then began the triumph to appeare. First there was a hill of wood, not much unlike that which the Poet Homer called Idea, for it was garnished about with all sort of greene verdures and lively trees, from the top whereof ran downe a cleare and fresh fountaine, nourishing the waters below, about which wood were many young and tender Goates, plucking and feeding daintily on the budding

THE TENTH BOOKE

CHAPTER XLVI

How a certaine Matron fell in love with Apuleius, etc.

trees, then came a young man a shepheard representing Paris, richly arrayed with vestments of Barbary, having a mitre of gold upon his head, and seeming as though he kept the goates. After him ensued another young man all naked, saving that his left shoulder was covered with a rich cloake, and his head shining with glistering haires, and hanging downe, through which you might perceive two little wings, whereby you might conjecture that he was Mercury, with his rod called Caduceus, he bare in his right hand an Apple of gold, and with a seemely gate went towards him that represented Paris, and after hee had delivered him the Apple, hee made a signe, signifying that Jupiter had commanded him so to doe: when he had done his message he departed away. And by and by, there approached a faire and comely mayden, not much unlike to Juno, for she had a Diademe of gold upon her head, and in her hand she bare a regall scepter: then followed another resembling Pallas, for she had on her head a shining sallet, whereon was bound a garland of Olive branches, having in one hand a target or shield: and in the other a speare as though she would fight: then came another which passed the other in beauty, and presented the Goddesse Venus, with the color of Ambrosia, when she was a maiden, and to the end she would shew her perfect beauty, shee appeared all naked, saving that her fine and dainty skin was covered with a thin smocke, which the wind blew hither and thither to testifie the youth and flowre of the age of the dame. Her colour was of two sorts, for her body was white as descended from heaven, and her smocke was blewish, as arrived from the sea: After every one of the Virgins which seemed goddesses, followed certaine waiting servants, Castor and Pollux went behind Juno, having on their heads helmets covered with starres. This Virgin Juno sounded a Flute, which shee bare in her hand, and mooved her selfe towards the shepheard Paris, shewing by honest signes and tokens, and promising that hee should be Lord of all Asia, if hee would judge her the fairest of the three, and to give her the apple of gold: the other maiden which seemed by her armour to be Pallas, was accompanied with two young men armed, and brandishing their naked swords in their

OF LUCIUS APULEIUS

hands, whereof one named Terror, and the other Feare; behind them approached one sounding his trumpet to provoke and stirre men to battell; this maiden began to dance and shake her head, throwing her fierce and terrible eyes upon Paris and promising that if it pleased him to give her the victory of beauty, shee would make him the most strong and victorious man alive. Then came Venus and presented her selfe in the middle of the Theater, with much favour of all the people, for shee was accompanied with a great many of youth, whereby you would have judged them all to be Cupidoes, either to have flowne from heaven or else from the river of the sea, for they had wings, arrowes, and the residue of their habit according in each point, and they bare in their hands torches lighted, as though it had beene a day of marriage. Then came in a great multitude of faire maidens: on the one side were the most comely Graces: on the other side, the most beautifull Houres carrying garlands and loose flowers, and making great honor to the goddesse of pleasure; the flutes and Pipes yeelded out the sweet sound of Lydians, whereby they pleased the minds of the standers by exceedingly, but the more pleasing Venus mooved forward more and more, and shaking her head answered by her motion and gesture, to the sound of the instruments. For sometimes she would winke gently, sometimes threaten and looke aspishly, and sometimes dance onely with her eyes: As soone as she was come before the Judge, she made a signe and token to give him the most fairest spouse of all the world, if he would prefer her above the residue of the goddesses. Then the young Phrygian shepheard Paris with a willing mind delivered the golden Apple to Venus, which was the victory of beauty. Why doe ye marvell, ye Orators, ye Lawyers, and Advocates, if many of our judges now a daies sell their judgements for money, when as in the beginning of the world one onely Grace corrupted the sentence betweene God and men, and that one rusticall Judge and shepheard appointed by the counsell of great Jupiter, sold his judgement for a little pleasure, which was the cause afterward of the ruine of all his progeny? By like manner of meane, was sentence given between the noble Greekes: For the noble and valiant per-

CHAPTER XLVI

How a certaine Matron fell in love with Apuleius, etc.

THE TENTH BOOKE

CHAPTER XLVI

How a certaine Matron fell in love with Apuleius, etc.

sonage Palamedes was convicted and attainted of treason, by false perswasion and accusation, and Ulisses being but of base condition, was preferred in Martiall prowesse above great Ajax. What judgement was there likewise amongst the Athenian lawyers, sage and expert in all sciences? Was not Socrates who was preferred by Apollo, above all the wise men in the world, by envy and malice of wicked persons impoysoned with the herbe Cicuta, as one that corrupted the youth of the countrey, whom alwaies be kept under by correction? For we see now a dayes many excellent Philosophers greatly desire to follow his sect, and by perpetuall study to value and revolve his workes, but to the end I may not be reproved of indignation by any one that might say: What, shall wee suffer an Asse to play the Philosopher? I will returne to my further purpose.

After the judgement of Paris was ended, Juno and Pallas departed away angerly, shewing by their gesture, that they would revenge themselves on Paris, but Venus that was right pleased and glad in her heart, danced about the Theater with much joy. This done from the top of the hill through a privy spout, ran a floud of the colour of Saffron, which fell upon the Goates, and changed their white haire into yellow, with a sweet odour to all them of the Theater. By and by after by certaine engines, the ground opened, and swallowed up the hill of wood: and then behold there came a man of armes through the multitude, demanding by the consent of the people, the woman who was condemned to the beasts, and appointed for me to have to doe withall: our bed was finely and bravely prepared, and covered with silke and other things necessary. But I, beside the shame to commit this horrible fact, and to pollute my body with this wicked harlot did greatly feare the danger of death: for I thought in my selfe, that when she and I were together, the savage beast appointed to devoure the woman, was not so instructed and taught, or would so temper his greedinesse, as that hee would teare her in peeces lying under mee, and spare mee with a regard of mine innocency. Wherefore I was more carefull for the safeguard of my life, then for the shame that I should abide, but in the meane season while my master

OF LUCIUS APULEIUS

CHAPTER XLVI

How a certaine Matron fell in love with Apuleius, etc.

made ready the bed, all the residue did greatly delight to see the hunting and pleasantnesse of the triumph, I began to thinke and devise for my selfe. When I perceived that no man had regard to mee, that was so tame and gentle an Asse, I stole out of the gate that was next me, and then I ran away with all force, and came to Cenchris, which is the most famous towne of all the Carthaginians, bordering upon the Seas called Ageum, and Saronicum, where is a great and mighty Haven, frequented with many a sundry Nation. There because I would avoyd the multitude of the people, I went to a secret place of the Sea coast, where I laid me down upon the sand, to ease and refresh my selfe, for the day was past and the Sunne gone downe, and lying in this sort on the ground, did fall in a sound sleepe.

THE
ELEVENTH BOOKE
of LUCIUS APULEIUS of
THE GOLDEN ASSE

THE ELEVENTH BOOKE

THE FORTY-SEVENTH CHAPTER
How Apuleius by Roses and prayer returned to his humane shape.

HEN midnight came that I had slept my first sleepe, I awaked with suddaine feare, and saw the Moone shining bright, as when shee is at the full, and seeming as though she leaped out of the Sea. Then thought I with my selfe, that that was the most secret time, when the goddesse Ceres had most puissance and force, considering that all humane things be governed by her providence: and not onely all beasts private and tame, but also all wild and savage beasts be under her protection. And considering that all bodies in the heavens, the earth and the seas, be by her increasing motions increased, and by her diminishing motions diminished: as weary of all my cruell fortune and calamity, I found good hope and soveraigne remedy, though it were very late, to be delivered from all my misery, by invocation and prayer, to the excellent beauty of the Goddesse, whom I saw shining before mine eyes, wherefore shaking off mine Assie and drowsie sleepe, I arose with a joyfull face, and mooved by a great affection to purifie my selfe, I plunged my selfe seven times into the water of the Sea, which number of seven is conveniable and agreeable to holy and divine things, as the worthy and sage Philosopher Pythagoras hath declared. Then with a weeping countenance, I made this Orison to

THE ELEVENTH BOOKE

CHAPTER XLVII

How Apuleius by Roses and prayer returned to his humane shape

the puissant Goddesse, saying: O blessed Queene of heaven, whether thou be the Dame Ceres which art the originall and motherly nource of all fruitfull things in earth, who after the finding of thy daughter Proserpina, through the great joy which thou diddest presently conceive, madest barraine and unfruitfull ground to be plowed and sowne, and now thou inhabitest in the land of Eleusie; or whether thou be the celestiall Venus, who in the beginning of the world diddest couple together all kind of things with an ingendered love, by an eternall propagation of humane kind, art now worshipped within the Temples of the Ile Paphos, thou which art the sister of the God Phœbus, who nourishest so many people by the generation of beasts, and art now adored at the sacred places of Ephesus, thou which art horrible Proserpina, by reason of the deadly howlings which thou yeeldest, that hast power to stoppe and put away the invasion of the hags and Ghoasts which appeare unto men, and to keepe them downe in the closures of the earth: thou which art worshipped in divers manners, and doest illuminate all the borders of the earth by the feminine shape, thou which nourishest all the fruits of the world by thy vigor and force; with whatsoever name or fashion it is lawfull to call upon thee, I pray thee, to end my great travaile and misery, and deliver mee from the wretched fortune, which had so long time pursued me. Grant peace and rest if it please thee to my adversities, for I have endured too too much labour and perill. Remoove from me my shape of mine Asse, and render to me my pristine estate, and if I have offended in any point of divine Majesty, let me rather dye then live, for I am full weary of my life. When I had ended this orison, and discovered my plaints to the Goddesse, I fortuned to fall asleepe, and by and by appeared unto me a divine and venerable face, worshipped even of the Gods themselves. Then by little and little I seemed to see the whole figure of her body, mounting out of the sea and standing before mee, wherefore I purpose to describe her divine semblance, if the poverty of my humane speech will suffer me, or her divine power give me eloquence thereto. First, shee had a great abundance of haire, dispersed and scattered about her neck, on the crowne of her

OF LUCIUS APULEIUS

head she bare many garlands enterlaced with floures, in the middle of her forehead was a compasse in fashion of a glasse, or resembling the light of the Moone, in one of her hands she bare serpents, in the other, blades of corne, her vestiment was of fine silke yeelding divers colours, sometime yellow, sometime rosie, sometime flamy, and sometime (which troubled my spirit sore)·darke and obscure, covered with a blacke robe in manner of a shield, and pleated in most subtill fashion at the skirts of her garments, the welts appeared comely, whereas here and there the starres glimpsed, and in the middle of them was placed the Moone, which shone like a flame of fire, round about the robe was a coronet or garland made with flowres and fruits. In her right hand shee had a timbrell of brasse, which gave a pleasant sound, in her left hand shee bare a cup of gold, out of the mouth whereof the serpent Aspis lifted up his head, with a swelling throat, her odoriferous feete were covered with shoes interlaced and wrought with victorious palme. Thus the divine shape breathing out the pleasant spice of fertill Arabia, disdained not with her divine voyce to utter these words unto me: Behold Lucius I am come, thy weeping and prayers hath mooved mee to succour thee. I am she that is the naturall mother of all things, mistresse and governesse of all the Elements, the initiall progeny of worlds, chiefe of powers divine, Queene of heaven, the principall of the Gods celestiall, the light of the goddesses: at my will the planets of the ayre, the wholesome winds of the Seas, and the silences of hell be disposed; my name, my divinity is adored throughout all the world in divers manners, in variable customes and in many names, for the Phrygians call me the mother of the Gods: the Athenians, Minerva: the Cyprians, Venus: the Candians, Diana: the Sicilians, Proserpina: the Eleusians, Ceres: some Juno, other Bellona, other Hecate: and principally the Æthiopians which dwell in the Orient, and the Ægyptians which are excellent in all kind of ancient doctrine, and by their proper ceremonies accustome to worship mee, doe call mee Queene Isis. Behold I am come to take pitty of thy fortune and tribulation, behold I am present to favour and ayd thee, leave off thy weeping and lamentation, put away all thy sorrow, for behold

CHAPTER XLVII

How Apuleius by Roses and prayer returned to his humane shape

THE ELEVENTH BOOKE

CHAPTER XLVII

How Apuleius by Roses and prayer returned to his humane shape

the healthfull day which is ordained by my providence, therefore be ready to attend to my commandement. This day which shall come after this night, is dedicated to my service, by an eternall religion, my Priests and Ministers doe accustome after the tempests of the Sea, be ceased, to offer in my name a new ship as a first fruit of my Navigation. I command thee not to prophane or despise the sacrifice in any wise, for the great Priest shall carry this day following in procession by my exhortation, a Garland of Roses, next the timbrell of his right hand : follow thou my procession amongst the people, and when thou commest to the Priest, make as though thou wouldest kisse his hand, but snatch at the Roses, whereby I will put away the skin and shape of an Asse, which kind of beast I have long time abhorred and despised, but above all things beware thou doubt not nor feare any of those things, as hard and difficill to bee brought to passe, for in the same houre that I am come to thee, I have commanded the Priest by a vision what he shall doe, and all the people by my commandement shall be compelled to give thee place and say nothing ! Moreover, thinke not that amongst so faire and joyfull Ceremonies, and in so good a company that any person shall abhorre thy ill-favoured and deformed figure, or that any man shall be so hardy, as to blame and reprove thy suddaine restoration to humane shape, wherby they should gather or conceive any sinister opinion : and know thou this of certaine, that the residue of thy life untill the houre of death shall be bound and subject to me ! And think it not an injury to be alwayes serviceable towards me, since as by my meane and benefit thou shalt become a man : thou shalt live blessed in this world, thou shalt live glorious by my guide and protection, and when thou descendest to Hell, where thou shalt see me shine in that subterene place, shining (as thou seest me now) in the darknesse of Acheron, and raigning in the deepe profundity of Stix, thou shalt worship me, as one that hath bin favourable to thee, and if I perceive that thou art obedient to my commandement, addict to my religion, and merite my divine grace, know thou, that I will prolong thy daies above the time that the fates have appointed,

OF LUCIUS APULEIUS

and the celestial Planets ordeined. When the divine Image had spoken these words, she vanished away! By and by when I awaked, I arose, haveing the members of my bodie mixed with feare, joy and sweate, and marvailed at the cleare presence of the puissant goddesse, and being sprinkled with the water of the sea, I recounted orderly her admonitions and divine commandements. Soone after, the darknes chased away, and the cleare and golden sunne arose, whenas behold I saw the streets replenished with people going in a religious sort and in great triumph. All things seemed that day to be joyfull, as well all manner of beasts and houses, as also the very day it selfe seemed to rejoyce. For after the hore-frost, ensued the hot and temperat sun, whereby the little birds weening that the spring time had bin come, did chirp and sing in their steven melodiously: the mother of stars, the parent of times, and mistres of all the world: The fruitful trees rejoyced at their fertility: The barren and sterill were contented at their shadow, rendering sweete and pleasant shrills! The seas were quiet from winds and tempests: The heaven had chaced away the clouds, and appeared faire and cleare with his proper light. Behold then more and more appeared the pomps and processions, attired in regall manner and singing joyfully: One was girded about the middle like a man of armes: Another bare and spare, and had a cloake and high-shooes like a hunter! another was attired in a robe of silke, and socks of gold, having his haire laid out, and dressed in forme of a woman! There was another ware legge-harnesse, and bare a target, a sallet, and a speare like a martial souldier: after him marched one attired in purple with vergers before him like a magistrate! after him followed one with a maurell, a staffe, a paire of pantofles, and with a gray beard, signifying a philosopher: after him went one with lime, betokening a fowler, another with hookes declaring a fisher: I saw there a meeke and tame beare, which in matron habite was carried on a stoole: An Ape with a bonet on his head, and covered with lawne, resembling a shepheard, and bearing a cup of gold in his hand: an Asse which had wings glewed to his backe, and went after an old man, whereby you would judge the one

CHAPTER XLVII
How Apuleius by Roses and prayer returned to his humane shape

THE ELEVENTH BOOKE

CHAPTER XLVII
How Apuleius by Roses and prayer returned to his humane shape

to be Pegasus, and the other Bellephoron. Amongst the pleasures and popular delectations, which wandered hither and thither, you might see the pompe of the goddesse triumphantly march forward: The woman attired in white vestiments, and rejoysing, in that they bare garlands and flowres upon their heads, bespread the waies with hearbes, which they bare in their aprons, where this regall and devout procession should passe: Other caried glasses on their backes, to testifie obeysance to the goddes which came after. Other bare combes of Ivory, and declared by their gesture and motions of their armes, that they were ordained and readie to dresse the goddesse: Others dropped in the wayes as they went Balme and other pretious ointments: Then came a great number, as well of men as women, with candels, torches, and other lights, doing honour to the celestiall goddesse: After that sounded the musicall harmony of instruments: then came a faire companie of youth, apparelled in white vestiments, singing both meeter and verse, with a comely grace which some studious Poet had made in honour of the Muses: In the meane season, arrived the blowers of trumpets, which were dedicated unto Serapis, and to the temple before them were officers and bedles, preparing roome for the goddes to passe. Then came the great company of men and women, which had taken divine orders, whose garments glistered all the streets over. The women had their haire annointed and their heads covered with linnen: but the men had their crownes shaven, which were the terrene stars of the goddesse, holding in their hands instruments of brasse, silver and gold, which rendered a pleasant sound. The principall Priests which were apparelled with white surplesses hanging downe to the ground, bare the relikes of the puissant goddesse. One carried in his hand a light, not unlike to those which we used in our houses, saving that in the middle thereof appeared a bole which rendred a more bright flame. The second attired like the other, bare in his hand an Altar, which the goddesse her selfe named the succor of nations. The third held a tree of palme with leaves of gold, and the verge of Mercurie. The fourth shewed out a token of equitie by his left hand, which

OF LUCIUS APULEIUS

was deformed in every place, signifiing thereby more equitie then by the right hand. The same Priest carried a round vessell of gold, in forme of a cap. The fift bare a van, wrought with springs of gold, and another carried a vessell for wine: By and by after the goddesse followed a foot as men do, and specially Mercurie, the messenger of the goddesse infernall and supernall, with his face sometime blacke, sometime faire, lifting up the head of the dogges Annubis, and bearing in his left hand, his verge, and in his right hand, the branches of a palme tree, after whom followed a cow with an upright gate, representing the figure of the great goddesse, and he that guided her, marched on with much gravity. Another carried after the secrets of their religion, closed in a coffer. There was one that bare on his stomacke a figure of his god, not formed like any beast, bird, savage thing or humane shape, but made by a new invention, whereby was signified that such a religion should not be discovered or revealed to any person. There was a vessell wrought with a round bottome, haveing on the one side, pictures figured like unto the manner of the Egyptians, and on the other side was an eare, whereupon stoode the Serpent Aspis, holding out his scaly necke. Finally, came he which was apointed to my good fortun according to the promise of the goddesse. For the great Priest which bare the restoration of my human shape, by the commandement of the goddes, approached more and more, bearing in his left hand the timbrill, and in the other a garland of Roses to give me, to the end I might be delivered from cruel fortune, which was alwaies mine enemie, after the sufferance of so much calamitie and paine, and after the endurance of so manie perilles: Then I not returning hastilie, by reason of sodaine joye, lest I should disturbe the quiet procession with mine importunitie, but going softly through the prease of the people, which gave me place on every side, went after the Priest. The priest being admonished the night before, as I might well perceive stood still and holding out his hand, thrust out the garland of roses into my mouth, I (trembling) devoured with a great affection: And as soone as I had eaten them, I was not deceived of the promise made unto me.

CHAPTER XLVII

How Apuleius by Roses and prayer returned to his humane shape

THE ELEVENTH BOOKE

CHAPTER XLVII
How Apuleius by Roses and prayer returned to his humane shape

For my deforme and Assie face abated, and first the rugged haire of my body fell off, my thick skin waxed soft and tender, the hoves of my feet changed into toes, my hands returned againe, my neck grew short, my head and mouth began round, my long eares were made little, my great and stonie teeth, waxed lesse like the teeth of men, and my tayle which combred me most, appeared no where: then the people began to marvaile, and the religious honoured the goddesse, for so evident a miracle, they wondred at the visions which they saw in the night, and the facilitie of my reformation, whereby they rendered testimonie of so great a benefit which I received of the goddesse. When I saw my selfe in such estate, I stood still a good space and said nothing, for I could not tell what to say, nor what word I shoulde first speake, nor what thanks I should render to the goddesse, but the great Priest understanding all my fortune and miserie, by divine advertisement, commanded that one should give me garments to cover me: Howbeit as soone as I was transformed from an asse to my humane shape, I hid the privitie of my body with my hands as shame and necessity compelled mee. Then one of the company put off his upper robe and put it on my backe: which done, the Priest looked upon me, with a sweete and benigne voice, gan say in this sort: O my friend Lucius, after the endurance of so many labours, and the escape of so many tempests of fortune, thou art at length come to the port and haven of rest and mercy: neither did thy noble linage, thy dignity, thy doctrine, or any thing prevaile, but that thou hast endured so many servil pleasures, by a little folly of thy youthfullnes, whereby thou hast had a sinister reward for thy unprosperous curiositie, but howsoever the blindnes of fortune tormented thee in divers dangers: so it is, that now unwares to her, thou art come to this present felicitie: let fortune go, and fume with fury in another place, let her finde some other matter to execute her cruelty, for fortune hath no puissance against them which serve and honour our goddesse. For what availed the theeves: the beasts savage: thy great servitude: the ill and dangerous waies: the long passages: the feare of death every day? Know thou, that now thou art safe, and under the protection of her, who

OF LUCIUS APULEIUS

by her cleare light doth lighten the other gods: wherefore rejoyce and take a convenable countenance to thy white habit, follow the pomp of this devout and honorable procession, to the end that such which be not devout to the Goddes, may see and acknowledge their errour. Behold Lucius, thou art delivered from so great miseries, by the providence of the goddesse Isis, rejoyce therefore and triumph of the victory of fortune; to the end thou maist live more safe and sure, make thy selfe one of this holy order, dedicate thy minde to the Obsequy of our Religion, and take upon thee a voluntary yoake of ministrie: And when thou beginnest to serve and honour the goddes, then thou shalt feele the fruit of thy liberty: After that the great Priest had prophesied in this manner, with often breathings, he made a conclusion of his words: Then I went amongst the company of the rest and followed the procession: everie one of the people knew me, and pointing at me with their fingers, said in this sort: Behold him who is this day transformed into a man by the puissance of the soveraigne goddesse, verily he is blessed and most blessed that hath merited so great grace from heaven, as by the innocencie of his former life, and as it were by a new regeneration is reserved to the obsequie of the goddesse. In the meane season by little and little we approached nigh unto the sea cost, even to that place where I lay the night before being an Asse. There after the images and reliques were orderly disposed, the great Priest compassed about with divers pictures according to the fashion of the Ægyptians, did dedicate and consecrate with certaine prayers a fair ship made very cunningly, and purified the same with a torch, an egge, and sulphur; the saile was of white linnen cloath, whereon was written certaine letters, which testified the navigation to be prosperous, the mast was of a great length, made of a Pine tree, round and very excellent with a shining top, the cabin was covered over with coverings of gold, and all the shippe was made of Citron tree very faire; then all the people as well religious as prophane tooke a great number of Vannes, replenished with odours and pleasant smells and threw them into the sea mingled with milke, untill the ship was filled up with large gifts and

CHAPTER XLVII

How Apuleius by Roses and prayer returned to his humane shape

THE ELEVENTH BOOKE

CHAPTER XLVII

How Apuleius by Roses and prayer returned to his humane shape

prosperous devotions, when as with a pleasant wind it lanched out into the deep. But when they had lost the sight of the ship, every man caried againe that he brought, and went toward the temple in like pompe and order as they came to the sea side. When we were come to the temple, the great priest and those which were deputed to carrie the divine figures, but especially those which had long time bin worshippers of the religion, went into the secret chamber of the goddesse, where they put and placed the images according to their ordor. This done, one of the company which was a scribe or interpreter of letters, who in forme of a preacher stood up in a chaire before the place of the holy college, and began to reade out of a booke, and to interpret to the great prince, the senate, and to all the noble order of chivalry, and generally to all the Romane people, and to all such as be under the juris-diction of Rome, these words following (*Laois Aphesus*) which signified the end of their divin service and that it was lawfull for every man to depart, whereat all the people gave a great showt, and replenished with much joy, bare all kind of hearbs and garlands of flowers home to their houses, kissing and imbracing the steps where the goddesse passed: howbeit I could not doe as the rest, for my mind would not suffer me to depart one foot away, so attentiv was I to behold the beauty of the goddesse, with remembrance of the great miserie I had endured.

OF LUCIUS APULEIUS

THE FORTY-EIGHTH CHAPTER
How the parents and friends of Apuleius heard news that he was alive and in health.

IN the meane season newes was carried into my countrey (as swift as the flight of birds, or as the blast of windes) of the grace and benefit which I received of the goddesse, and of my fortune worthy to be had in memory. Then my parents friends and servants of our house understanding that I was not dead, as they were falsely informed, came towards me with great dilligence to see me, as a man raised from death to life: and I which never thought to see them againe, was as joyfull as they, accepting and taking in good part their honest gifts and oblations that they gave, to the intent I might buy such things as was necessarie for my body: for after I had made relation unto them of all my pristine miserie, and present joyes, I went before the face of the goddesse and hired me a house within the cloister of the temple to the end I might continually be ready to the service of the goddesse, and ordinarily frequent the company of the priests, whereby I would wholy become devout to the goddesse, and an inseparable worshipper of her divine name: It fortuned that the goddesse appeared to me oftetimes in the night, perswading and commanding me to take the order of her religion, but I, though I was indued with a desirous good will, yet the feare of the same withheld me considering her obeysance was hard and difficile, the chastitie of the Priests intolerable, and the life fraile and subject to manie inconveniences. Being thus in doubt, I refrained my selfe from all those things as seemed impossible.

On a night the great priest appeared unto me, presenting his lap full of treasure, and when I demanded what it signified, he answered, that it was sent me from the

THE ELEVENTH BOOKE

CHAPTER XLVIII

How the parents and friends of Apuleius heard news that he was alive and in health

countrey of Thessaly, and that a servant of mine named Candidus was arived likewise: when I was awake, I mused in my selfe what this vision should pretend, considering I had never any servant called by that name: but what soever it did signifie, this I verely thought, that it was a foreshew of gaine and prosperous chance: while I was thus astonied I went to the temple, and taried there till the opening of the gates, then I went in and began to pray before the face of the goddesse, the Priest prepared and set the divine things of every Altar, and pulled out the fountaine and holy vessell with solempne supplication. Then they began to sing the mattens of the morning, testifying thereby the houre of the prime. By and by behold arived my servant which I had left in the country, when Fotis by errour made me an Asse, bringing with him my horse, recovered by her through certaine signes and tokens which I had upon my backe. Then I perceived the interpretation of my dreame, by reason that beside the promise of gaine, my white horse was restored to me, which was signified by the argument of my servant Candidus.

This done I retired to the service of the goddesse in hope of greater benefits, considering I had received a signe and token, whereby my courage increased every day more and more to take upon me the orders and sacraments of the temple: insomuch that I oftentimes communed with the Priest, desiring him greatly to give me the degree of the religion, but he which was a man of gravitie, and well renowned in the order of priesthood, deferred my affection from day to day, with comfort and better hope, as parents commonly bridle the desires of their children, when they attempt or indeavour any unprofitable thing, saying, that the day when any one should be admitted into their order is appointed by the goddesse, the Priest which should minister the sacrifice is chosen by her providence, and the necessary charges of the ceremonies is alotted by her commandement, all which things he willed me to attend with marvailous patience, and that I should beware either of too much hastinesse, or too great slacknesse, considering that there was like danger, if being called I should delay, or not

OF LUCIUS APULEIUS

called I should be hasty: moreover he said that there was none of his company either of so desperate a mind, or so rash and hardy, as to enterprise any thing without the commandement of the goddesse, whereby he should commit a deadly offence, considering that it was in her power to damne and save all persons, and if any were at the point of death, and in the way to damnation, so that he were capable to receive the secrets of the goddesse, it was in her power by divine providence to reduce him to the path of health, as by a certaine kind of regeneration: Finally he said that I must attend the celestiall precept, although it was evident and plaine, that the goddesse had already vouchsafed to call and appoint me to her ministery, and to will me refraine from prophane and unlawfull meates, as those Priests which were already received, to the end I might come more apt and cleane to the knowledge of the secrets of religion. Then was I obedient unto these words, and attentive with meek quietnesse, and probable taciturnity, I daily served at the temple: in the end the wholesome gentlenesse of the goddesse did nothing deceive me, for in the night she appeared to me in a vision, shewing that the day was come which I had wished for so long, she told me what provision and charges I should be at, and how that she had appointed her principallest Priest Mythra to be a minister with me in my sacrifices.

CHAPTER XLVIII
How the parents and friends of Apuleius heard news that he was alive and in health

When I heard these divine commandements, I greatly rejoyced: and arose before day to speake with the great Priest, whom I fortuned to espie comming out of his chamber: Then I saluted him, and thought with my selfe to aske and demand his counsell with a bold courage, but as soone as he perceived me, he began first to say: O Lucius now know I well that thou art most happy and blessed, whom the divine goddesse doth so greatly accept with mercy, why dost thou delay? Behold the day which thou desiredst when as thou shalt receive at my hands the order of religion, and know the most pure secrets of the gods, whereupon the old man tooke me by the hand, and lead me to the gate of the great temple, where at the first entrie he made a solempne celebration, and after morning sacrifice ended, brought out of

THE ELEVENTH BOOKE

CHAPTER XLVIII

How the parents and friends of Apuleius heard news that he was alive and in health

the secret place of the temple books, partly written with unknown characters, and partly painted with figures of beasts declaring briefly every sentence, with tops and tailes, turning in fashion of a wheele, which were strange and impossible to be read of the prophane people: There he interpreted to me such things as were necessary to the use and preparation of mine order. This done, I gave charge to certaine of my companions to buy liberally, whatsoever was needfull and convenient, then he brought me to the next bains accompanied with all the religious sort, and demanding pardon of the goddesse, washed me and purified my body, according to custome. After this, when noone approached, he brought me backe againe to the temple, presented me before the face of the goddesse, giving a charge of certaine secret things unlawfull to be uttered, and commanding me, and generally all the rest, to fast by the space of ten continuall daies, without eating of any beast, or drinking any wine, which thing I observed with a marvellous continencie. Then behold the day approached, when as the sacrifice should be done, and when night came there arrived on every coast, a great multitude of Priests, who according to their order offered me many presents and gifts: then was all the Laity and prophane people commanded to depart, and when they had put on my backe a linnen robe, they brought me to the most secret and sacred place of all the temple. You would peradventure demand (you studious reader) what was said and done there, verely I would tell you if it were lawfull for me to tell, you should know if it were convenient for you to heare, but both thy eares, and my tongue shall incur the like paine of rash curiositie: Howbeit, I will content thy mind for this present time, which peradventure is somewhat religious and given to some devotion, listen therefore and beleeve it to be true: Thou shalt understand that I approached neere unto Hell, even to the gates of Proserpina, and after that, I was ravished throughout all the Element, I returned to my proper place: About midnight I saw the Sun shine, I saw likewise the gods celestiall and gods infernall, before whom I presented my selfe, and worshipped them: Behold now have I told thee, which although thou

hast heard, yet it is necessarie thou conceale it; this have
I declared without offence, for the understanding of the
prophane.

When morning came, and that the solemnities were
finished, I came forth sanctified with xii. Stoles and in a
religious habit, whereof I am not forbidden to speake, considering that many persons saw me at that time: there I was
commanded to stand upon a seate of wood, which stood in
the middle of the temple, before the figure and remembrance
of the goddesse; my vestiment was of fine linnen, covered and
embroidered with flowers. I had a pretious Cope upon my
shoulders hanging downe to the ground, whereon were
beasts wrought of divers colours, as Indian dragons, and
Hiperborian Griphons, whom in forme of birds, the other
world doth ingender; the Priests commonly call such a habit,
a celestiall Stole: in my right hand I carried a light torch,
and a garland of flowers upon my head, with Palme leaves
sprouting out on every side: I was adorned like unto the
Sun, and made in fashion of an Image, in such sort that all
the people compassed about to behold me: then they began
to solemnize the feast of the nativitie, and the new procession
with sumptuous bankets and delicate meates: the third day
was likewise celebrated with like ceremonies with a religious
dinner, and with all the consummation of the order: when
I had continued there a good space, I conceived a marvailous
great pleasure and consolation in beholding ordinarily the
Image of the goddesse, who at length admonished me to
depart homeward, not without rendring of thanks, which
although it were not sufficient, yet they were according to
my power. Howbeit I could unneth be perswaded to depart,
before I had fallen prostrate before the face of the goddesse,
and wiped her steps with my face, whereby I began so greatly
to weepe and sigh that my words were interrupted, and as
devouring my prayer, I began to say in this sort: O holy
and blessed dame, the perpetuall comfort of humane kind,
who by thy bounty and grace nourishest all the world, and
bearest a great affection to the adversities of the miserable,
as a loving mother thou takest no rest, neither art thou idle
at any time in giving thy benefits, and succoring all men, as

CHAPTER
XLVIII
How the
parents and
friends of Apuleius heard
news that he
was alive and
in health

THE ELEVENTH BOOKE

CHAPTER XLVIII
How the parents and friends of Apuleius heard news that he was alive and in health

well on land as sea; thou art she that puttest away all stormes and dangers from mans life by the right hand, whereby likewise thou restrainest the fatall dispositions, appeasest the great tempests of fortune and keepest backe the course of the stars: the gods supernall doe honour thee: the gods infernall have thee in reverence: thou environest all the world, thou givest light to the Sunne, thou governest the world, thou treadst downe the power of hell: By thy meane the times returne, the Planets rejoyce, the Elements serve: at thy commandement the winds do blow, the clouds increase, the seeds prosper, and the fruits prevaile, the birds of the aire, the beasts of the hill, the serpents of the den, and the fishes of the sea, do tremble at thy majesty, but my spirit is not able to give thee sufficient praise, my patrimonie is unable to satisfie thy sacrifice, my voice hath no power to utter that which I thinke, no if I had a thousand mouths and so many tongues: Howbeit as a good religious person, and according to my estate, I will alwaies keepe thee in remembrance and close thee within my breast. When I had ended mine orison, I went to imbrace the great Priest Mythra my spirituall father, and to demand his pardon, considering I was unable to recompence the good which he had done to me: after great greeting and thanks I departed from him to visit my parents and friends; and within a while after by the exhortation of the goddesse, I made up my packet, and tooke shipping toward the Citie of Rome, where with a prosperous winde I arrived about the xii. day of December. And the greatest desire that I had there, was daily to make my praiers to the soveraigne goddesse Isis, who by reason of the place where her temple was builded, was called Campensis, and continually adored of the people of Rome. Her minister and worshipper was I, howbeit I was a stranger to her Church, and unknowne to her religion there.

When the yeare was ended, and the goddesse warned me againe to receive this new order and consecration, I marvailed greatly what it should signifie, and what should happen, considering that I was a sacred person already. But it fortuned that while I partly reasoned with my selfe,

OF LUCIUS APULEIUS

and partly examining the thing with the Priests and Bishops, there came a new and marvailous thought in my mind, that is to say, I was onely religious to the goddesse Isis, but not sacred to the religion of great Osiris, the soveraigne father of all the goddesses, between whom, although there was a religious unitie and concord, yet there was a great difference of order and ceremony. And because it was necessary that I should likewise be a minister unto Osiris, there was no long delay: for in the night after, appeared unto me one of that order, covered with linnen robes, holding in his hands speares wrapped in Ivie, and other things not convenient to declare, which then he left in my chamber, and sitting in my seate, recited to me such things as were necessary for the sumptuous banket of mine entrie. And to the end I might know him againe, he shewed me how the ankle of his left foote was somewhat maimed, which caused him a little to halt.

After that I manifestly knew the will of the god Osiris, when mattins was ended, I went from one to another, to find him out which had the halting marke on his foote, according as I learned by my vision; at length I found it true: for I perceived one of the company of the Priests who had not onely the token of his foote, but the stature and habite of his body, resembling in every point as he appeared in the night: he was called Asinius Marcellus, a name not much disagreeing from my transformation. By and by I went to him, which knew well enough all the matter, as being monished by like precept in the night: for the night before as he dressed the flowers and garlands about the head of the god Osiris, he understood by the mouth of the image which told the predestinations of all men, how he had sent a poore man of Madura, to whom he should minister his sacraments, to the end hee should receive a reward by divine providence, and the other glory, for his vertuous studies. When I saw my selfe thus deputed unto religion, my desire was stopped by reason of povertie, for I had spent a great part of my goods in travell and peregrination, but most of all in the Citie of Rome, whereby my low estate withdrew me a great while.

CHAPTER XLVIII

How the parents and friends of Apuleius heard news that he was alive and in health

THE ELEVENTH BOOKE

CHAPTER XLVIII
How the parents and friends of Apuleius heard news that he was alive and in health

In the end being oft times stirred forward, not without great trouble of mind, I was constrained to sell my robe for a little money: howbeit sufficient for all my affaires. Then the Priest spake unto me saying, How is it that for a little pleasure thou art not afraid to sell thy vestiments, and entring into so great ceremonies, fearest to fall into povertie? Prepare thy selfe, and abstaine from all animall meats, as beasts and fish. In the meane season I frequented the sacrifices of Serapis, which were done in the night, which thing gave me great comfort to my peregrination, and ministred unto me more plentifull living, considering I gained some money in haunting the court, by reason of my Latin tongue.

Immediatly after I was eftsoones called and admonished by the god Osiris, to receive a third order of religion. Then I was greatly astonied, because I could not tell what this new vision signified, or what the intent of the celestiall god was, doubting least the former Priests had given me ill counsell, and fearing that they had not faithfully instructed me: being in this manner as it were incensed the god Osiris appeared to me the night following, and giving me admonition said, There is no occasion why thou shouldest be afraid with so often order of religion, as though there were somewhat omitted, but that thou shouldest rather rejoyce, since as it hath pleased the gods to call thee three times, when as there was never yet any person that atchieved to the order but once: wherefore thou maist thinke thy selfe happy for so great benefits. And know thou that the religion which thou must now receive, is right necessary, if thou meane to persever in the worshipping of the goddesse, and to make solempnity on the festivall day with the blessed habite, which thing shall be a glory and renowne to thee.

After this sort, the divine majesty perswaded me in my sleepe, whereupon by and by I went towards the Priest, and declared all that which I had seene, then I fasted ten dayes according to the custome, and of mine owne proper will I abstained longer then I was commanded: and verely I did nothing repent of the paine which I had taken, and of

OF LUCIUS APULEIUS

the charges which I was at, considering that the divine providence had given me such an order, that I gained much money in pleading of causes: Finally after a few dayes, the great god Osiris appeared to me in the night, not disguised in any other forme, but in his owne essence, commanding me that I should be an Advocate in the court, and not feare the slander and envie of ill persons, which beare me stomacke and grudge by reason of my doctrine, which I had gotten by much labour: moreover, he would not that I should be any longer of the number of his Priests, but he allotted me to be one of the Decurions and Senatours: and after he appointed me a place within the ancient pallace, which was erected in the time of Silla, where I executed my office in great joy with a shaven Crowne.

CHAPTER XLVIII

How the parents and friends of Apuleius heard news that he was alive and in health

FINIS

www.ingramcontent.com/pod-product-compliance
Lightning Source LLC
Chambersburg PA
CBHW031938230426
43672CB00010B/1968